The Road to Kosovo

The Road to Kosovo

A Balkan Diary

GREG CAMPBELL

Westview
PRESS
A Member of the Perseus Books Group

Copyright © 2000 by Westview Press, A Member of the Perseus Books Group

Published in 1999 and 2000 in the United States of America by Westview Press, 5500 Central Avenue, Boulder, Colorado 80301-2877, and in the United Kingdom by Westview Press, 12 Hid's Copse Road, Cumnor Hill, Oxford OX2 9JJ

Find us on the World Wide Web at www.westviewpress.com

Library of Congress Cataloging-in-Publication Data
Campbell, Greg.
  The road to Kosovo / by Greg Campbell.
    p. cm.
  This book is an updated version of the 1999 edition of "The Road to Kosovo" with two new concluding chapters.
  Includes bibliographical references and index.
  ISBN 0-8133-3767-4 (pbk.)
  1. Campbell, Greg—Journeys—Yugoslavia—Kosovo (Serbia).
2. Campbell, Greg—Journeys—Bosnia and Hercegovina.   3. Kosovo
(Serbia)—History—1980–   .   4. Bosnia and Hercegovina—History—1992–   .
I. Title.
DR2086.C36 2000
914.971043—dc21   99-088252
                                                                      CIP

For Meg and Turner . . .
and a little boy named Fidan,
who will never know the reasons he died

Contents

Courtesy of Sarajevo Daily, Tom Gjelten

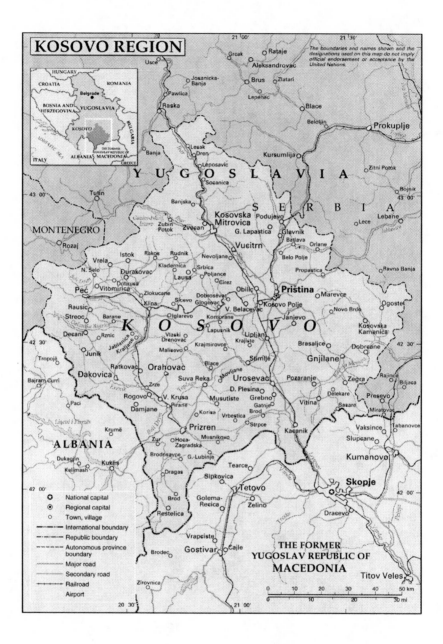

KOSOVO REGION

The boundaries and names shown and the designations used on this map do not imply official endorsement or acceptance by the United Nations.

Usce
Grcak Rataje
Aleksandrovac
Josanicka-
Banja
Pawlica Brus Zlatari
Raska
Lepenac
Blace
Belotjin Prokuplje
Lesak Kursumlija
Banja Dren
Leposavic Zitni Potok
Socanica

Y U G O S L A V I A

Tutin
Banjska Bojnik
Kosovska S E R B I A
MONTENEGRO Zubin Mitrovica Podujevo Lece Lebane
Potok Zvecan G. Lapastica Glavnik
Rozaj Batlava
Vueitrn Orlane
Vrela Istok Rakoe Rudnik Nevoljane Belo Polje
N. Selo Durakovac Kladernica Srbica Propastica Ravna Banja
Vitomirica Lausa Poljance
Dobrusa Cirez Obilc Pristina
Pec Zlokucane Skevo Marevce
Rausic Klina Glogovac V. Belacevac Kosovo Polje Novo Brdo Ogoste
Streoc Barane Olglarevo Komorane Janjevo Kosovska
Decani Rznic Vlaski Lapusnik Lipljan Kamenica
Jablanica Drenovac Krajmirovce Krajiste Brasaljce Dobreane
Junik Kraljane Malisevo Stimlje Gnjilane
Tropoje Ratkovac Orahovac Blace Urosevac Pozaranje Zegra Rajince
Bajram Curri Zrze Suva Reka Novljane Vitina Biljaca
Rogovo V. Krusa D. Plesina Grebno Delekare Presevo
Paci Damjane Pirane Musutiste Gatnje Sasare Miratovac
Korisa Brod Kacanik Tabanovce
Krume Prizren Vrbestica Strpce Vaksince
Zur Musnikovo Slupcane
ALBANIA Hoca- Kumanovo
Zagradska
Dukagjin Brodnsavce G. Lubinje Tearce
Kelimash Kukes Dragas Sipkovica Skopje
Brod Tetovo
Golema- Zelino
Restelica Recica Drasevo
Vrapeiste THE FORMER
Brodec Gostivar Cajle YUGOSLAV REPUBLIC OF
Zirovnica MACEDONIA Titov Veles

HUNGARY
CROATIA ROMANIA
Belgrade
BOSNIA AND YUGOSLAVIA
HERZEGOVINA
KOSOVO BULGARIA
ITALY ALBANIA MACEDONIA GREECE

○ National capital
◉ Regional capital
○ Town, village
—·—·— International boundary
— — — Republic boundary
- - - - Autonomous province
boundary
——— Major road
——— Secondary road
+—+—+ Railroad
✈ Airport

0 10 20 30 40 50 km
0 10 20 30 mi

Prologue

GRBAVICA, MARCH 1996

The civilian and military components [of the Dayton, Ohio, Balkan Peace Accords], through a coordinated approach to the protection of human rights, have the opportunity to create the foundation for reviving a multiethnic society in Bosnia and Hercegovina based on the rule of law. If this opportunity is missed, human rights violations will be the seeds of further strife and ultimately will jeopardize the entire peace effort.

—"Human Rights in Bosnia and Hercegovina Post Dayton:
Challenge for the Field," presented to the Human Rights
in Bosnia Roundtable, Vienna, Austria, March 4–5, 1996,
by Human Rights Watch/Helsinki

One

Dan Rather had made the announcement a few weeks before I first arrived in former Yugoslavia in March 1996: The Bosnian Serb siege of Bosnia's capital city, Sarajevo, was over.

But from the ground in Grbavica, one of the city's suburbs from which Serb gunners had laid waste to the metropolis over the previous three and a half years, it was hard to tell.

On all sides, buildings were burning unattended. Overhead, black-smoke towers filled the sky but still let through a desultory rain. Underfoot were mud, scattered belongings—books, plates, picture frames—and land mines. And swirling all around, through the drifting smoke and early-morning mist, people moved in all directions, slightly hysterical with fear and confusion, shifty eyes looking only

1

for signs of immediate danger, pockets crammed with ammunition and hand grenades, arms juggling logs and water bottles. There was no telling who they were, victim or aggressor; they probably didn't even know themselves.

It was a maze, the neighborhood, built of grim apartment houses and rivers of trash where there were once streets. It was also surreal, like a full-scale theater production, and it took me some time to grasp where I was and what was going on. A scream did it, cleaving the air like a bullet. The air was full of such sounds: shouting, edgy voices; the gassy chugging of truck engines; the panicked babble of foreign voices. Along with a gang of other reporters, I instinctively broke into a jog in the scream's direction, a mixture of dread and exhilaration enveloping me.

She was about sixty years old, dressed in a plain blue skirt and a featureless blouse. No one could tell what was wrong. She'd fled from her apartment, a grim concrete block with the same Swiss-cheese architecture of every other building in Sarajevo, flapping her hands and lunging at those nearby, pleading for someone to call off the demons tormenting her.

"What's wrong with her?" someone asked while snapping a photo. She was weeping hysterically, fallen against the bullet-ventilated door of her apartment building. Photographers were bucking for an angle—but their body language spoke volumes; the light was flat and all wrong and pictures of a woman sobbing were a dime a dozen. If only there were a burning apartment in the background . . .

But her terror frightened me. I breathed in each of her screams, absorbing her hysteria. I kept scanning the balconies and low rooftops for snipers, thinking she was trying to alert us to some imminent danger. Nothing.

"Can you *move*?" a photographer shouted at me from behind her camera. She'd stepped over the woman so that she was behind her, inside the apartment building, shooting out, going for a silhouette. I hustled off to the side. She took her shot and came out scowling. "This light sucks," she shouted.

I nodded sympathetically. Everything about Grbavica, this sordid suburb of Sarajevo, sucked.

A Serb soldier had sliced open his bare foot. His commander, a captain, was carrying him to an Italian Implementation Force (IFOR) medical truck, but he was too drunk to be of much help. He dropped the soldier onto the pavement, eliciting a pitiful shout of pain from his wounded counterpart.

We recognized this guy: about an hour earlier, the captain had been so dangerously drunk and unpredictable, he had had to be disarmed. We had run into him at the raging inferno that had become of the Grbavica market a few blocks away. While the ceramic tiles on the market roof overheated and popped into gray space as if a pistol were being fired through the ceiling, he lurked on the littered perimeter, muttering darkly about "American motherfuckers," and swigging purple wine from a greasy bottle. When a gang of us passed by to shoot the fire, he whipped an Asian photographer into a headlock and casually motioned for us to follow him into a secluded alley . . . which we did, fingers tight on shutter buttons in case he decided to murder the guy right there in front of us. He never unholstered his pistol, but he never let go of it either; perhaps realizing the potentially fatal predicament he was in, the Asian wiggled out of the headlock and shuffled away, resisting the urge to run. Italian IFOR soldiers took the Serb's weapon away.

But they couldn't take away his desire to try to help the troops. And try he did: so drunk that he could barely stand, he kept picking up and then dropping the soldier, whose foot was pouring blood, creating a paisley design in the mud. Finally, Italian medics shooed the officer away and lifted the wounded man into their truck. The captain slumped against the apartment building, fighting an imminent blackout, sweating booze and failure. No one bothered to wonder aloud why the soldier had been traveling barefoot over the mine-seeded detritus that made up Grbavica's floor.

Four stories up, silhouetted against the gray sky, an elderly man started swinging an ax into the roof of his apartment building. No one was sure what he was doing up there; he was either ventilating the roof so the building would burn better, creating holes to pour diesel fuel into (to be followed by a flaming rag or a grenade), or he was just run-of-the-mill out of his mind and deciding that now was the time to chop up his home and those of his neighbors.

A squad of Italian Rangers huddled in the mud with a radio, watching along with the rest of us. A German correspondent said later that one of the soldiers had joked about just shooting the man off the roof, a solution that would have fixed any one of the things that might have been wrong about him. Along with a small unit of French monitors also assigned to the area, the Italians were the only ones with any supposed official authority in Grbavica, about fifty ground troops assigned to monitor the safe and orderly withdrawal of hundreds of Serb soldiers and the safe and orderly return of Sarajevan refugees as outlined in the Dayton Accords. As anyone could see, they weren't having much success—nor, did it seem, were they trying very hard. In reality, Serbs still controlled the town until March 19— a full two days away—and not only were they not enforcing safe and orderly behavior by the people they were ostensibly in control of, but some of them had also decided to take one last shot at the city they'd tried unsuccessfully for three and a half years to conquer. Therefore, no one was in control.

Except the arsonists, that is, who stayed maddeningly busy bombing, looting, and robbing the neighborhood they'd called home for the past four years. The Italians took another look at the guy on the roof and decided that there were more pressing things to deal with— about a dozen apartments were already on fire and threatening to kill someone. If the lunatic on the roof torched the building, they'd just have to wait until later to handle it.

"How about all this shit, huh?" A U.S. Army colonel appeared, seemingly out of nowhere. "This is the whole deal right here, the whole ball of wax. This is crazy . . ." The smile he wore said clearly that the chaos and terror were nothing, actually, nothing but a morbid and wiggy epitaph, compared to the type of really crazy shit that had been going on in Sarajevo for four years. Small potatoes. He was with an army camera detachment to film the whole mess, perhaps for training purposes back in the States, *Chaos Management and the Role of NATO* or *How the Dayton Accords Look From the Ground.* I lit a cigarette and moved away from him, unable to handle the sight of yet another fully armed international soldier doing nothing but watch even though he had full United Nations Security Council approval[1] to use his weapons to protect the panicking civilians streaming all around us. Most of the other photographers had wandered off as well, looking for more action. I was trying to remain anchored, suffering from information and sensory overload and broken, disturbing sleep; everywhere I walked, there was the potential of losing my legs to buried mines, every soot-blackened apartment window was the portal to secret nightmares I couldn't even begin to comprehend, every person a possible killer and assassin.

Things weren't supposed to be this way . . . this was supposed to be the end of the violence and the terror. There were 60,000 international soldiers in this miserable country, for chrissake.

Two

Peace came to Grbavica with a bang, no joke. A hand grenade in a burning building blew out a wall with a horrific *blam!* making everyone leap and cringe with the type of sickening "too late" feeling that's involuntary when something blows up nearby, too late because you know that by the time you've reflexed, the shrapnel from the blast will already be sunk deep into something, hopefully not you. The only people who didn't flinch were the Serb soldiers bunched in motley formation high above the city on a mud-splattered residential street. They made a depressing assembly, purple camouflage combat gear untucked in and stiffening with mud, cigarette smoke uncurling high overhead, eyes hard but tired, staring somewhere into the middle distance, uninterested in the ceremonial removing of their country's flag hanging wet and limp over the city, waiting only for it to be done so that they could pack into a bus and be taken over the hill to Pale, where they could sleep. They weren't needed here anymore; the arsonists and looters would finish off Grbavica.

But the person most unfazed by the explosion, which was followed by the hollow patter of cinder and wood falling from the sky, was the Serb diplomat speaking to the troops. Imported from somewhere else, he moved in a tight little world that seemed very different from the one we were standing in, dressed in such fine clean clothing that a brighter sun seemed to shine on him. Where everything around him was monochromed in mud, smoke, and death, he stood out in Technicolor, low Italian loafers rubbed into a high shine, speaking at a podium too nicely polished to have been found in Grbavica. It was a world designed not to extend beyond the scope of a television minicam, through the lens of which he would demonstrate to the world that Republika Srpska, the Serb half of Bosnia, was happily complying with the Dayton Accords. In the background was the red, white, and blue flag of Serbia and one of the few homes that hadn't been firebombed. The only thing that would have alerted TV viewers that something was strange about the press conference was the casual, de-moralized slouch of soldiers in formation in the foreground and the fact that they were smoking cigarettes while supposedly standing at attention—but most viewers weren't astute enough to notice. Which is why the timing of the grenade was so well appreciated by those of us in the press corps.

"For those of you leaving, I wish you peace and happiness in your new place," said the diplomat. "For those of you staying, I wish you peace and happiness in staying—"

Blam!

"Did you *get* that?" whispered the CNN woman to her soundman. "Oh, yeah, we got it." The Serb got it too—there was the barest tick of loathing in his face, which was surely unnoticed by the television cameras, more of a vibration than an expression, and then he was off again with accolades for the troops and words of hope and peace for the citizens of the neighborhood, citizens who doubtless heard his amplified voice deep in dozens of blacked-out cellars nearby, where they waited for the arsonists and their very own firebombs.

The dead buildings of Sarajevo watched silently.

On paper, that was that. The Dayton Accords were ticking along ac-cording to schedule: the Serbs would begin to withdraw their forces today, and tomorrow the refugees would return. But everyone agreed that peace implementation wasn't supposed to look like this. Visions of burning homes, huddled and cold elderly, menacing men with hammers and hand grenades . . . they were to have been nothing more than a painful memory by then. The only thing that made Grbavica in March 1996 different from any of the other horrors in Bosnia over the previous four years was that this time, NATO soldiers had been superimposed on the grief. But for all the good they were doing, they may as well have been cardboard cutouts.

The General Framework Agreement for Peace in Bosnia and Hercegovina was negotiated in Dayton, Ohio, in November 1995. It was the child of U.S. envoy Richard Holbrooke, the instrumental point man who succeeded in milking a peace plan from Croatian President Franjo Tudjman, Bosnian President Alijza Izetbegovic, and Serbian President Slobodan Milosevic, who represented the Bosnian Serbs because their leaders were prohibited from the discussion, hav-ing been indicted for war crimes.

What have come to be known as the Dayton Accords created a deceptively simple arrangement for all three sides to stop battling and work toward achieving a durable cease-fire so that Bosnia could begin the mountainous task of rebuilding.

At that point, there was a lot to rebuild. Since 1991, television audiences have been witness to a spectacle of bloodshed that, thanks to modern media technology, was brought nightly into living rooms across the world. Unlike Desert Storm, which was fought mainly with remote-fired missiles and relentless air assaults, the violence in Bosnia went beyond conventional military warfare to that of medieval times. It was conducted with "ethnic cleansing," the complete eradication of different and enemy cultures, as its main goal, a goal that was pursued with fire, torture, and rape. Though thousands died from falling bombs, thousands of others died looking into the eyes of their killers, many of whom they knew. The people killing one another had been countrymen and neighbors before chaos broke out.

By the time Dayton was being negotiated, Bosnia was scorched-earth. Ancient places of worship were gone—bombed and then paved over. Village upon village had, indeed, been cleansed, the houses standing vacant, punctured with artillery during midnight assaults, the bodies of the dead withering in common graves. More than a quarter of a million people had been killed in three and a half years. Two million more had become refugees in countries across the globe.

To this genocidal residue the Dayton Accords were affixed. The agreement reads as innocently as a young child's prayer and, as the world was finding out with Grbavica and other Serb-dominated neighborhoods in Sarajevo, has about the same basis in reality.

To media audiences who knew no better, the agreement seemed sound, even revolutionary in terms of global politics and the role of the United States after the cold war. According to the agreed-upon plan, Bosnia would remain one country that was split into two semi-autonomous halves, Republika Srpska (or RS), hugging the country's entire northern and eastern sections, and the Bosnian-Croat Federation, comprising the rest of the country, keeping Sarajevo as its easternmost outpost and the capital of the country as a whole. Critics seized on this facet immediately: it amounted to nothing more than a partitioning of the country, they said, which is the very thing the Serbs were trying to do in the first place. Indeed, they were right: many prewar Muslim-majority towns were now under the control of the aggressors, and the ethnic cleansing that the world had roundly denounced had been legitimized.

To mitigate this troubling reality as much as possible, Holbrooke included another key facet in the agreement: the return of refugees. Ideally, this would mean that Muslim civilians, for instance, who'd fled their besieged homes would return en masse, thereby re-creating their majority status in their old hometowns. The security of this plan was to come through another Dayton provision: Free and fair elections. Theoretically, they would mean that the newly returned refugees could vote for a mayor and city council that would reflect their ethnic demographics, creating a Muslim-run town in RS, for instance. In this way, Bosnia would again become the multiethnic nation it had once been.

Other provisions included creating a UN International Police Task Force (IPTF) that would retrain the police in the methods of modern law enforcement, concentrating on respecting human rights and regaining the confidence of the locals, regardless of ethnic background. And just as before the war, Bosnians in either semiautonomous half were to be able to travel unhindered to anywhere else in the country.

At least, that was the theory.

Reality, as I quickly discovered, was quite different. The local warlords of the signing parties saw the division of the country much as the agreement's critics suspected they would: Federation land was for Croats and Muslims, and RS land was for Serbs. Immediately after the agreement was signed in Paris in December, Croat troops drove into the small village of Majdan with twenty trucks and forced Croat citizens to move to a nearby village because Majdan was slated to come under Bosnian Serb control. Dayton created another miniexodus of people who'd held out as the minority in lands that were to come under the governance of the enemy. This was especially so in Sarajevo, where thousands of Serb civilians fled Grbavica for the RS capital of Pale ten miles away.[2]

Of course, everyone expected this reaction to the new borders: After four years of brutal, nonstop war, few people held the illusion that the animosity and paranoia would evaporate simply because a paper had been signed in some American city they had never heard of. That's why hope for Dayton's success came in the form of two key provisions: The arrest of war criminals and the firepower of a diverse multinational military force.

Thirty-five countries, both NATO and non-NATO, deployed soldiers to an Implementation Force—collectively called IFOR—that had the primary task of securing a demilitarized zone between the country's two halves, to physically stop the fighting. And after that was accomplished, according to the agreement, IFOR had the power to enforce other aspects of the Dayton Accords with military might, if necessary. This part of the agreement is not ambiguous: "All parties understand and agree that they shall be subject to military action by the IFOR, including the use of necessary force to ensure compliance."[3]

IFOR, in other words, was in Bosnia to force compliance from people not inclined to cooperate. These troops would arrest encountered war criminals, assist the IPTF, and provide security to returning displaced persons.

Unfortunately, as I was discovering in Grbavica, IFOR was not holding up its end of the bargain. Tragically, fulfillment of its responsibilities provides the foundation on which the rest of the peace relies: Without vigorous dedication to its mandate, whatever fragile peace emerges from the Bosnian ashes is bound to disintegrate.

In Grbavica, the writing was on the wall.

Three

I didn't immediately notice Dayton's diplomatic flaws; I had enough problems of my own. I'd never been in an active combat zone before, and even though technically there wasn't any "combat" in the classic meaning of the term, there was enough menace and grief in the air to keep me nearly immobilized by a constant gripping fear and random flash floods of adrenaline. My mental stability reached its limits in Sarajevo when I casually glanced up at an apartment balcony to see a man in civilian clothes cradling an AK-47 and grinning down at me. At any other time over the past four years, this would have been an expected sight; but with international troops patrolling Sarajevo's streets, trying to enforce an international peace agreement, it was jarring, especially since the building he was in was a notorious sniper's nest. Minutes later, when the building was surrounded by Italian soldiers and the dreadful sound of snapping rifle bolts, I tried stuffing myself into the wheel well of an armored personnel carrier, sure that any second the sniper was going to start rattling bullets down on us and I'd be caught in the middle of a bloody, deafening firefight. Chris Morris, a photographer for *Time*, crouched next to me and asked with a smile, "So how're ya liking your first visit to Sarajevo?"

Most of those in the press corps had been in worse situations. During lulls they'd reminisce about Chechnya, Sudan, or Mogadishu, and even Sarajevo merely months before. They worked for places that paid them pretty well for their brand of work: the *New York Times*, the *Wall Street Journal*, *Newsweek*, ITN, CNN, AFP, BBC, AP, Reuters, and dozens more I'd never heard of. They spent their time on the road from one battle zone to the next, and it showed: their clothes were only a few degrees on the respectable side of Salvation Army handouts, and if it weren't for several thousands of dollars' worth of camera equipment hanging from their necks, they could easily be mistaken for heroin dealers or mercenaries.

I, on the other hand, was clearly of a different breed. The small newspaper I worked for had provided me with a budget of $1,000 for five weeks (money that had come mostly from private donations, particularly from the others in the editorial department)—chump change for an assignment like this. When I mentioned my paper, no one could figure out what I was doing there, including me. "Why would they send you *here*?" they'd ask.

Standard outfitting for an assignment like Bosnia included transportation, preferably a fully armored four-wheel-drive vehicle with friendly license plates from somewhere like neutral Hungary; a place to stay either with colleagues who had rented houses in key places like Tuzla or Sarajevo or a hotel room at the Sarajevo Holiday Inn, where almost every other journalist stayed; a translator to speak to the locals so that you don't have to live out the sick joke of shouting to a crowd of refugees, "Anyone been raped and speak English?"; a bullet-proof vest and a Kevlar helmet; and an expense account so that you can keep enough hard currency on hand for checkpoint bribes, last-minute hotel accommodations, and on-the-spot translation services.

All I had was a Vietnam-era flak jacket that wouldn't stop an AK round, a free bunk in Tuzla, and Mark Milstein.

Milstein is *Soldier of Fortune*'s chief foreign correspondent and a photographer for Atlantic News Service. I'd arranged to stay at his place in Tuzla through his boss, Colonel Bob Brown. Mark stands about six feet tall, speaks with brusque military precision, and is very high-strung, given to psychotic fits of temper, almost as if he suffers from Tourette syndrome. He apparently delights in scaring the be-jesus out of small-town reporters whose only previous foreign experiences have been in the discos of Tijuana.

"I'm going to go work for a while. Wanna come?" he said the first day we met.

"What are you going to do?"

"Go out and scope the ZOS. See what the situation is like there," he said, referring to the four-kilometer-wide Zone of Separation between the Federation and the RS, a border that looked like a giant cauliflower surrounding west central Bosnia.

"Sure," I said. "Is it safe?"

He gave me a look that I would come to know well over the course of my stay. "Of course it's not safe. How the hell do I know if it's safe?"

Mark's definition of work is to drive as fast as possible into the most worrisome trouble he can find, get some photos, and then get out, stopping along the way to interview American soldiers for his magazine. Bosnian roads aren't good for high speeds—four years' worth of neglect and artillery have turned them into dangerous, uneven crater fields. And they're too narrow to accommodate all the traffic, being permanently clogged with everything from beaten-up Mercedes and rancid buses to IFOR tanks and clumsy horse-drawn wagons. But we drove a Russian Lada Niva, a quick little truck painted quasi-military lime green, with pilfered IFOR insignia in the front and back windows and a profile high enough to keep us out of all but the worst potholes, good for fast maneuvering. Mark drove everywhere as if he were under mortar attack, and he warned me not to fasten my seat belt, which was my natural inclination; if I needed to get out of the car fast, he said, the time it takes to unsnap a seat belt might be long enough to get me killed.

So could his driving; during the five weeks I was there, we had two accidents. But there were none that first day, just run-of-the-Milstein terror, a quick jaunt out into Republika Srpska beyond the Zone of Separation and the IFOR perimeter, into territory ruled by Chetnicks, Serb paramilitary irregulars known for their savagery and utter disdain for non-Serb life. There was little traffic out on those roads, just creepy silence and ethnically cleansed villages, little collections of vacant whitewashed, red-tile-roofed farm houses full of bullet- and tank-shell holes.

Perhaps to prove his fearlessness, Milstein decided to heckle a Chetnick we encountered, a huge bearded man standing in the middle of a dusty intersection. The man was filthy, as if he'd been living in the woods all year, brown hunter's camouflage overalls so stained with dirt and his own body grease that you could probably peel them off in rotting strips, like wet wallpaper. A chain of machine gun ammunition was draped across his chest and a shiny AK-47 was slung over one shoulder.

He slowed down the Niva for reasons that I couldn't understand, his voice rising in a profane tirade directed at the Chetnick, which carried through the open window and was surely audible. What is he doing? I thought, staring straight ahead. Does he know this guy? I shot a quick look at the Serb, who was turning slowly toward us, wondering why in the hell a green truck with IFOR tags on it was harassing him on the side of the road, out in the middle of nowhere. We gunned it and left him wondering.

What was that all *about*? A few miles down the road, we sped around a curve, toward a destroyed restaurant being pillaged by a gang of freelance warriors. They had the same grimy look to them as the fellow we'd just left; wild hair, Viking beards, hot eyes. And more AK-47s. They'd heard the truck approaching at the last minute, and they began urgently flagging us down. Mercifully, Mark decided that taunting them would be deadly, and he floored it.

They saw the truck surge forward, and a few rifles swung down. "Watch it, get down," Mark murmured, almost to himself. He was humming now, walking some mental high wire I couldn't see, gripping the wheel, and slamming the truck into fourth gear. We streaked over a hill, out of sight.

Letting up on the juice, Mark said, "They think we're going to stop for *them*? Sheee!" Then quietly, reasonably: "Let's call it a day. I'm hungry."

It was like that for a week, a Balkan crash course of high tension and nauseating panic. It was a roller coaster of a learning curve, and I'd end each day by drinking no less than eight large bottles of Slovenian beer just to dilute the adrenaline so I could sleep. Mark may be a lunatic, I thought, but in his own weird way, he was teaching me what he knew, even though he did it by showing off and making me fear for my life.

Like many other reporters who'd made Sarajevo their life's work over the course of the war, he didn't look favorably on those of us who waited for the shooting to stop before showing up. His boastfulness was a way of proving to me that there was far more involved in war reporting than getting quotes accurate; it was also a means of proving to himself that I wouldn't do anything stupid that could get us both hurt.

Four

Grbavica was arguably the most deadly of the Serbs' Sarajevo outposts, high on Mount Trebevic and offering the best view of the city and the streets below. There had been a restaurant up there somewhere, I was told, that served some of the best food in Bosnia before the war, but people went there mostly for the view. It was perfect for sipping wine and lingering over dessert, the lights and gentle hum of the capital laid out below.

I hadn't gone to what had become of the restaurant, but one of the other correspondents had heard of it. The picture windows had been removed, he said, and the tables pushed to the side to make room for sandbags that protected a 12.7-millimeter heavy machine gun aimed down into the city. The view was indeed magnificent, so good that snipers in Grbavica could "get you anywhere. Anywhere. It was amazing," as one local put it.

Indeed, I'm no military expert, but standing on the hill, I felt confident that I could hit most buildings below with a Daisy air rifle or a well-tossed Frisbee. Off in the distance, I could see the Olympic stadium. With the right kind of rifle scope, I might have been able to see the bumps in the soccer field where hundreds of Sarajevans were buried.

The twin towers of the Unis Trade Corporation, the tallest buildings in the city, were among the first to go back in 1992, the most obvious targets, punched through with incendiary tank rounds until they burned like Roman candles; even though they had had the most advanced fire protection system of any building in the city, the residents had emptied the buildings' reservoirs for drinking water. Next door was the mustard-yellow cube of the Holiday Inn, a blunt and garish architectural nightmare before the shooting began, now arguably more pleasing to the eye full of holes and freckled with four years' worth of small arms fire. The Bosnian Parliament building was across the street from the Holiday Inn, on the very edge of Grbavica, so shelled you could see clear through it. Running past, right across the base of the hill, was the airport road, Sniper Alley.

I hadn't been around when the four-lane highway lived up to its name, but I was given a high-speed tour by Milstein. We were downtown, driving as fast as usual through the business district, walled in safely by four- and five-story buildings, approaching a curve where the buildings ended. Even though it had been months since the snipers were very active, limp black tarps spiraled down toward the street over the last of the buildings, barricades designed to block approaching cars from the deadly eyes on the hill. We were going eighty-five miles an hour when we shot through the curve.

"And you'd get here," Mark said, "and it would all start up. You'd have your helmet on, your bullet-proof vest on, and everyone would be shooting at you."

We rocketed out onto Sniper Alley, the hill of Grbavica *right there* off the driver's side window, the hollow homes staring like gnawed-clean skulls, every black window a comfortable sniper's nest, the next quarter mile to the Holiday Inn a gauntlet of high-caliber bullets and rifle-fired rockets.

"And you'd pull in here," he said, jerking the truck behind the hotel, cooling the speed because there was no real danger, not anymore, "and you'd better be half out the door before you stopped."

If you can see the hills, the saying goes, the hills can see you. Snipers looked down on you from deep within brick buildings flying skull-and-crossbones flags, none of this barrel-over-the-window-sill stuff of the movies: They aimed through holes punched through several walls to dilute the barrel flash and protect their positions from Bosnian snipers. Sometimes the machine gunners would rattle off rounds to the beat of a popular song, Madonna maybe, or Michael Jackson.[4] Veteran military scholars of the Vietnam era would call that *psyops*—psychologic operation—but the Serbs just called it boredom and fun. Other times, they'd use long silencers so that no one heard the shots coming. Technically, that's illegal according one of the many international conventions that say how war is supposed to be conducted. But so is sniping at civilians. Over 1,000 citizens were wounded by snipers and about 250 killed, including 60 children.[5]

Some of the people doing the shooting would tell you that they were defending the city from a Turkish army, the ghosts of Kosovo's Ottoman conquerors returned to finish their mission of Serb eradication, and where better to defend yourself from foreign invaders but the hilltops?[6] It's the first lesson of military strategy—seize the high ground—and the Serbs had almost all of it on every side of the city. On average, 4,000 artillery shells per day were poured into Sarajevo from these surrounding outposts.[7] Grbavica was the closest Serb po-sition to downtown. It was their crown jewel.

The Dayton Accords dictated the return of Sarajevo's Serb-held neighborhoods in clear, straightforward language, language that meant absolutely nothing on the ground. Serbs were determined to leave as little as possible for the refugees who were scheduled to return to their long-lost homes and to exercise a little last-minute revenge on those civilians who were planning to stay in Grbavica, a sort of reverse ethnic cleansing that convinced most Serb civilians to flee with the soldiers. Official word is that 200 non-Serbs survived until reunification.[8] Those who stayed were mostly old and had nowhere to go; leaving Grbavica meant becoming a refugee both be-fore and after the siege. They didn't leave their homes often, only peeking their heads out of windows long enough to make sure the building wasn't on fire, then hustling back into the dark to triple-check the locks and count down the minutes until the soldiers from the Bosnian-Croat Federation swept across the Brotherhood and Unity Bridge, spanning the Miljacka River, to save them. It was these people for whom the March 19 deadline could not come soon enough—they'd risked everything to stay in their homes, not neces-sarily out of courage, but because they had no other choice. During four years of occupation, they had lived in the abject terror that one night, a knock on the door would signify the end of their lives, either literally or figuratively by forcing them to leave their homes.

Now, the end was in sight, only days away, but what tense days they would be. When the Serbs rolled up their flag and packed into their buses for the short trip to Pale, they left the neighborhood in a dangerous no-man's-land, a limbo between aggressor and protector occupation, ostensibly protected by IFOR. But for that brief and ter-rible time, the town was run by Serb paramilitary punks and bearded Chetnicks who wore no uniforms. They were following orders from Pale, orders for all Sarajevo Serbs to burn their apartments to the ground, orders that went so far as to provide instructions on how to do it. They were told to pile all the furniture in the middle of the room, drench it with diesel, turn on the gas, and drop a match on their way out the door.[9] The arsonists were there to help along the re-luctant. They were clearly the most dangerous people in town that weekend—they were impossible to distinguish from the general pop-ulation, and they operated unburdened by any ethical code or stan-dard of conduct.

Chris Morris looked into the sky at the beginning of that dreadful weekend. "This whole town is gonna burn," he said.

He was right.

Five

The first building to get torched that weekend was an old office building that stored crates of relief food and medical aid from the United Nations High Commissioner for Refugees. Then the market-place was bombed, sparking a spectacular fire that did next to nothing to affect its small business trade. Everything was available, from German chocolate to American cigarettes to vile bathtub brandy in bottles clear enough to see the suspended matter swirling inside. The disheveled vendors just moved their tables and wares out into the rain when the market was firebombed.

It was easy to see that the place had been something of a focal point for the people of Grbavica, a place where you wandered to pick up some fresh fruit and fresher gossip, children scampering underfoot, the smell of made-to-order *chivapcici* heavy in the air. It was still a gathering place when it burned, but the people who milled through the smoke and lurked in the concrete shells of gutted storefronts had probably set the fire. These weren't soldiers. They were amateur urban guerrillas, though with their mud-caked civilian clothing they looked more like dangerous bums than anything else. Some were imported rowdies who had trekked to Sarajevo convinced by Belgrade propaganda that Sarajevo's destruction was instrumental to saving the Serbian race. Others had migrated from the country to claim a deserted home as their own. They were policemen, mechanics, and farmers, blue-collar folks mad with rage and violence, impotent to destroy the other Sarajevo across the river now that IFOR had arrived, so they settled for burning and booby-trapping their own turf so that nothing but rubble would remain for the refugees to return to.

And for the most part, IFOR did nothing about it, despite all the firepower and international mandates at its disposal. Though the soldiers had the authority to use deadly force to try to keep order, NATO leaders were reluctant to bring that force to bear. For one thing, deciding whom to use force against was a touchy call: Too much was happening at once for IFOR to identify a front from which to make a stand, or even an enemy to stand against. The arsonists generally moved too fast to catch, and they blended in perfectly with everyone else. The Italians seemed to realize the futility of enforcing order and instead busied themselves with preventing murder. They became glorified firefighters without water (the IFOR fire-fighting equipment was kept at headquarters to prevent "mission creep," an insipid term that means wandering from the narrowest possible interpretation of the military mandate of the Dayton Accords. It became a coded excuse for not doing anything at all). The Italians were relegated to dashing from one arson masterpiece to the next, trying to rescue the elderly from the flames—scooping them up and setting them down in the rain in their pajamas to watch their homes burn to the ground, then dashing off to the next crisis.

Once, the Italians actually caught a few Serbs with a satchel of hand grenades, a few pistols, and a big drum of gas. They'd been preparing a house high up on the hill when a woman popped out of a nearby hole like a wharf rat and flagged down a passing Italian patrol. She chattered in a shaky, high-pitched voice, telling the soldiers what the men had been up to, and after a short foot chase, the soldiers had three teenagers in custody. They looked as if they belonged to the varsity track team of the local high school. The Italians kept the arsonists at gunpoint until Serb soldiers arrived to lead them away. Until the Serbs removed their flag, it was, after all, still their turf, and they were still "in charge" of maintaining order. The arsonists walked uncuffed with the soldiers to a van, and they all drove off.

"What do you think they're gonna do to those guys?"

"Road to Pale's right over there, man. Arrested? Shit, they're just getting a free lift up to the border."

We all knew where the border was, even if we hadn't seen it for ourselves. It was where nearly everyone in Grbavica was eventually headed, whether on foot, with a Serb escort, or in a Zastava, scraping the ground under the weight of personal belongings. It was at the end of a steep road winding along the mountain, past a heavily mined Jewish cemetery overgrown with weeds and vines, around the bend to a sandbagged machine gun bunker that marked the way to Pale, the capital of Republika Srpska. For most of the weekend, the road was nearly impassable by car. A Fiat had died at the head of the line and could be neither repaired nor moved; it was too heavy with wood and water to be pushed out of the way. The motor of every vehicle backed up behind it was turned off to save precious fuel, each of these vehicles equally burdened with anything that could be lifted or pried free from its surroundings. The only thing to look at was the super-natural decimation of the Sarajevo skyline cloaked in mid-morning fog, each building looking like a giant, well-used dartboard.

These people on the move were civilians, mostly. It didn't matter if they were guilty or innocent of sieging Sarajevo—if they were Serbs, they were leaving whether they wanted to or not and regardless of whether they'd lived there their whole lives or for just the past month. Some believed the official propaganda that those flooding back across the river on the 19th would be the ghosts of bloodthirsty Turks from 1389 who would finish them off once and for all. Others were more pragmatic: they didn't want to wait around to find out if the people who'd lost their homes during the war might be inclined to seek some long-savored revenge after nightfall. Others still feared being bombed out by the arsonists and went along with the firebug instructions to avoid being killed by people who called themselves comrades. Of the estimated 70,000 Serbs in Sarajevo at the beginning of the month, only 10,000 remained after reunification.[10]

In the meantime, I was reaching the conclusion that Hollywood war movies are a bad preparation for the real thing. In the movies, explosions are always big, slow affairs that seem to leave plenty of time to duck for cover. In reality, a hand grenade exploding twenty yards in front of you is over and done with before you even have time to reflex. A loud, flat *bang!* and the simultaneous sound of shrapnel shredding leaves and air on all sides of you, the targets found before your brain even registers what happened. You wince and recoil anyway, even though it's a lifetime too late to change anything. The same thing with a bullet. As it passes close by, you hear a low-pitched whistle—*vvvwwwwwoooo!* You duck then, too, never mind that if you can hear it, it's already missed you.

The arsonists got creative with some of their fires, leaving grenades and ammunition in the apartments they burned so that it sounded like a mini war when the explosives started cooking off. It also made sure no one ventured too close to try to extinguish the blaze, but there wasn't any water in Grbavica anyway, so they needn't have bothered.

We thought the first arson like that was a firefight, the snap of gunfire attracting reporters like seagulls to a trash heap. We were in the truck, plowing over curbs and through the mud, past feral dogs and shattered souls creeping through the streets. But as always, Mark was driving too fast to put us at the scene safely; we bucked around the corner of an apartment building at about forty miles per hour, hydroplaning through the mud into the line of fire. *Vvvwwwwoooo!*

We were being closely followed by the Reuters crew in their fully armored Range Rover Discovery. Both trucks slid to a stop in the middle of the lawn, and we sprang from ours as if we'd been dyna-mited out, hugging the heavy steel of the other truck. The crack of grenades and the pop of small-arms ammo was deafening, but it took us a moment to realize that we'd arrived not at a firefight, but at an apartment fire that was like a compressed, indoor Fourth of July cel-ebration. It was right above our heads on the second floor.

Inside the building, people were trying to get out, away from the bullets that were punching through the walls into their homes, but the front door was locked, and no one had a key. A German doctor working for Médecins sans Frontières rammed his Toyota Land Rover through some heavy shrubs right up to the front door, leaping out to catch a set of keys that was heaved from a fourth-floor win-dow. He dashed over and freed the residents, who all looked as if they belonged in a retirement home.

Off to the side, in the mud, a huge plastic hand had been ripped from some cheap statue somewhere. Every finger had been hacked off except the middle one.

Six

"This makes *Apocalypse Now* look like *Ace Ventura, Pet Detective*," Mark said, repeating an observation he'd made at least five times that day. This time I agreed with him.

We were staring at each other wide-eyed. We'd just walked through a rotten cabbage garden on the edge of Grbavica to get to an apart-ment that was burning. By the time we'd made it halfway across, we had the shocked attention of the Italian soldiers on the other side, and they screamed for us to stop. We ignored them at first, thinking that they were telling us not to take photos, an order they yelled so con-stantly that we didn't even acknowledge them anymore. Then I heard them say, "Mee-nay!" Land mines. Sweet Jesus . . .

"Mee-nay?" said Milstein, looking at the ground as if it had grown teeth and tentacles.

The apartment that was on fire had been on the front line between Bosnian and Serb forces. The road was blocked by a shell crater that had turned into a ten-foot-deep sinkhole twelve feet across. The only way to get to the fire without driving completely around the block was to go on foot across the lawn. Unfortunately, the lawn was also a great place to dig a machine gun bunker and lay land mines.

It was only about ten feet back to the hard dirt path, which was probably too well packed to be mined. It was the longest ten feet I've ever walked, my eyes searching the ground for telltale triggers poking up through the muddy weeds, trying to remember where I'd stepped before. I cursed myself for being so stupid. I'd violated the first, most basic rule in a country seeded with an estimated 6 million land mines: Don't walk on the grass. Mines are evil weapons, completely indiscriminate, some capable of shearing off both legs in a blinding flash, turning the feet into fine clouds of bone and meat. Just days before, a man had stepped on a mine by the side of a well-traveled road near downtown Sarajevo, instantly losing his leg below the knee. As he hopped around screaming in pain, he stepped on another mine with his other foot, losing that one as well. Without skilled and immediate medical attention, the natural gases generated by an explosion force their way up into the torn muscles of the legs, souring and killing the rest of the appendage. These were not good things to ponder as I gingerly made my way back to the path, thinking that each step was going to be my last.

At the scene of the fire was an old woman who didn't care about land mines. Until about five minutes ago, she had lived in the first-floor apartment behind the machine gun bunker. The wall of the building spoke clearly enough about the insanity of staying in her home; it was almost punched through by four years' worth of gunfire aimed at the Serbs dug into her lawn. The only safe access to the apartment was through a hole in the outside wall and a meandering tunnel through the basement. Even though she was a Croat, it was clear why she stayed: her eighty-seven-year-old husband was feeble and weak, incapable of sneaking off into the night under the gun barrels of both sides, and since the hell in Sarajevo was arguably equal to the hell of where they were, why bother? So they cowered for four years, living balled up in dark corners like doomed animals, somehow surviving long enough for the Dayton Accords to take effect . . . and then they were firebombed out on the literal eve of peace.

The woman wailed and moaned, wandering through the minefield with an empty bucket, directionless. Her husband sat on a wooden chair wrapped in a ratty brown blanket, vacant and demented, unsure of what was happening.

•   •   •

Nighttime in Grbavica was twice as bad as the day—no lights, little movement, and the weight of a thousand eyes staring at us from the dark. After watching the police station burn, throwing orange light on the pallid faces of the elderly peering down silently from the balconies overhead, we decided to stay in the truck, too disconcerted by strange laughter and breaking bottles from the deep shadows. We were parked in a dark alley with the engine off, listening for trouble, feeling only the bass rumble of tank treads echoing up the streets.

"Who's starting these fires?" photographer Jim Lowney asked, as we watched an apartment across the street slowly start glowing orange. We'd been parked there for twenty minutes, and we'd neither seen nor heard anyone move on the entire block. Yet the fire started somehow.

"They're like ghosts. They come and go like ghosts," he said.

The echo of a grenade wafted down from the hill. Mark kicked on the engine, a thunderous sound in the dark, and we made our way up to Banjalucka Street, where a house was completely engulfed in flames. We arrived at the same time as a squad of Italians, who swept the area with laser sights mounted on their rifles, looking for anyone who might be waiting in the dark to ambush them. The only person they found was an old man who lived next door to the house on fire. He was moving burning rafters off his porch.

The fire was incredible; even the concrete seemed to burn. Jim and Mark helped the old man dump snow in the narrow alley between the homes, hoping that it would act as a fire break. The old man was terrified, on the brink of panic. He'd lived in his house since he was a boy; his wife was upstairs asleep. He hadn't slept himself in days, spending the nights at the window overlooking the street in case something happened. When they were finished moving the snow, he crept back inside, telling us to leave. He didn't want anyone lurking in the dark to know that his house was occupied.

We stood outside anyway. The Italians had left, and we were the only ones who seemed concerned about the people in the house. A few IPTF officers wandered from the darkness, their hands in their pockets, looking at the fire as if window shopping in a mall. They walked past the blaze without breaking their casual pace.

We took it upon ourselves to keep an eye on the old couple and their house, especially after the scene near the minefield. The next day, it was difficult to decide if Banjalucka Street was worse at night or during the day. Despite all the trouble that came with nightfall, at

least you couldn't see the rubble that the neighborhood had been reduced to. When we pulled up, the house on the *other* side of the old
man's was on fire. He was barely visible in the gloom of his upstairs
window.

"Se dobro?" (Are you OK?)

"Da, da," he answered, waving us off.

For some reason, despite all the people we'd seen throughout the
weekend, this man and his wife became an icon of survival that we
felt we needed to protect, even if that protection meant only driving
by every hour or so and offering him a thumbs-up from the open
window to let him know that we actually cared whether or not he
made it through one more night of fear and uncertainty. He obviously appreciated the gestures; toward nightfall, he invited us in for
coffee.

"Tomorrow," Mark said. "When this nightmare is over."

We only prayed that the house would still be standing when we
came back in the morning.

We got up early March 19. We dressed quickly in the predawn
light, nervous about what we'd find on Banjalucka Street. In my
dreams, I watched fire consume everything a Croat couple risked
their lives for, a rat-filled shit-hole apartment in a building as empty
as a parking garage, surrounded by staring vacant windows, an abandoned machine gun emplacement, and white sheep bones sucked dry
by wild dogs. I wanted to help the couple put out the fire, but I was
too afraid to move: the ground beneath me was seeded with land
mines. I couldn't take a step.

"Let's go get that cup of coffee."

We had to force the truck through a throng of refugees clogging the
Brotherhood and Unity Bridge, Bosnian Muslims ready to storm
back into their old neighborhood. It was going to be a long wait—
IFOR had decided to allow only people with legitimate proof of res-
idency back into former Serb outposts after the neighborhood of
Ilidza was thoroughly looted by a Muslim mob immediately after the
transition of power.

The couple living on Banjalucka Street had survived the night. We
were greeted at the door with hugs and kisses, strong coffee, and cigarettes. We were ushered into the living room, a dusty, mote-filled
chamber busy with battered antiques and threadbare doilies. It was
the room in which the husband had diligently kept watch, an old sen-
try guarding his wife's sleep against terrorists in the dark. Mark was

the only one with a passing knowledge of Serbo-Croatian, and we haltingly learned that the house we were in was truly charmed. When the Americans bombed Sarajevo during World War II, the air force had destroyed houses on either side of this one. And the houses that had been built in their place had been destroyed by Serb Chetnicks fifty years later. On both occasions, this man's boyhood home—as well as his life—had been spared.

We sat in the living room, smoking cigarettes and sipping strong coffee, which was served by the man's wife. She brought the drinks in from the kitchen on a thin wooden serving tray. Our muddy shoes were stacked by the door; we had traded them for soft slippers, traditional courtesy in Muslim households. If it hadn't been for the fact that wisps of smoke from smoldering homes still crept through the open window from the neighborhood below, it was as unremarkable a visit as any.

But that in itself is what made it so remarkable. Bosnian Serb snipers had lived on the street, we were told, because the hill made it easy for them to shoot Muslims across the river. The man and his wife had waited for this day since the siege began, fearing every minute that those doing the shooting might discover that there were targets close enough to kill with their hands rather than their rifles.

The couple was proud to host us due to the simple fact that they still had a home in which to host anyone. All victories are relative: in this case, that they were able to keep their home and their possessions in light of everything that had happened around them made them as heroic as any of Sarajevo's defenders.

We left when the next-door neighbors arrived, those whose home had vanished into a pile of ash.

We emerged on destruction that suddenly looked so vivid . . . and so overpoweringly melancholy. On one end of Banjalucka, Serbs had piled cars on top of one another to protect the street from Bosnian snipers. The pile sagged, the cars rusting. On the other end of the block, there wasn't anything at all, just a hint of muddy street under the rubble of homes that had once made up the neighborhood.

Welcome to peace.

1 Drvar, July 1998

For after their baptism, the Croats made a covenant, confirmed with their own hands and by oaths sure and binding in the name of St. Peter the apostle, that never would they go upon a foreign country and make war on it, but rather would live at peace with all who were willing to do so; and they received from the same pope of Rome a benediction to this effect that if any other foreigners should come against the country of these same Croats and bring war upon it, then might God fight for the Croats and protect them, and Peter the disciple of Christ gave them victories.

—Constantine VII Porphyrogenitus
(905-959 A.D.)
De administrando imperio

One

It was easy to forget where I was . . . zooming down a smooth four-lane expressway, the Crystal Method wailing from a cassette in the stereo, and getting lost in the quaint vista of red-roofed farmhouses, giant thimbles of hay, and the hazy profile of strange mountains crouching in the distance. The scene was reminiscent of Kentucky; but two years after leaving Grbavica, I was again speeding through former Yugoslavia, through the Croatian countryside south of the capital, Zagreb, toward Bosnia and beyond.

Once again, war had brought me there. In February 1998, after relative silence in the wake of the implementation of the Dayton Accords, the Balkans were again in the headlines. Serbs had started cleansing ethnic Albanians from the Serbian province of Kosovo, where Albanians comprised more than 90 percent of the population.

25

In comparison to what happened during the Bosnian and Croatian wars, the international community acted quickly to condemn the fighting and threaten Serbian President Slobodan Milosevic with military intervention if the fighting didn't stop. But by the time those pronouncements were made, it was too late for the decision to be entirely up to Milosevic. The Albanians, in the form of the Kosovo Liberation Army, had been preparing for this course of events as far back as the 1960s and by the summer of 1998, there seemed to be little hope of turning the tide.

So I was going through the Balkans to Kosovo by car, a means of travel that I'd tried hard to avoid. But since the only battling forces in Kosovo were local, there was no piggybacking with international troops or U.S. soldiers this time—and with the beating the Serbs believed they got in the press during the past war, they weren't about to make it easy for reporters to enter the new Yugoslavia, which had emerged from the ashes of the Bosnian war. A whittled-down version of the older, larger Yugoslavia, the country was now made up of Serbia and Montenegro only. It had come as little surprise that my application for a Yugoslavian visa was denied by the consular office in Washington several weeks before, as soon as the Serbian officials discovered I was a journalist. Flying into Belgrade or entering Kosovo by bus from Macedonia, to its southeast, was out of the question.

But getting to my destination wasn't, although it would be far more arduous than simply ordering plane tickets. A photojournalist friend of mine had just gotten back to the United States from Kosovo and knew of a secret way into Yugoslavia. Though legal, it was "sketchy," as he put it. "Sketchy" is a broad word to him; it can mean anything from life-threatening to mildly annoying. But he told me of the Montenegrin minister of information who, out of either spite for Belgrade or ignorance of its policies, regularly issues thirty-day Yugoslavian tourist visas to almost anyone who asks. Since Montenegro is the only Yugoslavian republic besides Serbia, this was the last hope of getting in quasi-legally.

Several weeks before I arrived in Zagreb to begin the journey, I reached the minister of information at home on a static-filled connection. Getting a tourist visa—good for one border crossing only—wasn't a problem. The only hitch was that I had to cross the border at a place called Scepan Polje, in Montenegro, a town so small that it took twenty minutes to locate on a map.

In order to get there, I had to drive, another problem, because the people at the Budget car rental agency in the Zagreb airport made it clear that I wasn't to take their vehicle outside of Croatia. To get the keys, I lied and said I was only traveling to Dubrovnik, an ancient coastal city on the southern tip of the country.

The truth was that the moment I got in the car, I was going to point it south along a meandering highway that led through Croatia, Bosnian Federation territory, Republika Srpska, across the Yugoslavian border at Montenegro, and finally into Serbia—into Kosovo, which Dayton negotiator Richard Holbrooke had recently proclaimed the "most dangerous place in Europe."

Technically, it wasn't a difficult drive; the distance between Zagreb and Pristina, the provincial capital of Kosovo in Serbia, would take about ten or twelve hours if I followed the narrow southern route through Scepan Polje and the tenuously approved border crossing. But several colleagues said that my plan to travel alone was ill advised, as I would be driving in Serbia in a car with Croatian license plates. But there was no other choice.

Besides, I wanted to go through Bosnia. Since Holbrooke and Christopher Hill, U.S. ambassador to Macedonia, were at that moment meeting with Milosevic and Ibrahim Rugova, president of the Albanian Kosovars, as they're called, I welcomed the opportunity to assess the American negotiators' earlier efforts to institute peace in Bosnia. I suspected that if the Dayton Accords had been an all-out success, there wouldn't have been rumblings in the press lately about the potential of violence in Kosovo leading to a "larger Balkan war."

So I secured a car under false pretenses and a United Nations press pass under legitimate ones, although both acquisitions presented similar bureaucratic red tape. First, the telephone didn't work at the UN office in Zagreb, my destination after the Budget desk. The press officer had to call the UN branch in Sarajevo, which is where reporters fax their information for approval. Then, a half hour later, when the phone came back to life on its own, she called the wrong number . . . which had been the right number to call yesterday. But today, it seemed, the phone company in Sarajevo had arbitrarily reassigned the number to a florist. Then, after I retreated for a long lunch while they sorted things out, the people in Sarajevo said they had never heard of me, even though I had faxed my documents more than two weeks before from the United States.

I'd been dealing with the press people for five hours and I was on the verge of giving up. The little laminated paper you're issued isn't anything more than an elaborate ID card, good for admittance into any of the dozens of international Stabilization Force (or SFOR, as IFOR has been renamed) encampments throughout Bosnia and Croatia, or for wangling an interview with administrators of the

Organization for Security and Cooperation in Europe. In tangible terms, the card is really only good for comparing and contrasting the military discipline of the different NATO forces. It's greatest value is little more than being able to bum a meal and a cup of good old Western drip coffee in SFOR mess halls.

But those perks were quickly looking less and less valuable. I had no intention of spending much time with peacekeepers en route to Kosovo. But I knew if I got into trouble, the card would allow me to flee into the nearest SFOR base to cower behind the tanks and firepower of, say, Egypt. The ID card might also come in handy at checkpoints, where the greater the volume of official-looking things you thrust at someone who has trouble even reading his own language (much less English), the more apt he is to think you're someone of international importance who shouldn't be hindered in his travels. At least that's the theory.

Finally, just before the press office closed for the day, Sarajevo called the press officer with the go-ahead for my accreditation. Five minutes later, I walked back to the car with a newly pressed media pass dangling from my neck. I roared back through Zagreb to the Esplanade Hotel to get my bags and check out so I could make it to Bosnia before sunset.

Two

The Esplanade Hotel is the portal for all journeys into the Balkans and, in many ways, it's also the end point.

I had almost passed on a night at the famous hotel when I landed at the airport the night before; even with my United Nations media discount, it was still an expensive night's stay. But I was exhausted from more than two days of travel, and after I had made my way through the spooky vacancy of the airport, I didn't feel like making the effort to communicate with the cab driver to find a cheaper place to stay. I ordered him to drive me to the Esplanade, and after twenty minutes, I was dropped in the hush of far-off traffic at what looks more like an imperial keep than a hotel, a massive edifice bathed in golden light that seems to emanate from the walls themselves rather than the small flood lamps buried in the shrubbery. I was instantly glad I hadn't tried to go elsewhere.

My memories of the Esplanade as a surreal haven are preserved within its walls, mixed into the common psychic batter that every guest has contributed to, a palpable déjà vu given as a gift by the phantoms of history crowding the halls and ballrooms. In 1996 it had been my paradise after five weeks of drowning in the anarchy of Bosnia. I'd staggered into the black-and-gray marble lobby in clothes that had lost all color from being stuck to my unwashed body the entire time, dragging a 100-pound backpack like a hobo who lived in a coal pit. No one even gave me a second glance when I asked for a room . . . and no one thought it odd when I drank the entire minibar in an effort to wash away the nightmares keeping me from a peaceful sleep.

The people behind the desk were also the same, at least in presence if not in identity. They spoke flawless English accented with equal parts of condescension, conspiracy, professional pride, and empathy. They moved and behaved like arms dealers, diplomatic peacemakers, and high-dollar pimps all at the same time. How could I not stay there?

I eschewed the elevator to the third floor and instead trudged up the hushed master staircase under the weight of my bags. The bellhop gave me a quizzical look when I politely begged off his insistent attempts to help carry my things, finally relenting when I shoveled a fistful of kunas into his gloved hands. He backed off with a shrug . . . it was not the strangest thing to happen there, by far.

Which is why I wanted to move slowly to the sanctuary of the room, to allow the visitant history, sometimes nearly as tangible as a ghost spotted for just an instant from the corner of one's eye, to seep into me. The voices of the long-withered dead were nearly audible in the late-night hum: Nazi SS soldiers drunk in the ballroom, partisan spies whispering of revolution . . .

From this cluttered crossroads, the most important aspect of conflicts both modern and ancient can be discovered. But that discovery is anything but simple: the pieces of history scattered in the cobbles and architecture within an easy stroll of the hotel, and in some cases within its very walls, give the illusory promise of quick understanding and easy fulfillment. But even the slightest misreading can lead into blind alleys of confusion. History is far less a tapestry in the Balkans than it is the scattered pieces of a million jigsaw puzzles. Anyone wishing to embark on an understanding of Bosnia must first pay homage to such chaos. But this time, examining history's clues would have to come later; sadly, I didn't have time to waste in Zagreb wandering the streets, discovering its secrets. I was due at Scepan Polje in less than three days, and there was no telling what sort of tactical trouble I would experience along the way.

According to the theory of the Dayton Accords, I shouldn't have any problems whatsoever. Bosnia has barely been in the news since Sarajevo was reunified, except for a rare wire service piece detailing some vague atrocity, a bombing clouded in confusion, or a quick and violent shooting, incidents that could just as easily happen anywhere else in the world. Bosnia might be weird, but it should be neutralized.

But I'd been there before and knew better. I remembered all too well the palpable hatred that emanated from people and the unmistakable look in the eyes of those who've experienced more horror than Western minds can easily comprehend. Most of all, I remembered the blind gaze of the mountains, land that had seen enough vicious death to warp any human mind but that had somehow remained staid and unfazed throughout centuries of bloodletting. It would take everything the Dayton Accords had and more to jerk Bosnia up to any level even within sight of what was considered normal in civilized countries. And I knew, from my time in Grbavica, that almost no one with the power to make a difference cared very much about pulling out all of Dayton's fail-safes.

Three

By accident, I found the highway I was supposed to be on and made it out of the city at precisely what would have been rush hour anywhere else in the world. But once I made it past the suburbs, there was very little traffic. The tollbooth attendant seemed shocked to see a car when I pulled up for the ticket. And just like that, I was in the country.

But unlike Western rural lands, the fields and farms south of Zagreb were preternaturally empty and lonely, as if they'd been abandoned in the middle of the night. Indeed, many of them had been. The still homesteads seemed quaint in their loneliness . . . until you realized that they were lonely because those who'd made their homes there had fled in fear to the city. The buildings were just beginning to lose their modernness to the corruption of time and weather, facades flaking like skin rot and roof tiles falling to the earth one by one like bad dentistry. The few cars on the road between Zagreb and Karlovac moved at speeds that kept the reminders of the war in the driver's mental periphery.

I found out why soon enough: evidence of the war's impact on the Croatian people became far more acute beyond Karlovac, a depressing city of big empty factories and boulevards turned nearly yellow by the sun.

A few miles farther is a sort of monument different from the ones standing nobly in Zagreb, one that speaks to events that, though they happened in 1991, are considered current by Balkan standards: the ethnically cleansed village of Turanj. It's the first indication one gets that the warfare that engulfed the former Yugoslavian republics was anything but ordinary. Houses in Turanj look, from a distance, as if they're constructed of sponges, their surfaces so totally pocked with craters that it's hard to imagine them ever having been smooth and clean. The air has been still for seven years, but it used to be deadly, full of screaming lead, smoke, and the lunatic linear designs of tracer bullets racing over the Korana River in both directions. Material damage was not incidental, as anyone can see. Buildings and houses of worship were as valuable as targets as the Croatian militia. As I crept the car through the vivid destruction, a lone man stood in his undershirt in front of what used to be a tire repair shop. There was a pile of broken bricks and rubble at his feet, and he was leaning on a push broom as if wondering where to start cleaning or whether it was even worth it. A gray cow skull was hung over the building's front door, twisting like a nefarious wind chime.

Village buildings throughout the former Yugoslavia are simple affairs: four walls, two stories, a balcony, and a blood-colored clay-tile roof supported with sturdy timber beams. A bullet blown into the soft stucco-over-brick walls creates a hole Hollywood would be proud of: deep and perfectly round surrounded by a halo of missing mortar. Artillery rounds fell easily through the roofs to explode inside, leaving Three-Little-Pigs-style destruction overhead, beams askew like hands imploring the heavens. Tank shells did the same type of puncture damage, but these came right in through the walls, creating jagged holes big enough to crawl through. Mortar rounds left the most dramatic structural damage, however: they were usually fired from too high a trajectory to penetrate the walls, so they exploded on the outer surface, leaving a frozen diorama of action imprinted forever on the stucco, like a fan of hot coal dashed into white snow. The impact design even has a nickname: the Sarajevo rose.

Turanj has all this in abundance even though there are only a handful of buildings in the town, lying as still as the corpse of anything else there that used to be full of life, a new chapter of history to regret. A brand-new hand railing on the bridge with a sharp coat of blue paint does nothing but make the ruin more acute.

   No degree of knowledge about wartime atrocities is sufficient to prepare you for such a sight. You can read all the reports generated about war crimes against civilians, about how, night after night, teenage girls in Foca detention camps were chosen by drunken paramilitary groups to be raped up to fifteen times in a row and then sent back to be selected by another gang.[1] You can know all about the Omarska concentration camp, where Bosnian prisoners were beaten to death by the feet and fists of common civilians.[2] You can be familiar with the special degeneracy of "Serb Adolf," a twenty-five-year-old ex-mechanic who would instruct his victims to place their heads on a mesh grill feeding into the Sava River in Brcko before telling them that they were seeing their hometown for the last time and then blowing their brains down the drain with his Scorpion pistol.[3] You may have heard about the massacre of the people of Srebrenica, where thousands of unarmed civilians ended up in mass graves, either dead or alive, before the dirt was pushed on top by bulldozers.[4] You can know all of this and more . . . but when you first see the scars left by ethnic cleansing, the buildings that have been decimated, the chunks of concrete spilled into the streets like guts, the very ground that hides the patient evil of land mines, you realize with crushing despair that you're entering a dimension very different from the one you're used to. There the evidence of violent death abounds, trumped only by the sorrow and heartache of people who've long ago forgotten any Western definition of a normal life. Under that thin crust of anguish, however, is a far more ominous life force, one that has been hardened and forged by four years of bloody anarchy—it's the cold heart of vengeance, carefully stoked and primed for the time when it's needed.
   The palpable closeness of easy violence and lingering dread lasts all the way to the border, a collection of graffiti-spoiled sheds where a woman in uniform waves a pistol at the car for me to pull over, the look on her face telling me not to try anything tricky.
   And just like that, with a flash of the passport, I was back, sucked again into the vacuum of Bosnia.

Four

Ahead, in the arc of the headlights, was nothing. The road stretched into the gloom unobstructed; geometric patterns of fresh black tar over mortar scars and bomb craters rolled by beneath. With the bright lights on, there were no stars, only darkness above the road.

Finally, a stop sign appeared, glowing brightly in the headlights. I turned right and could make out buildings, faint silhouettes outlined with yellow backyard utility lights, standing far back from the road, as if trying to stay out of sight. The road narrowed, and there were more cars, parked helter-skelter on the sidewalks for the night. A dog skipped across the road at the edge of the high beams, and I made an unsure left turn. Dim glow ahead, dusty lighted signs teetering over a carport protecting the entrance to a pitted concrete box called the Hotel Grmac. I pulled the car into the empty parking lot, not expecting much. Things close up early when the sun sets in Bosnia.

To my surprise, the door was open, though there was no one in sight. The only light came from the signs outside. I walked through the linoleum-floored lobby, uncertain.

Straight ahead was something of a dining room, clumsy wooden doors in various stages of openness, a television's blue radiance weakly shining through. There, a lone man sat in the dark at a table for six, watching TV with the sound off. Cigarette smoke bunched around him in a neon cloud that reflected the colors from the screen. A small glass sat next to the ashtray, two fingers full of brandy. The scene was so romantically sad, I could barely bring myself to disturb it.

"Dobro veche" (Good evening), I said at last.

He looked away from the TV slowly, not really pulling himself away from whatever was on but from some deep rumination that had permanently creased his face with worry, an expression made all the more garish by the deep shadows hanging from his nose and chin. He got up slowly to take my bags upstairs.

Hotel Grmac was cheap and pathetic, but in a way that was somewhat endearing. The stairs to the second floor were carpeted in some sort of pinkish fabric, and at every ninety-degree turn in the wall, a full stand-up ashtray slumped in the corner. The lights on the second floor didn't work. I followed my guide through the murkiness of the narrow hallway, my knees popping like walnuts from being in the car all day. The room was all the way at the end.

Since the doorway was as cramped as the room itself—so crowded that only one person at a time could go from one end to the other—I waited outside in the darkness as he carried my bags inside, and then I tried to tip him for his efforts. He only gave me a tired smile and waved off the dinar. It was the first time I looked in his eyes: they were as black as the night outside, as unrevealing as a shark's. He shut the door on the way out.

There wasn't much to the place. The bed was ironing-board narrow out of necessity; nothing bigger would have fit into the room. With a low table and a chair as crude as stick drawings, there was nowhere left to stand except in an area just inside the door, a half a step from all the furniture. The window was broken; the bullet that had come through was still lodged deep in the wall over the bed, another un-needed reminder of where I was and what had happened here. If the lack of cars in the parking lot was any indication, I was the only guest.

I unzipped my duffel bag and stripped off my clothes, slipping into baggy shorts and a clean T-shirt. I lined up two warm cans of beer I'd bought in Zagreb and, after checking that the door was locked, stared for a while at the dark painting of a farm boy holding a clay jug. It was meant to be quaint, but I found it gruesome, entertaining the thought, only for a moment, of heading down to the dining room to sit in the dark with the innkeeper. I felt we could communicate perfectly.

There was no time to debate the pros and cons of that, though—the sudden jackhammering sound of gunfire came wafting over the hills into the room, the unmistakable "sudden-rain-on-stiff-canvas" tattoo of an automatic rifle, carrying for miles through the still air. I stepped to the window, not worried about the silhouette I made with my back to the lighted room. The gunman was nowhere near. The sound came from over the mountain to the south, under a low-slung crescent moon, from Drvar.

Five

I hadn't planned to spend the night at the Grmac, but by the time I had to make a decision, there were no other choices . . . I'd driven too far through the night, relying on the unwise assumption that there would be someplace to bed down outside Bihac, the first major town across the border from Croatia, where I had stopped for dinner. It became clear only miles from the lights of the city that I was making a foolish move. I'd driven from life and vibrancy into death and despair, into a town that had been "cleansed," a term that's deceptive because there's nothing clean about the violent extermination of a whole village. It was like driving into a lake, a sudden splash of jolting fear that came from nowhere. On both sides, hiding in the semi-obscurity, were buildings that lurked like crazy animals in overgrown glades, reaching out to the passing car with groaning whispers of pain and torture, each one worse than the last. The only people there were the unseen dead; but they made themselves known as well as if they'd staged a parade on the highway.

I'd lost track of how far I'd driven, and I knew that I needed to stop for the night soon—the border of Republika Srpska dipped down briefly across the highway somewhere up ahead. I'd thought that I would just pull over and sleep behind the wheel, hiding the car in some field if a hotel didn't present itself. Such possibilities had been easy to entertain a mere mile back, with the casual experience of dining in the sunset by the Una River fresh in my mind. But I hardly wanted to pull over here, in this bog of wraiths and spooks, to spend the night tortured by spirits intent on reminding me of their fate. But I also didn't want to drive across the RS border in the dark.

About fifteen miles farther, a lighted building emerged from the gathering fog. You approach these kinds of things cautiously; no telling if it's a Chetnick brothel or an all-night gas station. But I slowed and pulled over anyway, the little oasis of light my last hope for the night.

The place was called the Motel 9. The motel itself was closed, but a surprisingly busy bar-and-restaurant that had obviously been built since the end of the war, constructed of clean imported timber and fresh concrete, was full of action. The inviting glow of neon beer signs was like a laser light show in the thick night. The place acted as a truck stop of sorts: the parking lot was full of battered vehicles and smoke-blackened trucks parked in typical Balkan style, that is, wherever they'd fit, whether on the patio of the restaurant, the sidewalk, blocking the front door, no matter. The result was that all parking lots everywhere looked like the aftermath of Hurricane Hugo with vehicles wedged together and pointed in all directions. This quirk was convenient for me, since I wanted to keep an eye on the car at all times, in case anyone decided to start the war again by torching one with Croatian license plates. I pulled up right onto the patio, feet from a gang of wrought iron tables filled with Bosnians drinking in the night.

The place was a relief. I was jangled from the last thirty miles of hollowed homes, feeling like I'd run through a gauntlet of electrified death, a sort of Balkan Bermuda Triangle. Anyplace with legitimate life, no matter how depressing or menacing, was a welcome distraction. The Motel 9 fit the bill: there were high ceilings, an aquarium, a not-so-bad mural of farm life overlooked by angels, and smart red leather chairs. All the swinging front windows were propped open to allow the breeze to wash in and try to convince the twenty or so gathered people that they were somewhere else.

I sat at the bar and waited for the Balkan Stare to subside—this is the uneasy phenomenon experienced by any stranger, regardless of origin, in this country. My entrance anywhere caused a sudden cessation of conversation, an ominous silence that made me immediately want to flee back to the car and never make the mistake of stopping ever again ... it was the type of glare that could kill weeds. None of those staring seemed ashamed about being so blatant in their mistrust of strangers. Maybe years of never knowing where death was going to come from had taught them that it was less important to be polite than to be prepared. Or maybe they had always been like that.

The stare eventually abated. The slowly reemerging babble of soft conversation was the only indication that I'd been accepted. By then, I'd learned not to waste time trying to blend in, hoping to avoid all that discomfort; the technique I'd adopted for most places was to be as boldly foreign as possible and then to ask loudly if anyone spoke English. This set the stage right away and deflated any curiosity. But so far, I'd tried that approach only in the cafés of Zagreb, where the biggest threat to a foreigner's health is the fact that the cook is smoking while he's frying your dinner. The Motel 9 had a very different vibration. And at that point, I didn't know where the hell I was. It had been too dark to glance quickly at the map in the car, and for all I knew, I had crossed the Inter-Entity Boundary miles ago and was sitting in the first Serb stronghold, having just driven halfway into the restaurant in my Croatian car. So I abandoned my normal strategy and didn't announce that I was American.

Except to the bartender, if only to ask him where I was. But he didn't speak English and didn't seem inclined to entertain anyone who did. After twenty minutes of awkward sitting, I was given the beer I ordered. Finding out where I was became something of an obsession, a critical gap in my knowledge that I needed to fill before I could relax. But taking out the map and trying to figure it out alone was out of the question. Being a foreigner is bad enough. Looking like a *lost* one, laden with expensive photo gear and a flashy new car, could be catastrophic. It was important, I thought, to appear supremely confident of everything I was doing.

Which is hard in such a situation. It was dangerous naïveté to assume that everyone wandering Bosnia was a hapless victim—there were plenty of restless perpetrators about who would have had little or no compunction about sticking a homemade blade between my shoulders if they thought I had the cash on me to justify it.

So it was a serious jolt when someone blurted into my ear, "I hear you speak English."

Jesus Christ! I whipped my head around, setting the beer glass down with a bang. A heavy girl with short black hair had crept up to my elbow.

"What?"

"The bartender . . . he tells me you speak English," she said.

"That's right . . . "

She turned and walked toward the door. "Come with me. There are people you should talk to."

I was in Bosanski Petrovac, eleven kilometers on the safe side of Republika Srpska. Edina, the young woman who'd rescued me from the bar, and Paul, a young British OxFam relief worker, looked on me with suspicion. A reporter who doesn't know where he is?

We didn't go far, only across the outside patio, in fact, to a Tuff-Shed-like square that held another little bar, a pool table, and some tall stools, the whole thing lit by stark red lightbulbs. They were playing horrid Bosnian music very loudly, but several people spoke English so I didn't complain. This was where international aid workers came to relax, Paul said. Relaxation was an amenity they didn't enjoy working in Drvar, just down the road, on the other side of the mountain.

"You go over that hill and there you are—a whole 'nother world," he said. "NGOs [nongovernmental organizations] seem to be the target of the month."

The picture they painted of Drvar was not pretty. It had been a Serb village until 1995, when the Croatian army (in federation with Bosnian Muslims) rolled all the way into western Bosnia during an operation that was intended only to reclaim Croatia's Krajina region from the Serbs' grasp. The momentum was powerful enough so that they just kept on going, with no one but the Serbs trying to beat back the offensive, even though Holbrooke and his gang were trying to cobble together a plan that would end the war. The Croatian offensive was, in fact, more than tacitly condoned by Holbrooke. In his memoirs, he wrote:

I told [Croatian President Franjo] Tudjman the offensive had great value to the negotiations. It would be much easier to retain at the table what had been won on the battlefield than to get the Serbs to give up territory they had controlled for several years. I urged Tudjman to take Sanski Most, Prijedor, and Bosanski Novi—all important towns that had become worldwide symbols of ethnic cleansing. If they were captured before we opened negotiations on territory, they would remain under Federation control—otherwise, it would be difficult to regain them in a negotiation.[5]

Thanks to the U.S.-approved offensive, Drvar is now another worldwide symbol of ethnic cleansing. When the Federation forces cascaded into the valley, swallowing up Bosanski Petrovac, Drvar, and even Jajce a little further to the east, most of the Serb families were driven to Banja Luka and other Serb strongholds. Drvar was completely repopulated by Croats, who were not about to welcome the old residents back with open arms.

"But don't quote me on all that," said Paul.

"Me neither," said Edina.

"Why not?" I asked. They weren't telling me anything I wasn't going to see for myself.

Paul shrugged. "Because I'm not an expert on the area," he said.

"How about you?" I asked Edina.

"Because I *am* an expert on the area," she said.

Yes, a Muslim expert, at that. Worse, a Muslim who was also a returning refugee, two things you didn't necessarily want to be in a place like Drvar, she explained. She had just moved back after spending years in Scotland, where she had fled the war, and she didn't need to be making enemies so soon. Even though the Croats and the Muslims ruled half the country together, there were no illusions about how well the two groups got along. In fact, Edina pointed out, here in Bosanski Petrovac, two Muslim soldiers had been killed after the Federation had liberated it from the Serbs in 1995. With no one left to fight, the Croats and the Muslims had turned their weapons on one another. With so many fans of Croatia around—not to mention Croatian soldiers, which was illegal under the Dayton Accords—it wouldn't do, she said, to have one's name published next to critical or embarrassing comments about those who might decide to burn your house down for the effort.

It had already happened to a lot of people, most of whom had never set eyes on a reporter. Drvar was a lost and hardened little town operating under a Lord of the Flies system of justice. Paul told me that everyone is armed, adding that it was only because of blind luck that there had only been two murders in the past month or so.[6] Most of the internationals who worked in Drvar had found somewhere else to be that night—Croatia and Romania were competing in the World Cup tournament in France, and regardless of the outcome, there was bound to be gunfire. It would not be good, they said, to try to drive into Drvar tonight. Instead, they gave me directions to the Hotel Grmac, a place they said was quiet and safe if not luxurious.

"Things are very bad there," Edina lamented. "People are terrified. There is no government, and all the Serbs who go there are afraid they'll be killed."

"Maybe SFOR should put in a base there," I suggested.

They both stared. "SFOR *has* a base there."

Six

Even in a hotel, there was no escaping the crow of a rooster at day-break. I was mostly awake anyway, having been jolted throughout the night by the lunatic with the machine gun. He was eventually joined by another reveler who seemed to have an endless supply of shotgun shells and, with the canvas of stars overhead, an equally end-less number of targets. I couldn't tell from the shooting whether Croatia had beaten Romania in the World Cup or not.

Drvar would be a small spot on any map, far from the main thor-oughfares. After getting coffee and directions, I headed south, over a tall mountain through evergreen forests. Before the previous April, only one notable thing had ever happened in Drvar: the Luftwaffe had dropped German paratroopers into the hills to kill a communist revolutionary named Tito, who was leading the antifascist, anti-Nazi revolution from a camouflaged house high up on a rocky cliff. The Germans almost succeeded—they poured withering machine gun fire into the hideout, chopping up large trees and chunks of cliff. Tito, along with some officers and his dog, escaped through a natural tun-nel in the mountainside, using ropes to climb through the dark, nar-row opening and emerging on the flat plateau on the other side of the valley. Tito's name is still spelled out in hillside shrubs on the north-ern road into town.

There was little sense of such heroics in Drvar when I arrived, though; it was just another shattered village coated in the fine dust of bad feelings and exploded bricks, cradled in the lap of a shallow mountain valley. Its citizens wandered the littered streets consumed with a vague menace and a penchant for quick and brutal violence. They were shadows of real people, flitting in and out of sight behind bullet-scarred walls and hollow homes. Only a hitchhiker seemed real, a lonely young woman looking for a ride out of town, eyes of hope turning to disappointment when she discovered the only reason for a roadside stop was the need for directions.

It took some time to find Camp Drvar, the Canadian SFOR base. Perhaps they didn't want to advertise their location; maybe they didn't expect outsiders to be looking for them. Whatever the reason, the only indication of direction came from a tiny white sign, maybe eight inches square, with a maple leaf stenciled on it. It was propped in an intersection roundabout, threatened by six-foot-high weeds that obscured a statue that must have been of some note . . . from there, a visitor had to follow rutted dirt roads through screeching marsh weeds, over a barely reconstructed footbridge, to the lonely outpost where everyone who was not a local had moved closer to the protection offered by Canadian guns. This, along with another base downtown, was the only vestige of peace evident in Drvar. It was the type of peace known to prisoners, one that comes in the lulls between violence. Drvar was a dangerous place.

"No one's in charge here. I like to call this place the wild, wild West," said Ben Jillett, a walrus-looking man with a sunburned forehead and a droopy handle-bar mustache. "And you're in Indian territory."

Jillett was a little testy. His office in town had been burned down by a mob of angry Croatians five weeks before, after they had looted and trashed the city's municipal building to get at the Serb mayor inside. The Canadian SFOR armored car that had driven to the rescue had taken only Canadian soldiers and Serb refugees to safety, leaving him stranded in a violent riot without a weapon, a memory that still made him shudder weeks later.

"How well equipped are you to deal with something like that?" I asked.

"I'm not!" he moaned.

Jillett was no refugee. He was the Canadian commander of Drvar's International Police Task Force station, which had occupied a vacant building downtown before the violence relocated it to safer environs outside Camp Drvar's gates. The IPTF had the unenviable job of re-

structuring the local police force to keep its members from terroriz-
ing and killing refugees who wanted to return to their homes. In January 1998, the State Department told Congress that the IPTF's job
would be done by July, but Jillett wasn't having much luck meeting
that deadline: The police force was atrocious, he said. There had been
three chiefs in three months, the last one kicked out for "corruption,"
hardly an unusual allegation; the previous year the police chief and
the chief of homicide investigations had both been fired for helping
burn down Serb homes.[7] While the cops waited around for a replace-
ment chief to arrive, no one was in charge except the IPTF, an organization with little authority and even less success deterring violence.
There had been fifty-three house burnings in the past two months,
culminating in the murder of two elderly Serbs, who had been beaten,
shot to death, and left in their burning home.[8] The IPTF had prodded the police into making an investigation, and they ended up arresting two suspects, the victims' next-door neighbors. But the men
were turned loose by the Croat prosecutor, who told the Croat judge
that there wasn't enough evidence to charge the Croat suspects.
Whether this was true or not was immaterial, Jillett explained. Everyone got turned loose by the prosecutor, with or without evidence. Jillett had no one to complain to about his problems except visiting reporters; the two platoons of Canadian SFOR soldiers in town
wouldn't have anything to do with him because police matters were
civilian in nature and didn't fall under SFOR's military mandate, they
argued. The only other avenue for help was through the mayor, but
he was a Serb, elected by absentee ballot by Drvar's prewar refugee
population. And the Croats took care of the mayor and many of the
people who had put him in office. Now Jillett was all alone, relegated
to a dusty shack in the scorching heat of a sand parking lot next to the
SFOR base.

Ironically enough, it was Holbrooke's Dayton Accords that had
burned down Jillett's office. Since the town had been won by Croatian forces and resided safely in the Federation half of Bosnia, displaced people were supposed to be returned to their prewar homes.
In the case of Drvar, that meant that almost everyone who had lived
there since 1995 must move out so that the prewar majority population of Serbs could return. As anyone could have predicted, that
wasn't going to happen without violence. Captain Scott Mc-
Corquedale, Camp Drvar's SFOR administrative officer, explained it
simply: "The way these people think is that they fought to take this

town during the war. They don't want to turn it over to people they see as the enemy when they had a lot of their people die and get injured for them to be here in the first place."

On April 24, 1998, at about eleven in the morning, a surly gang of drunks had gathered downtown at the municipal building to protest the return of the rightful residents, some 160 Serb-registered heads-of-household. Depending on how many people were in each family, the number of actual refugees probably numbered several hundred.[9]

The gathering got out of hand real fast despite the presence of both an SFOR unit and IPTF personnel. The crowd grew from 60 people to 600 in "literally minutes," McCorquedale said. Once they'd frothed themselves into a savage rage, the mob had rushed the building and jerked Serb mayor Mile Marcheta out of his office, pummeling him with fists, feet, and sticks until he lay still in the gutter, presumed dead. By then the thing had a life of its own, and the Croats turned against the UN building, torching the IPTF offices, the OxFam offices, and those of Impact Team International (an implementing partner of the UN High Commissioner for Refugees [UNHCR]). When the Canadians roared up to the scene in armored cars, rifles snapping warning rounds into the air, they quickly realized that they couldn't handle the situation and evacuated everyone they could to a compound in the center of town, ironically named Camp Utopia, where they huddled with the terrified refugees.

Meanwhile, the rioters burned cars belonging to international groups and just about anything else they could get their hands on. The mob collapsed the compound's outer perimeter, which was where the Serb returnees' temporary apartments were located, and the Canadians were forced to withdraw into a tight little circle, trapped in the remains of a schoolhouse that was being rocked with a hail of thrown debris. The rioters stormed the Serb apartments and looted them before setting them on fire. At the apex of the mayhem, a British helicopter throbbing fifty feet over the violence-mad crowd reported seeing a "long-barreled rifle," a sure sign that things were going downhill very fast.[10]

"We thought for sure there was going to be a firefight," said McCorquedale. But before things could get that far, the crowd dispersed when tank reinforcements ripped over the hill to evacuate the international representatives. The Serbs stayed at Camp Utopia for two days until things cooled down. Then they caught the first ride back to Republika Srpska. Only recently had they begun to trickle back under military escort, holing up in the less-damaged apartments until they could move from the ring of barbed wire into their old homes.

Ostensibly, the riot had been retaliation for another riot the day before in Derventa, where Serb residents had stoned Croat returnees trying to attend St. Mark's Day mass in a destroyed Catholic church. The violence had escalated to the point where the parishioners had to hide in the basement for six hours until a local SFOR unit could rescue them.[11]

But McCorquedale and a number of other Canadian soldiers were convinced that the fires, the riot, and the two murders several days before were connected, part of a larger politically condoned effort to make Drvar as unappealing as possible to its former residents in order to preserve its current ethnic demographics—that is, 100 percent Croatian in the town of Drvar.

"I believe that they met their political and civil aims with these incidents," McCorquedale said. "The Croatians feel like this is the frontier, this is where the war will be fought if there's another war. . . .

"I absolutely thought we were going to have to use force," he went on, looking at his hands.

There was certainly no lack of force to be used. Camp Drvar was home to two platoons of Canadian soldiers, at least four tanks, and enough ordinance and ammunition to make military enthusiasts drool. Over the hill was another rifle company, and ten minutes to the east was SFOR Strategic Reserve, a British helicopter division. You'd think that with all the resources available, such violence would never occur and that Drvar would be one of the safest places in the country for a refugee to return to—but it was never as simple as comparing hardware.

"This is where all the Serbs were living," said Captain Tom Mykytiuk, in a distinctive Canadian accent. "These are the temporary returnee barracks."

The barracks he was referring to were actually apartment buildings, standing in a loose L shape around a parking lot that the apartments shared with Camp Utopia's schoolhouse headquarters. The apartments had once been Croatian military barracks, he said, and had been vacated only months before the Serbs had moved in. The Croatian soldiers had moved to the apartment building right next door, their very presence disturbing for a number of reasons, but mainly because we weren't in Croatia and they shouldn't have been here at all. Dayton demands that all foreign forces be withdrawn.

We wandered around the parking lot to the back of the apartment/schoolhouse complex, past a field wired with trip flares and antipersonnel mines the Canadians had laid to protect the refugees—and themselves—from violent civilians. Black fire streaks stretched to the heavens from some ground floor apartments. The stairwells were enclosed in glass tubes, like a California mall, but all the glass had been kicked out by the rioters and lay on the pavement like dangerous jewelry. Trash was scattered everywhere . . . charred auto parts, the paper litter of everyday life chucked into the street as an indication that life is no longer "everyday," a wooden door that had been pried off its hinges and set aflame.

"We're pretty much back to our normal level of tension now," said Mykytiuk. "For a while there, we didn't even leave the base except for our standard patrols."

Up on the third floor of one building, a door stood ajar, but it was obvious no one lived there; the door was charred like a campfire log, the walls around it stained black from smoke. I crept forward and pushed it open . . . the apartment's hardwood floors were buckled and curled from the heat. There was a partly burned mattress, and the floor was scattered with the cinders of clothes and sheets. I started to walk in, but the translator I had borrowed from the base stopped me. "Don't go in there. You don't know if someone maybe put in a mine. To keep the Serbs away."

Out on the sidewalk, a woman maybe seventy years old stepped gingerly through the destruction carrying a big brown purse. She was on her way to the United Nations office in the next building to ask about getting an escort into town. She was a Serb who used to live in Drvar, and although she now had a place in Banja Luka in Republika Srpska, she wanted to move back. At the moment, she was running an errand for another former Drvar resident who also lived in Banja Luka and wanted her friend to see if anyone was living in her old apartment.

"But I'm not going to go over there by myself," she said with a shrug. "Too dangerous. I'm going to see, if there are people living there, if they want to trade for her apartment in Banja Luka."

The look on her face said enough about the possibility of a Croat family's accepting an apartment in the RS, so I didn't bother to ask. She gave me the same look when I asked if she felt safe with so many peacekeeping soldiers around her.

She hobbled off and we tried another building. This time, on the last apartment we rapped on, the door opened slowly. A huge woman in her sixties stood in the doorway, pouring sweat like a faucet. She invited us in for a drink of hot brandy poured from a plastic Coke bottle, assuring us that we weren't interrupting her, that she was just doing the same thing she'd been doing for the past twenty-five days, sitting at the window, looking over the tanks in the parking lot to the corner of her prewar apartment, which was visible through the thin trees dying in the heat. She was supposed to be able to move in there anytime, she said. The UNHCR had assured her that all the paper-work for reclaiming her house was in order and had been approved. But there was some problem convincing the people who had moved into it to get out. So she sat there, day after day, in a hot little cell that was completely empty except for a Sterno stove and a mattress, star-ing across the littered asphalt to the building across the way. I looked to where she was pointing. The building was bile green, and the roof was caved in from a direct artillery hit.

"But it's my home," she said. "I lived and worked here. I earned that apartment. When the Croats came, I had to move to Banja Luka. I lived for three years in Banja Luka. . . . I don't feel like a refugee . . . but when I move back into my apartment, I'll feel like a king in his palace.

"I don't care if I get shot or killed. If I die, at least I'll die in my own town. My soul will be full when I can live again in my home. I don't care if I get killed then."

Her daughter was with her, a woman about thirty-five years old, visiting from Banja Luka. She was so overpowered by the heat that she didn't bother putting a shirt on over her bra in the presence of strangers. "I'm scared for her, but it's what she wants," she said with a shrug. "I'm more worried that no one will give her the medicine she needs; she's diabetic."

The talk had gotten the older woman worked up—the sweat com-ing in a flood now—and she began belting down brandy and speak-ing quite animatedly: "This is my town and to hell with anyone who says I cannot live here. All I wait for is the UN to tell those Croats to give me back my home."

We left after choking down half a drink out of courtesy. The apart-ment was an inferno, a mixture of body odor and brandy fumes. Back out in the sunshine, the translator, who was a Serb, mused, "She says she will die for her apartment, that one with the big bomb hole. . . . I think she's a little crazy."

Seven

I wheeled through the littered streets of Drvar, under the dusty trees, past the colorless people trudging along with balled fists, until I found myself at the green apartment building with the exploded roof, the Serb refugee's home.

Across the street was a newer-looking café, although there were no customers. I spun the car into the parking lot (pulling up onto the curb again, just to fit in) and crossed the street to the apartment building.

The front doors were open . . . but the doorway was a narrow fit, like the dimensions of a coffin. The stairs were dusty with pulverized plaster, and the distinct ammonia smell of urine emanated from the darkness behind the stairwell. From somewhere up above came the refracted sound of Metallica. All the mailboxes had been ripped out, and there were two bare wires jutting from where the foyer light should have been. Like everything else in Drvar, the hallway was clogged with garbage . . . a dead rat lay flattened half out of one pile, obviously stomped by someone while digging for filth.

As I mounted the stairs, that mental buzz came back—the same one I had first felt driving through that first ethnically cleansed village the previous night, seemingly years ago. The staircase took on a life of its own, the steps in front leading to who-knows-what, the ones below leading to that beer I'd been craving and the safety that comes from not trying to know everything all at once. But I kept climbing, past the narrow second floor landing, on up to the third floor, the music getting louder until I had gone as high as possible. The roof had caved in above, raining rebar and concrete slabs onto the stairs, pieces of red tile crunching underfoot like spilled cereal.

There were two doors, one on each side. I knew that the one on the right was the one that belonged to the Serb in the apartment across the courtyard; it led to the only apartment that could be seen from her lonely perch. There was a red swastika painted on it, signifying the Ustashe, the Croatian insurgency that had sided with Nazi Germany during World War II.

This was her home, the place she'd worked her whole life to buy. It was where she'd raised the daughter who was worried about her diabetes. Now strangers lived there, people who'd earned it only by threatening to kill her and other Serbs. And as defaced as it was, as shattered as her life with the artillery hole overhead, she wanted it back for no other reason than that it was hers. It was her home. And she said she would die for it.

Tragically, if others wanted to kill her for claiming what was rightfully hers, even with two platoons of Canadian SFOR soldiers within earshot, they probably could get away with it.

2 Mission Creeps

One cannot speak about the protection of human rights with credibility when one is confronted with the lack of consistency and courage displayed by the international community and its leaders. . . . Crimes have been committed with swiftness and brutality and by contrast, the response of the international community has been slow and ineffectual. . . . The very stability of international order and the principle of civilization is at stake over the question of Bosnia. I am not convinced that the turning point hoped for will happen and cannot continue to participate in the pretense of the protection of human rights.

—Tadeusz Mazowiecki, special rapporteur
for the former Yugoslavia for the UN Commission on
Human Rights, letter of resignation in the wake of the fall
of the UN-declared "safe area," Srebrenica, July 27, 1995

One

The waiter at the café across the street from the Serb refugee's home was mean and powerful-looking, resembling Lurch from the Addams family, but he brought me a drink without delay once he saw that my car was from the motherland. I had to pay for it with kunas, Croatian currency. Fortunately, I had some left and, after some fumbling trying to sort them out from the soft wad of Bosnian dinars, handed them over with a less than hearty "Hvala," which means thank you in both Serb and Croat. But they each pronounce it differently—one of them says it like "vala," the other like "fala." I couldn't remember which was which, though, and sort of mumbled it, hoping to cover both bases at once. The waiter just walked away.

Which was a pleasant surprise. I'd been led to believe by both SFOR and IPTF that walking around without an armed bodyguard was deadly. "Everyone is armed," I'd been told, "but don't worry if you hear gunfire; these bastards are always shooting at something." In fact, I found out, the automatic fire I had heard the previous night from the hotel was indeed celebratory: Croatia had beaten Romania and had advanced to the next round of the World Cup. The Canadian soldier guarding the front gate at Camp Drvar said he had even left his barracks to see if there were any streams of tracers flying into the sky, as though he was looking for the northern lights. Nothing bad happened in Drvar (there was no one but Croats in town and there-fore no targets), but in Mostar, about fifty miles to the east, Muslims were shot at and terrorized during the festivities.[1] So much for Day-ton's dampening violent nationalism. One can hardly blame SFOR for not wanting to tangle with such people.

"How are you going to stop stuff like that?" McCorquedale had asked. "There is a limit to what the military can do. I can't point a gun at someone and order him to stop hating his neighbor."

That's certainly true. The military can't construct a happy and free government out of thin air—and anyone who's ever been in the mil-itary will tell you that you wouldn't want it to even if it could. But there are many people who believe that the military can do a whole lot more than cower in the dark and make excuses about "civilian ver-sus military" tasks.

Cowering in the dark, however, is at least a means of ensuring that the peacekeeping force won't stray from its stated task and embroil itself in side issues that may make an eventual pullout all the more difficult. SFOR was charged with keeping the enemy forces apart and preventing the outbreak of future war. Depending on your definition of war, SFOR has been a complete success. There have been no major clashes with enemy forces since the first troop transport plane touched down in Tuzla in December 1995. Led by the U.S. military, SFOR (IFOR at the time) swooped into Bosnia, erected forts and bases seemingly out of thin air, established the Zone of Separation within weeks, supervised the cantonment of heavy weapons, and continues to raid suspected illegal munitions stockpiles, seizing

weapons and ordnance on nearly a monthly basis. When I first arrived in Bosnia in 1996, on the heels of the troops, it was taken for
granted that the military would indeed use whatever means it had at
its disposal to ensure that the warring parties would comply with the
peace agreement. I remember one day Milstein returned to the house
flushed and giggly like a schoolgirl. He'd run into a U.S. tank brigade
in the RS that was a whisker away from blowing up a bunker they'd
discovered behind a restaurant. The local Serb Chetnicks had argued
futilely that the bunker was nothing more than a storage pantry for
the restaurant's dry wares. The U.S. soldiers weren't listening. They
had orders, they said, to destroy bunkers. The men had the choice of
doing it themselves or letting the tank take care of the task. No one
budged. The lieutenant in charge decided to give a count of three before he ordered a round fired into the bunker that would have taken
half the restaurant away as well. On the count of two, a woman ran
screaming out of a nearby house, yelling to the effect that the men
were idiots and that yes, of course, they would dismantle their
bunker. The soldiers supervised as it was taken apart sandbag by
sandbag. Three years into the mission, not a single U.S. fatality has
occurred because of a hostile act.[2]

This is an impressive record for any military, but it's one that
shouldn't surprise anyone: thorough fulfillment of the military aspects of the Dayton Accords is precisely the job of militarized forces,
and it was one that was almost tailor-made by the Pentagon and the
Joint Chiefs of Staff when Dayton was being drafted and the mission
goals were being outlined.[3] "This is our bread and butter, man," a
young sergeant told me in 1996. We were standing on the mined bank
of the Sava River, watching the U.S. Army Corps of Engineers build
a new permanent bridge atop one that had been practically vaporized.
"We'll be done in three days, and this sucker will be impenetrable,"
he said with the pride of a father talking about his newborn's future
football career.

But other than maintaining the status quo it had worked hard to establish, SFOR's mission all but stops there. There is a vague phrase in
the Dayton Accords mentioning that additional duties that fall beyond the military scope of the agreement can and will be conducted
by the soldiers "as needed." Naturally, that phrasing is open to interpretation, one that's never been broadened to agree with SFOR's critics that it includes such things as arresting war criminals and vigor-
ously defending the safety of returning refugees. In theory, of course,

the soldiers are committed to providing a secure environment and preventing casualties, but SFOR commanders are ever vigilant against "mission creep," a term that means doing anything that falls beyond Dayton's direct military mandate.[4] It's an interpretation of their peace agreement mission that the soldiers grudgingly agree with. In 1996, a U.S. Army captain told me that his troops had been ordered not to help the locals by handing out extra rations or providing medical care except in times of emergency. "It breaks my heart to see these starving kids begging on the side of the road," he said. "And besides, as soon as word gets out that American troops are giving out MREs (Meals Ready to Eat), we'll have kids jumping into the middle of the road to get us to stop. And the last thing we need to do is run over some villager looking for food."

Camp Drvar suffered under the same yoke, but it was jobs people want rather than food. "They are hard workers," Mykytiuk had said earlier. "The guy we have cooking today is one of the hardest-working people I've ever seen. If there was work for everybody, no one would care who lived here." As it was, he said, SFOR was the city's largest employer. As much as the citizens despised its presence, the waiting list for employment at the base was "as long as your arm," he said. On Canada Day, the troops extended the holiday to their local employees. "We're giving the Croats a half day off today," McCorquedale said. "We're going to have a little appreciation ceremony for them before the cookout, give 'em a plaque and tell them how much we appreciate their work."

He paused, a sad smile passing his face. "It's a tragedy. They're all great people, really hard workers, but as far as I know, some of them might have been out there throwing bottles at us at Camp Utopia."

"But we can't get involved in things like [creating civilian jobs] because if we did, how would we get back out?" Mykytiuk added. "We have to avoid mission creep."

"So what do you have?" he asked rhetorically. "You have a military force waiting around for a war to break out."

Two

It's quite clear that that won't happen anytime soon—the warring parties might be violence-prone, but they're not stupid. No one's going to start shelling anyone while SFOR's around. The people who are most likely to start trouble—the organizing forces behind the

April riots, for instance—are well aware of SFOR's self-imposed re-
strictions. As they're reasonably sure that all the military will do is
"threaten force," a threat that diminishes with each incident in which
angry civilians get away with ethnic cleansing on a low-intensity
scale, such occurrences are likely to happen more frequently, especially now that refugees are beginning to return in greater numbers
because some European countries, most notably Germany, have
begun expelling Bosnians and sending them back to their homeland.
It's been demonstrated that SFOR places responsibility for such civilian disturbances as midnight firebombings, murder, and mayhem on
the shoulders of the IPTF and the local power structure. But again, as
Drvar demonstrated, the local power structure is committing the
crimes.[5] Even though the Croatian soldiers living near Camp Utopia
participated in the riots, because they were dressed in civilian clothing and technically not acting in the role of conventional soldiers,
SFOR considered it a civilian disturbance. Even if they had wished to
act, the Canadians didn't have crowd control gear like tear gas, riot
shields, and batons, a fact that baffled and frustrated them because
their outpost's volatility was well known to their commanders in
Sarajevo.[6]

Responding to this criticism in a press conference in Sarajevo a few
days after the riots, SFOR representative U.S. Major Peter Clarke
told reporters:

> Riot control is not an SFOR task. We're not there as a civil disorder
> control team. . . . It is not a military matter to stop the initial incidents
> that start this. Unless you want me to put SFOR soldiers with every
> single person in Bosnia, there will always be someone who is unsuper-
> vised who could start it. Our job is to make sure that it does not esca-
> late. I think we did a pretty good job there. The situation could have got
> a lot worse. It didn't. Casualties were kept to a minimum. At the end of
> the day, the emphasis is on the civilian authorities and the people. They
> are the only people who can stop these incidents flaring up. It's their
> country. They've got to take control of their own destiny.[7]

Clarke was right: it's impossible to expect SFOR to eliminate all
threats and neutralize a country that's seen the worst bloodshed and
population displacement in Europe since World War II. It's hardly
feasible to expect SFOR to stand armed guard at the doorstep of each
and every returning family and to blow holes in every drunken punk

who can hurl a rock. However, if the riots have been politically and militarily coordinated, as the Canadians suspect, it might be safe to declare Dayton a failure because it's obvious that SFOR will do nothing in such a situation except allow the mayor to get killed (as everyone thought he had) and the refugees to be run out of town. Expecting other organizations like the IPTF to succeed in their missions in the face of such obstacles is futile.

Being engaged with an army intent on masking its aggression as civil unrest is a sticky matter, the same one faced by the Italians in Grbavica two years before. McCorquedale pointed at the surrounding hills overlooking his base:

> This is a lot like Northern Ireland here. We could go out and dominate this valley if we had to; we've got a much higher level of assets than they do. But think about who we're going to fight. Our most likely enemy would be terrorists—it'd just be some guy up in the hills with a hunting rifle who decides to take a shot at us. . . . As a professional soldier, I want to face a threat with my aggression. There's a definite effect on morale. *Hopelessness* would be a reasonable adjective in this case.

When Major Clarke faced reporters after the riots, he punctuated nearly every statement with the qualification that it's the people of the country who need to work harder to get along, and if they won't, well, there's really not much else that can be done. Short of throwing everyone into a dungeon, there's little more that can be expected of even the most skilled military organization if people are determined to rape and pillage.

Clarke was not alone in his assessment. The sentiment is a favorite among international peacekeepers determined to absolve themselves of responsibility—and to justify not doing anything—by pointing to the Bosnians and saying, "If only they'd stop fighting, we'd have peace." Nicole Szulc of the Organization for Security and Cooperation in Europe (OSCE) put it in nearly those terms at the same press conference when she said, "It is the responsibility of the people who run this country to make sure that laws are obeyed and people can live in peace."[8] Indeed, the Dayton Accords make it clear that the responsibility for carrying out the agreement's provisions falls to the signing parties, not outsiders. But the people who drafted the peace plan weren't stupid, either: they realized that if it were as easy as simply demanding compliance with a list of tasks, there would hardly have been the need for such deep international involvement in the first place. If it were only a matter of telling the Serbs, Croats, and Muslims to shape up, we wouldn't have an SFOR or an IPTF or a High Representative or a slew of other acronymed organizations in the country to compel compliance. The last time the people leading the three nations were given the sole responsibility of making sure that their citizens could live in peace according to the rule of law, more than seventy of them ended up being summoned to The Hague for crimes against humanity. Forty-nine of them were still at large as of March 13, 1998.[9]

But it's an easy way out to blame the military's failures on the people of the country: clearly the three ethnicities do not like one another and will flaunt Dayton as much as they can get away with, particularly if the people indicted by the International Criminal Tribunal for the former Yugoslavia—a collection of judges in the Netherlands—are allowed to roam freely, spreading the same message of hatred, fear, and paranoia that instigated the fighting in the first place. By insisting that the international community—in particular, the military—is doing all it can do and seeing limited success, SFOR's commanders are washing their hands in advance of Dayton's failure. They're also promoting the attitude that Bosnians are all criminally insane murderers who, even though they look identical, are slaughtering one another because of ethnic crimes, real or imagined, that happened more than ten generations ago. Such people are beyond help, they argue. Being passionate about history is one thing, but to burst suddenly into a violent killing frenzy that knows no moral bounds because some Serbian prince named Lazar failed to defend his homeland against invading Turkish hordes in 1389, well, that just points to a serious defect in the people in that part of the world, some serious weirdness we had no idea existed. SFOR might be powerful, but it can't perform miracles . . .

This argument is easy to make because there's certainly no lack of evidence to support it. The Bosnian war (and the related one in Croatia that preceded it) was conducted at a level of brutality that made it seem as if it were happening on another planet between species that only superficially resembled humanity. But as a war, it wasn't terribly more brutal than World War II and was far smaller in scale. And it was probably less horrific than the killing frenzy happening at the same time in Rwanda. The difference was television. Never before have audiences had the opportunity to see the effects of full-blown conventional warfare with the bluntness provided by satellite video feed. People whose only experience with war comes from the mind of Oliver Stone were appropriately stunned. This is the very reason the U.S. military heavily restricted media access to the battlefields of Kuwait during Desert Storm. As one unidentified Pentagon official reportedly explained when justifying the censorship of some footage, "If we let people see that kind of thing, there would never again be any war."

There were no such filters on the death in Bosnia, especially during the three-and-one-half-year siege of Sarajevo, an event that was unsurpassed in reportorial drama: a thoroughly modern metropolis that had once hosted the Winter Olympic Games was reduced to piles of masonry that used to be buildings and a population of mostly unarmed citizens who lived in cellars like cave dwellers. From the hills above town, Serb gunners poured rockets and shells into the downtown high-rises and pounded the streets with tank rounds. None of the people could leave for food or water without taking their lives in their hands; snipers overlooked the city, their main targets civilians.[10] The siege was the perfect icon for the war, the seat of multicultural harmony under fire from former countrymen whose only goal was the complete eradication of anyone who wasn't a Serb.

Then there were the concentration camps. There were dozens of them, but the ones around Prijedor, north of Banja Luka, became the most infamous, the same way everything else does in a television culture: through video images. The pictures of starving, battered Bosnian prisoners behind razor wire at Tronopolje—the "good camp" compared to its counterpart at Omarska up the road—were enough to send sane people over the edge. The prisoners were like walking dead, identical to ghostly images from Auschwitz and Dachau, figures of torture we'd all assumed were from some dark and worse past. The tales that emerged from the camps were even more stunning, nearly to the point of anesthetization because they pointed to an insanity that almost no one could fathom. A Muslim prisoner from Omarska was forced by Serb guards to castrate another prisoner with his teeth; others told of their captors' hammering nails into prisoners' heels, threatening them with death if the nails were removed.[11] One prisoner died anyway from the pain. One guard would nonchalantly ask a captive which of his eyes or testicles he liked best. The loser was gouged out or ripped off. Other prisoners were forced to strip naked and lap up puddles of motor oil like dogs while the guards leaped onto their backs until they were dead. The torture wasn't perpetrated by just the soldiers. Local Serb residents of Prijedor would go to Omarska, a former iron mine ringed with a heavy steel fence, after work for a night of drinking and torture, regular-looking men dabbling in this hideous form of recreation.[12]

And of course, there was Srebrenica, the little UN-declared "safe area" bloated with Muslim refugees fleeing Serb bullets from areas all around. The death of the town acted as another icon of the war, one that exposed both the extremes the Serbs were willing to go to and the utter uselessness of the United Nations. General Ratko Mladic, the military leader of Serb forces in Bosnia, began shelling Srebrenica just five months before the Dayton Accords were initialed, an act that was a middle finger in the face of international interventionists. Srebrenica had been a designated "safe area" since 1993; that is, it was supposed to be free from hostilities.[13] Thus it was a magnet for everyone within fleeing distance. When the Serb forces started their assault, nearly 30,000 people were crammed into a village that had an original population of perhaps 4,000. Full-scale shelling began on July 6, 1995, with so many detonations happening at once it was impossible for the UN to count. Slowly and methodically, the Serbs advanced, capturing UN observation posts and eventually taking more than forty Dutch soldiers hostage. The Dutch continually asked for close air support from headquarters, but the requests were consistently denied by UN officials who either didn't realize the urgency of the situation or were hesitant to use force, concerned that air strikes would anger the Serbs and escalate the situation. By the time limited, pathetic air strikes were ordered, the Serb soldiers were literally walking into Srebrenica. The Dutch and the refugees evacuated to the hamlet of Potocari about a kilometer to the north, but by then, there was nothing the UN could do. The Serbs took the uniforms off their Dutch prisoners and stole their vehicles. Chetnicks in UN outfits wandered among the civilians huddling inside the barbed wire, sometimes grabbing women to cart off and rape. The peacekeepers did nothing but stand and watch, reduced to impotent bystanders. When people began to realize that some of the soldiers they were relying on to help them were actually Serbs, hysteria broke out. Seven people hanged themselves inside the compound, using scarves or other items of clothing. One of them was a fifteen-year-old girl who had been raped.[14]

Meanwhile a column of 12,000 to 15,000 men and boys were trying to escape through heavily mined woods to Bosnian Federation territory fifty kilometers away. Very few survived the journey. The Serbs had the column virtually surrounded the entire time, cutting it into smaller and smaller sections with surprise ambushes in which they used mortars, antiaircraft machine guns, and grenade launchers to scatter the survivors into the woods. One survivor told his tale to a Human Rights Watch/Helsinki researcher:

> We walked for about twenty-four hours. Then our column began to di-
> minish because people were breaking off and running into the woods
> and mountains individually and in little groups. Along the way, we saw
> bodies and wounded people and a few who had just lost their minds.
> We encountered our first ambush at Nova Kasaba. We were in the
> woods where our column had to stop and leave our wounded. The
> Chetnicks started shelling the woods with mortars and calling for us to
> come out and give up. They told us that they would send the elderly to
> their families and that they would keep the younger men for exchanges.
> When we realized that we were surrounded, people from the column
> started killing themselves, committing suicide; some threw themselves
> on top of grenades, others shot themselves in the mouth and others
> were shooting themselves in order to wound themselves in the hope
> that maybe their injury would somehow save them after they were cap-
> tured by the Chetnicks. We ended up surrendering.[15]

There followed a week of horror and massacre that's all but impossible to comprehend. Eight thousand Muslims were eventually classified as "disappeared," most of them underground after having been systematically executed. Some were simply shot dead, others were forced to dig their own graves before being blasted into them, and still others were terribly alive when bulldozers shoved tons of dirt over their heads. When asked if the fall of Srebrenica represented the greatest failure yet of the UN's mission in Bosnia, Secretary-General Boutros Boutros-Ghali told reporters, "No, I don't believe this represents a failure. You have to see if the glass is half full or half empty. We are still offering assistance to the refugees . . . and we have been able to maintain the dispute within the borders of former Yugoslavia."[16] U.S. Speaker of the House Newt Gingrich had a very different view, calling the fall of Srebrenica the "worst humiliation for the Western democracies since the 1930s."[17]

What made things all the more difficult for foreigners to grasp was the astonishingly normal appearance of most of the combatants.

More than once I overheard people looking at a newspaper photo-graph and asking, "That's what a Serb looks like?" Hearing such stories, one can't help but picture bearded hillbillies with red eyes and the crude features of a cartoon villain dressed in a suit of armor pillaging with flaming arrows and blood-soaked long swords. But the Serbs were professional soldiers—even though they didn't conduct themselves as such—with training in the most modern of conventional weaponry.

Yes, international observers seemed to suggest, there's something very wrong with those people. But whatever it is, we forcefully concluded, usually in front of the bathroom mirror, you won't find any of that in *me*.

And the more willing people are to believe that, the easier it is for SFOR to get away with a shrug, saying that there's little that can be done. Of all the things in the Bosnia of 1998, the fact that this international attitude hasn't wavered an iota is perhaps the most astonishing. And the most damaging.

Three

If anything, understanding of the Bosnian war suffered from simplified overanalysis, purified by the "ancient Balkan hostilities" theory that originated with the combatants themselves. There is no simple explanation for this theory because it changes with each person you ask about it. But in simple terms, it goes something like this: the Serbs have always hated the Croats because they're really Nazis at heart. Thousands of Serbs were killed by Croatian Ustashe murderers at the Jasanovac concentration camp near Zagreb during World War II, and when Croatia declared independence along with Slovenia in 1991, Milosevic mobilized the Yugoslavian National Army (JNA) to fight for Croatian Serbs living in the Krajina region claiming that he feared that they would be targeted for extermination. The Croats hated the Serbs because they were aligned with Russia and communism and they were enemies during World War II. The Bosnians hated them both because there was never any telling, from one century to the next, which of them was going to invade Bosnia at the behest of their imperial leaders in Vienna to the west and Byzantium to the east. And both Serbs and Croats hated Bosnians because they succumbed to the Turks so easily in the fourteenth century, converting to Islam without so much as a fight. The Turks, of course, were the hated enemies of everyone: they had paved over the Serbs at Kosovo in 1389, and for nearly three centuries, they had kept warfare alive at the Croatian border ... where, just to add another twist to the maze, they had fought the Croatian Serbs in Krajina, as opposed to the Croatian Croats, refugees from Kosovo who'd outrun the Turks across the Balkans to join an ad hoc Croatian militia hastily organized by an Austrian general to keep the Islamic hordes at bay. In the current war, all of this ugly, tangled history was embraced and borne out by the combatants themselves: Croatian soldiers decorated their jeeps with swastikas and called themselves Ustashe; the Serbs began calling themselves Chetnicks after the World War II guerrillas who had sometimes fought Tito's partisans and sometimes fought the Allies, depending on what deals they could cut at any given time; and the Bosnians fulfilled everyone's worst stereotypes by appealing to Islamic nations like Iran for weapons and mujahideen guerrillas.

This sordid history just couldn't be reconciled, the "ancient hostilities" theorists argued. The strict rule of communism that Tito had imposed after World War II had done nothing but keep a lid clamped firmly over a pot boiling with hatred and tension, one that was bound to explode given enough time and the right combination of circumstances, they said. Tito had tried to eradicate ethnic strife by making it illegal; in the fashion of the Kremlin, if he needed to quash a pocket of Croatian nationalism, for instance, he would also punish the Serbs for no reason other than to be "fair." This worked about as well to foster interethnic cooperation as anyone who's ever had siblings and lazy parents might suspect. The people of former Yugoslavia are preconditioned to violence; nothing can be done to help them. The most we can hope for is to contain the violence and let it run its course.

There's a ring of craziness to this theory. For one thing, the history of the Balkans may be violent, but it's not any more twisted and atrocity-filled than that of other countries, the United States included. The other thing that isn't unique about Bosnia, Serbia, and Croatia, but that seems to have been greatly overlooked, is that it also had demagogic leaders who used these valid strifes and tensions to spark a war that had far less to do with long-sought revenge than it did with maintaining and consolidating political power.

The question that remains is whether either the Dayton Accords or the 33,000-man-strong SFOR will lead to lasting peace or will simply provide a lengthy and expensive cease-fire.

That's a difficult question to answer, and it drives right to the heart of the matter. It's obviously within the ability of a multinational military force to stop outright warfare . . . but can it stop hatred and the insidious effects of nonstop propaganda? That doesn't seem likely, since the factors that led to warfare in the first place—hypernationalism on all fronts perpetrated by three ethnic leaders who each has the sole desire of consolidating and maintaining political power—have remained more or less intact even though the fighting has stopped. Ending a war, but leaving the leaders that began the war in power, de facto or otherwise, is merely reactionary, like treating a child for parental abuse, but returning her to her parents after the hospital visit. Of course, forcing a coup d'état is less than democratic (although not unheard of in U.S. foreign policy); it would be far preferable if the people of Croatia, Bosnia, Republika Srpska, and Serbia elected less radical leaders on their own. Dayton allowed for this— but without the vigorous assistance of SFOR, elections aren't likely to work very democratically.

Listening to the spin doctors tell it, an outsider would think that the multinational troops were delivering babies and cooking dinner afterward for the people of Bosnia. Robert Gelbard, Special Representative of the President and the Secretary of State for Implementation of the Dayton Accords, told Congress in January 1998 that SFOR was producing "tremendous results" on the ground, working in partnership with the civilian implementation organizations. Whether the results are "tremendous" or not is debatable, but there are indeed some positive results. Bloodshed, at least on its previous scale, has stopped. Elections, though seriously crippled with fraud, corruption, and the continuing influence of war criminals, are hobbling along more-or-less according to schedule. In 1997, there was a victorious split in political ranks in Republika Srpska when moderate politicians wrested official party control from former Bosnian Serb leader and indicted war criminal Dr. Radovan Karadzic. The new politicians moved the RS capital from Pale to Banja Luka. Many of the houses around the country are being repaired. Unemployment dropped from 90 percent in 1996 to 50 percent by the end of 1997, and average wages quadrupled over the same period of time.[18]

But it's a loose peace that's prone to serious problems, as Drvar demonstrates. No one has bothered to keep track of how many acts of violence, arson, intimidation, false arrest, and death there have been since the signing of the Dayton Accords, but it's safe to say that there

have been far more than should have been expected with such an impressive military force in such a small country with an international
mandate to do everything in its power to keep the peace. The current
situation is well summed up in the opening paragraph of Amnesty International's 1998 Annual Report on Bosnia-Hercegovina:

> More than a million refugees and displaced persons were unable to re-
> turn to their homes because of continuing human rights violations.
> Scores of people, including prisoners of conscience and possible pris-
> oners of conscience, were detained on account of their nationality. Most
> were detained without charge or trial. Dozens of people charged with
> humanitarian law violations received unfair trials before courts in
> Bosnia-Hercegovina; trials of people from minorities within the sepa-
> rate political entities were also unfair. The whereabouts of more than
> 19,000 people, many of whom had "disappeared" in the custody of the
> police or armed forces, remained unknown. More than 100 people were
> ill-treated by police, and attacks on members of minorities appeared to
> be carried out with official acquiescence. At least one person was un-
> lawfully killed by police. Scores of war crimes suspects remained at
> large.[19]

A brief sampling of incidents in the first six months of 1998 offers
a little more clarity to those general observations: in April 1998 alone,
in addition to the incidents in Derventa and Drvar, there were several
other notable acts of violence. A bomb exploded in an abandoned
house in Velika Bukovica near Travnik just up the road from Drvar.
Two Bosnian Croats were injured; they were visiting the town to see
if they wanted to return to their prewar homes. Five Bosnian Serbs
were wounded by a hand grenade in a village near Doboj during a
confrontation with returning refugees. That incident led to an illegal
roadblock, which was later dismantled. In Mostar, it was business as
usual, with observers reporting seven fires, eight explosions, and several stoning incidents since the end of March. And in Zepce, the Social Democratic Party's municipal branch chairman, Faruk Hruskic,
and four party members were injured when someone opened fire on
them as they sat in an outdoor café.[20]

The Office of the High Commissioner for Human Rights attrib-
uted this troubling record to increased refugee returns, noting that of
the nearly 2 million displaced Bosnians, several hundred thousand of
them had been able to return home successfully—aid organizations

quickly put the damper on that good news, however, by pointing out that only about 30,000 had returned to areas in which they're now the minority and therefore at greater risk.[21] But with European countries beginning to kick out Bosnians seeking asylum, the returns are anything but voluntary in many cases. And with incidents like the Drvar riots fresh in everyone's mind, questions are being asked about what SFOR is going to do now that it's become obvious that clashes between returnees and the people they find living in their homes seem inevitable.

The answer from SFOR is "not much." Remember, riots, burnings, and lootings are matters for the police, not the army, to handle. It's a self-imposed Catch-22: mission success is defined as the time when SFOR can pull out, leaving Bosnia a stable country whose government is based on the rule of law and democratic elections. People will be able to live anywhere they want to regardless of their ethnicity because security is guaranteed by a democratic, multiethnic police force committed to the protection of human rights.

The hitch in this plan is that if any of the above can be reasonably expected to happen, the people who planted the seeds of hatred in the first place must be flushed from the country: the war criminals. And until very recently (more on this in Chapter 5), apprehending war criminals was considered mission creep. Therefore, despite many people's best efforts, the police forces remain corrupted, refugees are terrified of returning home, and the rule of law and the results of elections are meaningless. So there's no end in sight for SFOR's mission, which was extended into 1999 for those very reasons.

Four

One need only look at the IPTF to see the immediate, firsthand results of this conundrum. Undersupported Jillett, in his shabby cabin in the middle of a free-fire zone, is doomed to failure. His problems—and the problems of people like him—are myriad, not the least of them being a thorough lack of respect. If people who are determined to disrupt peace and flaunt the Dayton Accords don't fear SFOR, why should they fear something far more benign, like the IPTF? This was a rhetorical question raised by Jillett himself as we stood in the sun under a Canadian flag that seemed to have died of heatstroke. Jillett was pouring out his soul, mostly voluntarily.

"Everyone on the police force is a criminal," he griped. SFOR does nothing for him. All he has to go by is a cryptic, but simple-sounding sentence or two from the Dayton Accords: the IPTF is charged with "monitoring, observing and inspecting law enforcement activities and facilities . . . advising law enforcement personnel and forces [and] training law enforcement personnel."[22] Interpreted, this means that the IPTF is supposed to ensure that police officers will respect human rights and protect the return of refugees. The IPTF also has to make sure no war criminals serve on the force and to renew civilians' confidence in their boys in blue. These goals won't even begin to be reached until Jillett can hire Serbs on the Drvar police force so that the refugees will have someone to complain to other than people who'd rather see them dead, but in the third year of the peace agreement, he's having a tough time finding volunteers. Maybe some will come next week, he muses. Or the week after. No one's sure.

In the likely event that the IPTF discovers human rights violations happening within the police ranks, its responsibility is equally clear: "When IPTF personnel learn of credible information concerning violations of internationally recognized human rights or fundamental freedoms or of the role of law enforcement officials or forces in such violations, they shall provide such information to the Human Rights Commission . . . the International Tribunal for the Former Yugoslavia or to other appropriate organizations."[23]

Right. In fact, Jillett said, he was working on a report then, one he had to fax off to the appropriate organizations, detailing his near-death experiences and his utter disbelief that no one had been killed during the riot. Therefore, there was no time to talk, none at all, he said, as he proceeded to spend the next half hour telling me all his troubles.

And what troubles they were . . . I could hardly blame him for his near-hysteria; of all the things that are impotent about the Dayton Accords thanks to SFOR, the IPTF seems to be the most flaccid of them all. The idea behind it is a sound one—send in cops from NATO countries to teach the local police how to enforce the law—but it was born from the assumption that Bosnia's complexities could be solved through bureaucracy. The first flaw is that the IPTF personnel lack the one thing that everyone in Bosnia understands: weapons. The second is that the organization is independent of SFOR, so it can't appeal to the military for help in carrying out its duties. The third is that the only thing it can use to intimidate—a report to the "appropriate organizations"—is the adult equivalent of tattling, with more-or-less the same effect: the organization being reported to rarely does anything about the reported wrongdoing, at least not anything that has lasting merit. But the nail in the coffin is that troublemakers are smart enough to realize how suicidal it would be for them to attack civilians and continue ethnic cleansing using military means . . . therefore, they seem to have infiltrated the ranks of the police force to do it under a "civilian" umbrella that ensures they won't cross paths with international troops.

The situation with the police is by no means unique to Drvar. In late April 1997, two buses full of an ethnic mixture of refugees came to the town of Brcko near the northern border of Croatia under United Nations escort. The refugees on the buses were visiting to see if they wanted to return to their former homes, to cautiously walk around their old streets to get a sense of the type of animosity they might have to endure, and to see if there was anyone living in their houses, if in fact they were still habitable. They didn't even need to disembark to have the answers to these questions: Serbs who'd moved to Brcko stoned the buses before they even came to a halt. Off to the side, watching the attack with bemused interest, as if watching two dogs fight over a scrap of food, were several Brcko police, who did nothing. IPTF, perhaps threatening a report to the "appropriate organizations," asked the police to intervene and keep the crowd at bay, which had by then grown to a legitimate mob of about 130 angry people. Instead, as the UN hosts eyed the situation and wisely called for a retreat, the police directed a local transit bus to pass in front of the lead UN vehicle . . . a bus that was barely moving, inching along foot by foot, while the mob took advantage of the situation to continue pelting the stranded, terrified passengers with anything at hand. The subsequent report filed by the IPTF noted that the police had been notified of the trip and had given approval and an assurance of safety. The attack, the report noted, was most likely an organized ambush.

In that case, four cops were reprimanded. Their pay was cut by 30 percent for three months, and six civilians were charged with participation in the stoning. But when the IPTF appealed to the Republika Srpska minister of the interior seeking further disciplinary action, it received no response.[24]

In Jajce, just up the road from Drvar, the police force is so inadequate as to be nonexistent. In a six-day period in August 1997, between 400 and 550 Bosnian returnees were forcibly evicted from their homes. In fact, there was a string of late-night arsons and broad-daylight acts of violence by Bosnian Croats against the returning civilians. In that one-week period, the IPTF recorded twenty arsons and the murder of a Muslim who was shot dead and then set on fire. After a torturous investigation, the chief was dismissed, and one of the deputies was demoted to a nonsupervisory position for one year. Other officers indicted by the IPTF report were docked 20 percent of their pay for three months.[25]

The tales go on, one of the most blatant examples of the police continuing to carry the flag of ethnic cleansing occurring in February 1997 in Mostar. A procession of several hundred Bosnian Muslims from the east side of the city marched through Croat territory in the west to visit a cemetery during the celebration of Bajram, a Muslim religious holiday. They were promptly stopped by police at the "border" of the Croat half of the city and warned that things would get ugly if they decided to continue. They continued, nevertheless, at which point the police themselves, aided by plainclothes officers, started whipping the marchers with batons. Even though the unarmed civilians began to retreat, the police opened fire into the crowd, killing one and wounding twenty. The violence in western Mostar continued throughout the day and night, with human rights organizations recording ninety-one incidents of violence between Muslims and Croats, including a series of forced evictions.

The alphabet soup of international organizations overseeing the implementation of the Dayton Accords was horrified and acted relatively firmly. Letters of recommendation and reports flew about Europe in a tizzy of incredulous outrage. The UN Secretary-General sent a letter to the Security Council demanding that the chief of Mostar police be replaced by an outside professional police officer, and every international implementation agency with a finger in the Bosnian pie signed a letter to the IPTF and the Human Rights Coordinator of the Office of Human Rights demanding a full investigation. With such a reaction, you would think the police officers involved would have been hanged in the public square for their involvement in the violence and the death of an unarmed civilian.

But the international community obviously has little to do with the local system of justice. Five cops were fired from the force, but they were immediately granted licenses to carry personal firearms. The Office of the High Representative, another United Nations concern, which oversees implementation of Dayton's civilian aspects such as the IPTF, dealt a blow to three other officers by denying them the ability to get travel visas out of the country. Three others got suspended jail sentences. One was transferred to other duties within the police force. No charges were ever brought for the shooting or the forced evictions.[26]

So the IPTF's challenge of reinstilling confidence in the local cops is not only uphill but overhanging. This situation is compounded by the fact that the IPTF force is woefully understaffed. There were just over 2,000 IPTF officers from forty-two countries as of March 4, 1998, with oversight of police forces several times that. Only 119 IPTF officers are human rights monitors responsible for identifying and reporting abuses by the police, even though this is one of the main priorities of the IPTF mission. In November 1997, then–Special Representative of the Secretary-General Kai Eide told reporters at a press conference that the IPTF is "to ensure that each and every citizen of Bosnia and Hercegovina will have a democratic police that serves the public without discrimination and which is not an instrument of individual politicians or political parties. The most important of IPTF's goals is to see that human rights are being respected without regard to ethnic or religious belongings."[27] This is an absurd task, given the reported evidence that it's the police themselves who are committing, or allowing to be committed, the majority of recorded human rights abuses since the signing of the Dayton Accords, and given the fact that most IPTF personnel couldn't tell a human rights violation if they were ethnically cleansed themselves. When investigators from Human Rights Watch asked several IPTF monitors if they could define a human rights violation, the investigators reported:

We received responses ranging from shrugs to "everybody knows what that means" to "every case is a human rights case" but where only one monitor was aware of Operational Bulletin 0001, which describes "high profile violations" and refers monitors to human rights instruments which define various human rights. The experience of a Human Rights Watch researcher demonstrates the consequences of this lack of clarity on the effectiveness of the work of the IPTF. The researcher made several attempts over several months in 1997 to relay information to the IPTF regarding human rights violations allegedly committed by local police officers. This information was reported to Human Rights Watch by individuals in the course of interviews. However most of the IPTF monitors the researcher approached were completely unprepared to accept information gathered from victims about alleged police abuses, writing the information down on tiny scraps of paper and having to be repeatedly reminded to take the names of local police officers involved in the incidents.[28]

Five

Obviously, it's not the military's responsibility, even in the broadest interpretation of its Dayton mandate, to sort out all of these problems. But the document's authors were right to call it a "framework": consider it the frame of a new house, with each provision being a different load-bearing wall. Free and fair elections would be one wall, for instance, and the return of refugees another. A democratic police force would be the roof, and the arrest of war criminals would be the concrete foundation. SFOR is the main contractor in charge of making sure its subcontractors do the work properly. The subcontractors, of course, are the signatories to the agreement. And their employees—the carpenters, plumbers, and electricians—are the people of Bosnia themselves. But looking at the house that's been built so far, one would think that the construction workers are both drunk and retarded. No one seems to follow the blueprint, and the different subcontractors' employees constantly sabotage each others' work or begin construction on new rooms and different wings that aren't in the plans. Also, there doesn't seem to be any organization at all ... they've started raising the walls before they've even dug the hole for the foundation. And when the people who are supposed to live in the finished product—the wives and children of the workers—complain to the contractor, they're greeted with a shrug. "I'm not a carpenter, lady. If I went in there and started nailing boards for them, I'd never get out of here. . . . "

At the conclusion of the now-infamous Drvar press conference, *Washington Post* reporter Colin Soloway asked the question that sums up Bosnia's current situation perfectly:

For as much as we've been griping about SFOR's response, in a way, the fact that SFOR had to become involved (by evacuating refugees) signals a failure of political and civilian leadership, both on the local side and from the international community in this. I mean, the civilian administration in Drvar is majority Serb. Milo [*sic*] Marceta is the mayor of the executive council, majority Serb. The majority of the council members are Serb. Why were conditions in Drvar not such that . . . there was not a police force which could be seen to actually be protecting all the citizens of Drvar? Why were Croatian police involved in the cleansing of Serbs from the villages around Drvar Saturday night, according to UNHCR reports? I'm just curious, you know; have we reached the limits in terms of the powers that the international community is willing to use now? Have you reached the limits of those powers? Because what more can you do in Drvar? Who else can you fire? What—you know, I'm just curious—what options remain open to the international community, other than having SFOR shoot people?

Aisling Byrne, a spokesperson for the Office of the High Representative, responded, "Well, I think I've already made the essential points that we think are important in this respect. We do not want to look at the events in Drvar as the end of any process. Everything will continue. The return plans remain the same. The commitment to multiethnic administrations and police forces remain the same, although they're not within our direct mandate."

"The tactics don't seem to be working, do they?" Soloway asked.[29]

3 On the Road

It will have blood, they say; blood will have blood.

—Shakespeare, *Macbeth*

One

Of all the fears I had about Bosnia, driving on its roads wasn't one of them. Until I actually started doing it. Navigating Zagreb had been hard enough: I had been duly warned of its perils by a British UN officer who had directed me to the press office. "These people simply can *not* drive," he said gravely. "If you go too slow, they'll pass you regardless of where you are. If you go too fast, you'll come around the bend and meet up with someone passing from the other direction. Your options are crash or go off the road. More people die from car crashes these days than from mine injuries. Be careful."

He was right to warn me: beyond Zagreb the autobahn fed right into the type of road I was doomed to travel for the remainder of the journey: a narrow ribbon of crumbling asphalt that was barely wide enough for two cars abreast, much less the dense traffic of cargo trucks that are constructed more of lumber than of steel, buses that look like something that was just pried off the *Titanic,* and horse-drawn wagons carrying four-story haystacks. Of course, there are other obstacles, such as steep mountains, shoulders seeded with PMA-2 antipersonnel land mines, random police checkpoints that always seem to be located at the end of a patch of road-top gravel on a blind curve, sudden narrow business districts springing from the hill-

71

sides as if from a children's pop-up book, and a motley collection of pedestrians in various stages of fatigue-induced dementia staggering in the roadway . . . usually leading a herd of goats and hens and carrying a stack of 2-by-4s. All this is navigated at breakneck speeds and a thorough disregard for safety and curves.

The rules of the road are simple: do anything you want, but try to avoid getting killed. You drive as fast as reasonable to keep the lunatics behind you off your back, scanning the stretch of pavement ahead to provide some latitude for the reflexes to jerk the car between gaping holes and shabby patchwork, constantly monitoring the oncoming traffic for crazies rounding the bend at 150 kilometers an hour in your lane . . . and soon enough you come whaling up behind a two-ton cargo truck that seems to be going backward in a cloud of black smoke, struggling to climb a 2 percent grade. You lean out into the oncoming lane without easing up at all, praying for even a marginal opening because there's a column of speeding BMWs four inches from your rear bumper. If you feel immortal, which you must in order to get anywhere, you fling the car out to pass, drop it into second gear, and stomp on the gas, eyes bulging, staring at the fifty feet of pavement remaining in sight before the ninety-degree left-hand turn directly ahead. But even safely back in your lane with the truck now long gone, there's no cooling it . . . everyone following you has passed as well, and the driver behind is so close you can see your reflection in his sunglasses through the rearview mirror. Even tapping on the brakes now would cause a rearguard panic that would result in a cartwheeling loss of control, smoking tires, and maybe one of those high silent plunges out into space through the right-hand guardrail. So you whip the car into the turn, praying that the frame can withstand the torque and that the tires won't explode into little bits of showering rubber. And right at the apex of the curve, you notice someone's passing *you*.

Yes . . . by the time I left Drvar for Sarajevo, I'd gotten used to this kind of driving. But I spared nothing trying to avoid the potholes. I knew firsthand what they were capable of doing to a car.

In 1996, after watching IFOR and the Serbs in Grbavica get the Dayton Accords off on the wrong foot, I was riding back to Tuzla in the small green Lada Niva with *Soldier of Fortune* correspondent Mark Milstein and photographer Jim Lowney. Milstein was at the wheel, barreling us through the night at a consistent 120 kph. There was no traffic at that hour . . . but it was nighttime, and Milstein had worked in Bosnia long enough to know what that meant. The only people wandering in the dark were those with no reason to fear it. After a full weekend of exhaustive work, we didn't fit into that category, so we took no chances poking slowly through the night, giving anyone lurking in the woods the chance to hustle into the road to stop us at gunpoint. Even though the Dayton Accords were ostensibly in effect, we didn't want to be the experiment to see if the Chetnicks were taking it seriously. So we banged along a road that hadn't even begun to be repaired by the U.S. Army Corps of Engineers. In some places, entire sections of asphalt had been washed away and there was nothing but uneven patches of red clay dirt. The driving was tense, but it was a normal tension that was like a Caribbean vacation compared to what we'd just been through in Sarajevo the previous three days. We were all tired. So maybe Milstein wasn't paying the best attention . . .

"Shit!" The Niva jerked to the left and my head went into the glass of the passenger door with a wet smack. We had missed a bomb crater by inches, but now we were in the wrong lane going into a right-leaning curve at high speed. Milstein wrenched the truck back to the right. "Did you see the size of that hole?"

He was looking at me instead of the road . . . and I was staring at another hole, twice as big, rolling into the headlight beams. We were still going 100 kph. There wasn't even time to scream. *Ka-bam!* Milstein later said he thought that we'd hit a mine; the whole truck pitched forward to the left, and a shower of white sparks bounced across the hood. The savage grind of metal on asphalt was the only sound for the next fifty yards as Milstein locked the wheel, trying to keep us from sliding off the road and into the trees. We came to a rest on the side of the highway, up to the front bumper in soft, wet mud. Milstein turned off the engine.

This wasn't the first accident we'd had. A few days earlier, we hit an American M1-A1 Abrams tank on an ice-covered road in RS. Damage was slight, just a few shattered headlights and a bent grill. Milstein had looked at me then with a smile, "That could have been bad. RS is the last place you want to get stuck."

Indeed . . . and there we were. Stuck. The damage was serious this time. The hole had sheared the wheel joint completely off, and the tire on the driver's side was nearly on its side, twisted ninety degrees from where it should have been and sucked under the frame, sinking steadily into the mud.

"Great," Lowney said. The woods were still home to paramilitary guerrillas; just before we hit the crater, Milstein had pointed out an abandoned plywood shack that had been a Chetnick roadblock only a few weeks before.

We weren't quite sure what to do. We briefly entertained the idea of trying to rig a repair ourselves, an idea that was killed quickly when we tried lifting the front end of the vehicle out of the mud. It didn't budge. So we waited, flagging down the few random cars that passed with a flashlight. That was dangerous, too . . . no one was pleased by the sudden sight of three mud-coated men trying to stop cars in the middle of the night on a lonely road. Most people didn't stop, which despite our situation was something of a relief since there was no telling who might be coming to "help."

About an hour later, with the dawning prospect of having to spend the night in the car, a towering Mack truck pulling a full trailer emerged from the settling mist like a UFO, gears grinding and air brakes hissing. It was heading toward Tuzla.

We didn't expect to see a big rig on that little road, but no one was prepared for the fellow who climbed down from the cab.

"Choo fellas doin' out here?" He was a little black man, about sixty years old, wearing a mechanic's shirt with the name "Cliff" stitched on the pocket.

"Donchoo speak English?" We did, obviously, but we hadn't expected *him* to . . . it took a minute for us to quit gaping and tell him what happened.

When it came time to draw straws to see who was going to go back to Tuzla for help, I was nominated. "Me?" I said. "I don't know if that's a good idea . . ." Not only didn't I speak the language, but I had no idea where to find a tow truck in Tuzla during the day, much less in the middle of the night. But I didn't relish the idea of staying with the car, either.

"Just knock on the neighbors' door and get them to help . . . they know where to find a tow truck," Milstein said. Yes, the neighbors, a gang of drunken Muslim mechanics who spent their days playing darts and drinking beer. I knew that by the time I got there, they would all be deep in an alcoholic slumber. But it needed to be done. I reluctantly got in the cab with Cliff.

Cliff worked for Brown and Root, the U.S. military contractor hired to build all the bases and camps. He was from Spring Lake, North Carolina, a small town just outside Fayetteville, where I had grown up. "I'll be damned," I said. "It's safe to say that you're the last person I expected to meet here."

We almost hadn't met . . . Brown and Root was very strict in its policies about no contact with the locals. Insurance reasons, Cliff said. As a result, even though he'd been there for a month, he had to read the American papers delivered to the barracks to get an idea of what Bosnia was like, even though he worked there every day. Brown and Root had well-defined rules that included no leaving the barracks, no alcohol, no socializing with the locals, and no straying from desig- nated roads. And no picking up hitchhikers, he added, but he hadn't known we were Americans when he stopped. He had been hoping to pick up a Bosnian, just to get to know one.

He was one of those rare people who wanted to see for himself what people were like, not satisfied taking the media's version of events, which, though more or less accurate, was necessarily generalized to mean Muslim equals victim, Serb equals aggressor, Croat equals a lit- tle of both.

I discovered the shortcomings of this simplistic summation when I tried to describe to Cliff a typical Bosnian. Imagine trying to describe to a foreigner a typical American; it's impossible. There was Rijad, for instance, the nineteen-year-old Muslim translator for the U.S. Army in Tuzla. Rijad was like any kid his age anywhere on the globe—he loved rock and roll, played a little guitar from time to time, couldn't choose between two sixteen-year-old girlfriends who seemed, to me, to be equally beautiful and innocent. What made him different was the fact that he was lucky to be alive. On May 31, 1995, a Serb artillery shell, the only one fired at Tuzla all day by encroaching forces, which were attempting to besiege the city as they had Sarajevo, landed in a narrow intersection of the cobblestoned downtown pedestrian dis- trict. It fell literally at the feet of dozens of people Rijad's age who were crowded at an outdoor cafe drinking coffee in the balmy night. Rijad was standing 50 yards up the street when the explosion killed more than 70 people and injured about 150; it slammed him flat to the pavement, amazingly untouched by shrapnel that sliced into buildings and people on all sides. Even though he immediately stepped in to help the dying and wounded, and soon thereafter joined the Bosnian Army for a brief time to defend the city, he told me he didn't hate the Serbs. Instead, he hated the Croats, who'd never fired a shot at Tuzla.

With the Serbs, he said, he knew where he stood—they hated Mus- lims and would kill them if they had the chance, he said. In a weird way, he respected the clarity of their position. But he saw the Croats as a nation of Iagos—back-stabbing and untrustworthy, constantly taking advantage of the Muslims' military weakness to forge a larger country for themselves out of western Bosnia. He fought nonstop at the press office with a Croatian reporter who insisted on filing her articles to Zagreb under a "Hercog-Bosna" dateline, a designation that put the name of the Croatian-dominated region of Bosnia (Hercogovina) in front of the Muslim-dominated portion (Bosnia). Such details tend to make enemies of people.

There was the Croatian *Newsweek* photographer who was beaten by Croatian authorities for three days straight until he signed a confession that he'd been spying on Croatian military installations instead of simply photographing them for *Newsweek*. Of course he wasn't a spy, but after three days of torture, with no sleep, he said he would have admitted anything for it to stop.

Then there was the Serb couple who continued to live in their apartment in Sarajevo despite the fact that the Serbs were the least popular people in the world among their neighbors. They stayed, they said, for the simple reason that they believed in a multicultural Bosnia, and that such a thing could only remain a reality if the Serbs who didn't believe in the war made the brave decision to stay in communities where they found themselves in the minority. They never had any trouble from their neighbors, they told me, but other Serbs, the ones firing guns into the city, were another matter. Once, a tank shell exploded just outside their second-floor apartment window, vaporizing the glass and the window frame, sending hot spikes of shrapnel through several walls inside the apartment. They were fortunate to have been in the kitchen at the time, away from the direct blast, and they only suffered temporary hearing loss and minor cuts.

I tried to explain to Cliff as best I could that it wasn't always so easy to identify an enemy based solely on ethnic identity.

It took us an hour to get to the cloverleaf interchange at Tuzla. Cliff had to drop me off there because he didn't want to take the chance of getting caught with the truck off-route. It could cost him his job. I understood, but I wasn't happy. It was only about three more miles into the city ... but they were through a mist, which was quickly becoming a fog, and past the city's power plant, where Three-Mile Island–type turbines expelled unregulated exhaust into the air around the clock, giving the city a jaundiced cloak of sickly-sweet pollution.

The joke was that everyone smokes in Tuzla in order to get a breath of fresh air. There were no lights on the road at all.

Hopping along at a lazy jog, I quickly got paranoid. The lack of light was so complete that I may as well have been in a grave. And there were people around me, it seemed, though I couldn't quite see them. Every once in a while someone would cough softly or pull on a cigarette that illuminated his face in a small orange circle of light. These people were just feet away, standing in the dark by the side of the road, all but invisible. But I had this panicky notion that they could see me perfectly. I shook my head, thinking that I was hallucinating from fatigue and fear . . . then I nearly ran smack into a formless figure that suddenly shouted a long string of Serbo-Croatian at me that carried through the night like a foghorn. In my state of mind, it was impossible to tell if it was a man or a bus stop kiosk come to life in some sort of Alice in Wonderland acid-trip fantasy. I ran faster, breathing heavily, the machinery of the power plant shushing and clanging to the right. Who were these people? Refugees with nowhere to go but this trash-filled highway? *Were* there people there? Or just the ghosts of Srebrenica doomed to slog along in the afterlife toward the city? At the height of these thoughts, I tripped over something dead, a small soft corpse in the gutter. My foot came down squarely on it, breaking it open in a sigh of releasing gases. Pitching forward, I sprawled in the street for only a microsecond before launching forward in a full-blown sprint, barely resisting the urge to scream. It was probably only a dog or a goat killed in traffic . . . but at the moment I was sure it was a dead child, a little girl I could see vividly, lying in the gutter with her eyes open, reaching out in the gloom to grab my leg and beg for deliverance.

Two

Out in the bright daylight of summer two years later, at a café in Travnik where a friendly dog climbed up in the seat opposite mine hoping for a handout, it was hard to regain that feeling. The mountains stood as dormant as mountains anywhere, unconcerned with me or anyone else. I ordered a burek—a huge pastry filled with cheese and some sort of meat—and a Coke.

"Burek and . . . slivovitz?" the café owner said, repeating my order.

"Ne, ne," I said, pointing to the 1960s-era tin Coke sign in the window. "Coca-Cola."

"Da, da . . . slivovitz." There was a sly smile on his face, but he disappeared into the café before I could mount further argument. He returned promptly with four glasses, two little ones like those they serve orange juice in at Denny's and two bigger ones full of water. He put one of each down before me and the others in front of himself . . . where he settled down in a chair (chasing off the dog) and raised the small glass in a toast. "A day like today is too hot for Coca-Cola," he said in flawless English. He winked and tossed back the liquor after clinking my glass.

Slivovitz is made from plums, and though it's called *brandy,* it tastes more like the type of moonshine I used to buy in West Virginia, the kind with the brown paper label that guaranteed the contents were "less than thirty days old." I've done as much to avoid slivovitz as I have moonshine in recent years, but I grabbed the glass and heartily squeezed down a thimbleful. I hardly wanted to appear impolite at such an unexpected social opportunity. But it was hardly a shocking turn of events. Slavic people, regardless of their religious creed or ethnic identity, have consistently surprised me with their kindness, in light of everything I'd ever heard otherwise; an unknown shop owner breaking out the brandy to sit on the sidewalk with a perfect stranger, in fact, had come to be as expected as police checkpoints.

"You are from where?" he asked. "Not Croatia, eh?"

"I'm an American," I said. "I'm a reporter."

"An American reporter. My brother-in-law lives in Cleveland." Everyone seems to have a brother-in-law in Cleveland. Or Boston. Or Chicago. It's a reminder that former Yugoslavia had been—and was trying to be again—a country of modern, cosmopolitan people, who traveled, relocated, and took vacations just like the people of any other country. It was all too easy to forget that Bosnia wasn't always as "Third World" as the war had made it.

"You're going to Sarajevo, yes? Everyone comes for Sarajevo, all reporters. During the war it was very terrible there. Here was bad, too. But Sarajevo . . ." He shook his head and stubbed out a cigarette.

I tried a little more slivovitz, going slowly because if this encounter was anything like the others I'd been in like it, the liquor would continue to flow if I finished too soon. "How are things here now?" I asked.

"Fine now," he said. "Things are . . ." he tilted his head and scratched at his beard, searching for the right words, ". . . still difficult. No one has any money. But, it's better."

But what about that bomb that had injured the two Croats last month? That didn't sound too good.

He waved at that, as if people were making more of it than it warranted. "Some people, they are still crazy and stupid. Who knows why that happened? There are people like . . ." his words escaped him for a moment as he gestured at the passing crowd. "See these little children. They don't want to fight. We must be sane for the children so that their Bosnia is not like our Bosnia. Some people, they are still . . ." He groped.

"Angry," I suggested.

"Not angry," he said, leaning forward to pronounce the next word carefully so that it hung in the air like a bubble: "Crazy."

It was bound to happen: one glass of slivovitz led to another and another. Then he started bringing out beers in bottles that had been recycled so often you could barely see through them. We were joined by a steady procession of friends who wandered by on the streets and ended up joining us. Everyone looked rather scruffy, unwashed, in bad need of a shave and a haircut, and dressed in threadbare aid-organization clothing, much of which apparently came from the United States. One man wore a "Melrose Place" T-shirt that looked as if it had been found in someone's trunk before being turned over to the Salvation Army. One was a Serb and one a Croat, and two were Muslims, and I found out the café owner was part Croatian, part Slovenian ("Like Tito!"). At one point, he put his arms around his friends and said with a smile, "This is Bosnia!"

That may be true or it may not, depending on your frame of reference. In abstract terms, he was absolutely correct. The only thing that could have made him more accurate would have been if we were also joined by a Jew, a Gypsy, a Hungarian, an Albanian, a Montenegrin, and all their combined offspring. Bosnia is the literal crossroads of empires that has—or had—a population as diverse as its landscape.

I remember an assignment in social studies class in the third or fourth grade in which we had to argue that America was either a "melting pot" or a "tossed salad." The first theory was that by adopting American culture, immigrants lost their ethnic identities and were assimilated into their new society; therefore, they melted into the population and were Americans rather than Italian immigrants, for example. Whatever ethnic characteristics and customs they had brought with them were added into the universal mixture of what would come to define the American people as a whole. The "tossed salad" idea was that immigrants kept their culture and identity largely intact, creating a diversity of ideas and traditions that are distinct from others, just as tomatoes stand out in a salad. It was a trick question, though. Both answers were right; America was a salad tossed into a melting pot, with first- and second-generation immigrants as easy to pick out of a crowd as croutons are from a salad. With successive generations, the distinctions get less and less noticeable as children lose touch with ancestral roots and become content with identifying themselves simply as Americans.

The same is true of Bosnia.

When Serbs and Croats first settled on the Balkan peninsula, they were believed to have been from the same tribe, worshipped the same pagan gods, and spoke the same language.[1] The Holy Roman Empire to the west, the Byzantine Empire to the east, and the Kingdom of Hungary to the north grew in size and influence across the countries of Europe and Asia, spreading their spheres of influence farther and farther with each passing century . . . the frontierspeople were sometimes missionaries, who laid the seeds of imperial loyalty by spreading their faith to the people outside the kingdoms, and sometimes invaders, who came over the mountains on horseback with clothing and jeweled weaponry of colors and textures never before seen. The land stuck between these colliding empires was Bosnia.

In 880, Rome dispatched nomadic priests Cyril and Methodius to the Balkans to complete the conversion of the western Slavs—the Croats—to Catholicism. This mission was an extension of the practice that had started in 660 as a reward for the Croats' defeating and routing the troublesome Avars from Dalmatia and Bohemia, an act Byzantine emperor Heraclius was thoroughly grateful for. So grateful, in fact, that he made the Croats Catholics and Pope John VII allowed them to practice mass in their native tongue, a perk not extended to other countries until the Second Vatican Council, in 1962. The Croats, then as now, considered themselves European because of this early Western alliance with the Vatican, an alliance that fostered an infatuation with the power, beauty, and influence of places like Vienna, Rome, and Paris that lingers today. (Flying into Zagreb, the passengers on my plane were offered newspapers from England, France, Germany, Spain, Italy, Austria, and Croatia ... but there were no copies of *Oslobedenja*, the Sarajevo daily that became famous by publishing throughout the siege. "That's not a *European* newspaper," I was told rudely by the stewardess.)

Not far away—less than a modern half day's journey by car—the Byzantines were busily wielding the same religious influence over the eastern Slavs, the Serbs. The Serbs adopted Christian Orthodoxy, the dominant belief system of countries beyond the orbit of Rome; but there was a vast difference between the Serbs and the Croats in regard to their relationship with the larger imperial leaders of the world: Serbia became its own kingdom, one that eventually grew larger and richer than that of Byzantium (the seat of the Byzantine Empire, later named Constantinople and now Istanbul).

And what a kingdom: Serbia could be the impetus for every bedtime story ever told that featured a "magical kingdom," and indeed, there's an urge to tell of Serbian history by beginning, "Once upon a time ..." It had all the proper ingredients for such a tale. There were richly adorned monasteries embedded with gold and jewelry that were so exquisite in their spirituality that Rebecca West, British journalist and travel writer of the 1930s, was inspired to write, "Our cup has not been empty, but it was never full like those in this world, at the spot where Asia met Europe." There was a short dynasty of kings descended from the founder of the Serbian Orthodox church, including one reckless leader who was occupied, like all great kings of legend, with ensuring his immortality through monuments to God, donations of jewels and treasure to palaces and churches all over the East, and an appetite for procreation that knew few bounds. His royal predecessor brought promise and civility to the kingdom with decrees of religious freedom and a rule of law that included trial by jury. And the story has the one thing that makes a fairy-tale worth repeating from generation to generation—tragedy at the zenith of its majesty delivered by the sacking armies of an invading nation.

At the height of its glory, the Serbian Empire dominated nearly the entire Balkan peninsula, right up to the borders of Croatia and including Bosnia, Montenegro, Macedonia, northern Greece, and Bulgaria. As Robert Kaplan noted, at one point it was more civilized than the Roman Empire: Serbia's founding king could sign his own name "while the Holy Roman Emperor in Germany, Frederick I Barbarossa, could only manage a thumbprint."[2]

Thus were the foundations laid. To the west was a nation of Catholics whose aspirations to greatness were little more than inclusion in an empire that tolerated and exploited them because of their position on its eastern border. Croatia never really got beyond simply having a foot in the European door—one that Croats seem constantly paranoid about slamming shut. In the east was a nation of Christians, autonomous and rich, with visions that went beyond simple recognition to full-blown cultural greatness. The Croats were seen by the Serbs as guided by a religion that was too busy for its own good: Catholics were characterized by community action, ideas, and intellectualism. The Serbs were identified by the Croats as lazy because of the Orthodox church's emphasis on meditation and spiritual fulfillment rather than daily work. "Such differences, over centuries, engender conflicting approaches to daily life," wrote Kaplan.[3]

Forever stuck in the middle was Bosnia, a mountainous region that buffered the two conflicting ideologies. Nobles and landowners in Bosnia knew of their value to both the eastern and the western empires, and missionaries from both poles courted them, not unlike lawyers from competing developers wooing the holders of valuable ocean-front property. Each side came with its own incentives, and the landowners played one off against the other, defecting over time to whichever side presented the best offer. They never really held the upper hand—either empire could enforce its will with knights wielding rapiers and lances—but for centuries, the hazy border between the East and the West shifted and consolidated according to political rather than military maneuvering. The influences of both interests washed over Bosnia like a crazy tide, dominated by Croat and Bulgar beliefs one century and Serbian Orthodoxy the next. Conversions and shifting loyalties happened so often that none really took hold.

Until the Turks gave the Bosnians an offer they literally couldn't refuse.

Three

At first, it's odd to see mosques in Bosnia even though, clearly, one of the three warring parties is Muslim. Still, the domed buildings with their rocket-shaped minarets stand out from the rest of the architecture, religious icons that are deemed peculiar simply because few people in sight stand out as Islamic. Very few women wear traditional head coverings. Alcohol is consumed with an abandon that leads one to believe that it's as necessary as water to sustain life. Pornographic magazines and posters plaster the news kiosks. The call to prayer can literally bring a foreigner to a dead stop, the lilting Arabic sounds echoing on the wind as out of place as a grove of palm trees.

But it soon becomes apparent that a lot of what's called Bosnian is actually Turkish. Take coffee for example. There isn't a hot cup of Maxwell House within 1,000 miles: for caffeine addicts like myself, there are only two options: espresso or "Bosnian" coffee. After tense sleep, neither is very appealing at 7 A.M. when the temperature is already in the nineties—but certain traditions have to be followed.

I've never been one for espresso, so the Bosnian coffee is the only choice: it comes heavily sweetened in a little tin pot with a handle that you use to pour it carefully into a ceramic shot glass. You're supposed to sip it, but I always end up slugging it like a stereotypical rushed American. You have to be careful with this technique, though—the bottom of the cup is filled with fine grounds like volcanic sand. Swallowing this putty is a mistake only first-timers and drunks make—and you only make it once. There's nothing quite like choking hot grit through your nose in sputtering surprise to make you feel supremely stupid.

You find the same coffee in Romania, Serbia, and Greece—where it's called Romanian coffee, Serbian coffee, and so forth. But it's origin is Turkish. And so is a great deal of architecture deemed by locals to be "typically Bosnian" in Bosnia and "typically Serbian" in Serbia, when in fact it's the result, like the mosques, of 500 years of Turkish rule.[4]

In the fourteenth century, the Serbian kingdom was strong enough to contemplate moving on Constantinople. Nervous, the rulers of the Byzantine Empire invited massing Ottoman Turks to establish a military buffer at a strategic location at Gallipoli. The move held off invasion by the Serbs—but gave the Turks the territorial opportunity to invade Bulgaria and Greece, sweeping finally into Serbia a few decades later. Serbia was the last Christian stronghold between the Turks and the Western nations of the Romans and the Hapsburgs, an imperial dynasty based in Vienna—yet no support was offered the Serbs. Standing alone against a powerful nation that would conquer the fortress city of Constantinople a hundred years later, they met their enemy on the bumpy plane of Kosovo Polje on June 28, 1389. The Serbs were slaughtered, their bodies left steaming under the sun, covered by scavenging black birds like a velvet sea. Pockets of resistance and suspected opposition strongholds were eradicated by a method that became familiar 600 years later as ethnic cleansing: when Turkish knights sacked a village, they raped the women, pillaged the fields, and torched the homes, whipping up a frenzy of panic that translated easily into crazy flight.[5]

By this time, the Bosnians had tired of unwelcome advances from both the East and the West and had established their own kingdom based on a puritanical religion called Bogomilism. It was a highly superstitious Christian cult, its central belief being one of good versus evil that championed virginity as the highest level of pure living. It was decried by Pope Pius II as heresy, and he called for a Christian crusade into Bosnia in the late 1450s. The pope's bull—the legal document authorizing the crusade—listed Bogomilism along with Islam and Eastern Orthodoxy as his warrior-missionaries' targets. In probably the simplest alliance ever forged in the Balkans, the Turks, who had dug in across the Bosnian border, simply asked the Bosnian king if he would welcome their forces into his territory. Because both Islam and Bogomilism had been named as enemies of Rome, the sultan argued, the Turks would defend Bosnia on the condition that the Bosnians convert to Islam and not attack the Ottoman forces.

It was an easy decision to make. Not only would Turkish occupation defend against marauding missionaries, but the sultan also promised that Bosnian nobles would keep their land and their influence. Besides, converting to a new religion had become so common throughout history, what was one more conversion?

The Croats, eyes wide at this sweeping mountain of Mongolian-ponied invaders suddenly advancing upon their very border, were spared the same fate as the Serbs at the last minute when the Austrians dispatched a general to drum up a defense at the border of Bosnia. To supplement his garrison of mercenaries and ragtag defenders, the general recruited Serb refugees and settled them in a crescent around the Bosnian border, in the area that became known as the Krajina. The Turks dug in where Bihac is today.

The plate tectonics of political power ground like this for centuries: the Serbs dismal and enslaved by the Turks, the Croats thoroughly exploited as a population of military slaves to the Austrians, and the Bosnians hosting the westernmost outpost of Islam in Europe.

That's the easy history, the part most people in Bosnia can agree on. Therefore, no one ever discusses it. But they'll discuss everything from that point to yesterday if you allow them. The filters people put on the past (filters that have been forged from generational myth telling by stone fireplaces, political propaganda from state-run media that's so fictionalized it could have been scripted by Stephen King, and collective reinforcement that conveniently excludes conflicting historical fact) are what caused the war in 1991. And the near impossibility of figuring it all out and agreeing on even the most general of events and intentions was what led to the war's getting worse by dumbfounding international leaders into a stupor. Finally, the importance of that history was overblown by everyone involved—by the political leaders of Serbia, Bosnia, and Croatia and by President Bill Clinton and his team of foreign policy experts, who may have known better but used the complexities as an excuse not to get involved.

It's easy to see why with just a cursory glance behind the curtains of history.

Just this century alone, aside from the general unrest inherent in occupied and confused nations suffering under the yoke of terminal poverty, the Croats, Bosnians, Serbs, Montenegrins, and Macedonians (to say nothing of the Slovenians, Romanians, Bulgarians, Greeks, Albanians, and Russians) have seen five wars on their soil. In almost every one, there was no telling who was fighting whom and for what reasons because loyalties and alliances changed with the wind and different bands of armed groups sprang from the mountains like mushrooms after a wild rain. World War II was particularly baffling, splitting the Slavs into Croatian Ustashe fascists, who were aligned with the Nazis and who fought Communists and Serbs; Tito's partisans, composed of guerrillas and farmers who took their influence from Joseph Stalin and fought the Ustashe, the Nazis, and the Italians; and Serb Chetnick paramilitary units, which never seemed able to decide whom they were fighting for or for what reasons, but who were mostly against the Germans and sometimes the partisans. Meanwhile, dabblers from the United States, Great Britain, Italy, Germany, and Russia whispered in the ears of all the combatants for their own reasons. And all the while, Luftwaffe airplanes carpet-bombed Belgrade, and American artillery was smuggled to Yugoslavia's future Communist leader. Tito's partisans were the only winners to emerge from this mess, even though that statement's qualified by the fact that over a million Slavs were dead once the fighting ended. Most had died at the hands of their neighbors. Under communism, Tito managed to stifle the different ethnic groups' seemingly congenital urge to kill one another until his death in 1980.

But even calling the Slavs Serb, Croat, or Bosnian was never more than a matter of convenience by that point. Prior to World War I, Yugoslavia had more than once been conquered, overrun, occupied, liberated, defended, oppressed, and colonized to varying degrees by nearly every country within cannonball range. Not only was there a nearly endless flow of new people to the region, but each war, battle, uprising, opposition group, and terrorist organization also caused massive population movement in all directions almost constantly. And under communism, with the game of musical chairs on pause for more than three decades, the people of the region had time to settle down and marry those around them, who were likely from a different ethnic background.

Four

It's not unlikely that President Clinton received this tortured history with something like relief. He never seemed too interested in U.S. involvement in Bosnia, even though he ran for the American presidency in 1992 on the promise of heightened intervention, and this complicated history gave him the out he needed: the past was too entrenched and too confusing to risk intervention in the present.

According to Richard Holbrooke's memoirs, *To End a War*, Clinton's Bosnia policy was deeply affected by Kaplan's *Balkan Ghosts*, a moving journey through Balkan history. It fleshes out all of the above in detail that gives the impression of an intractable morass in which violence is inevitable and diplomacy would be, at best, a shot in the dark. Though Clinton is accused of being many things, no one's ever called him dumb when it comes to policy decisions—if *Balkan Ghosts* affected his policy, it was probably on a level that was secondary to a number of other things facing him at the time. Domestically, he received a regular beating in the press and the public opinion polls about the U.S. military mission in Somalia.

Somalia was the big smack in the face of post-cold-war U.S. foreign policy. Without the Soviet Union or the spread of communism to worry about any longer, members of the U.S. State Department and the Pentagon were left with the puzzling question of how and when to use the U.S. military when conflict arose that was troubling but didn't quite threaten direct American interests. *Time* magazine summed up the conundrum this way: "Murky wars like Somalia and Bosnia—complicated local fights with a potential for international spillover—are a growth industry now that the cold war no longer imposes a rough order on world politics. The Clinton Administration is faced with redefining when the U.S. should intervene abroad and whether it should be done alone, through the UN or through permanent or ad hoc alliances."[6]

It's a complicated question. When the threat of nuclear annihilation hung over the heads of Americans, it was easy to justify troop deployment to "contain" communism in areas like Korea and Vietnam; even though the policies polarized the nation, those in charge never doubted their own intentions. It was easy to define a "good guy" and a "bad guy." That became infinitely harder to do after the cold war. Somalia, for instance, looked good on paper—with the end of the Soviet threat, America could busy itself with humanitarian causes like feeding the starving thousands in Somalia. It made sense not only in moral terms—it was the right thing to do—but in the character of the president himself. Using U.S. Marines to deliver flour is just what one would expect from a baby boomer Vietnam protester.

But things are never that simple, as policy makers found out too late in Somalia. What began as a humanitarian effort soon turned into quicksand. No one was eating because the local warlords were stealing all the food from the bowls of the hungry. So the military started hunting the warlords. Eighteen U.S. soldiers were killed. One helicopter pilot's nearly naked corpse was dragged through the streets of Mogadishu by a kicking, spitting crowd, and suddenly people who had been all for this newer, friendlier U.S. military started asking, "What the hell are we *doing* over there?" The term *mission creep* was coined.

While the Bosnian war was being fought, there were massive changes in the geopolitical world that rightly captured the attention of the U.S. diplomats and policy makers, most notably the collapse of the Soviet Union. The U.S. State Department turned its attention to the USSR's demise, attempting to mitigate any negative friction it might cause either within the former USSR or in Europe where, with the fall of the Berlin Wall, local political leaders were figuring out how to forge themselves into an effective international alliance that would be strong enough to solve its own problems without the United States. For an American president who had run on a campaign platform that consisted of little more than a domestic economy plank, this couldn't have been better news. Let the Europeans handle Bosnia.

By the time the wisdom of that stance proved indefensible, it was too late to do much else for Bosnia than damage control. When the United States stepped in finally and bombed the Serbs to the negotiating compound at Wright-Patterson Air Force Base, there was little left to negotiate. The Serbs had solidified their positions in the north and the east, and the Croats and Muslims tenuously held onto the rest. Populations had shifted drastically, with people moving from towns and villages where they suddenly found themselves the minority into safer areas, or they fled the country altogether. Partitioning Bosnia along ethnic lines seemed inevitable. But Holbrooke and the other negotiators were determined to re-create Bosnia as a single, multiethnic nation. However, the resulting Dayton Accords, coupled with the international community's by-now-trademark unwillingness to commit fully to the little bloody country, have done just what everyone was trying to avoid: divided the nation in half. Anyone who thinks that Bosnia is anything less than two distinct ethnic nations should spend an afternoon traveling between Sarajevo in Federation territory and Pale in RS. Though they are divided by a mere ten or twelve miles, the difference is profound.

4   Welcome to Sarajevo

I demand and I want just as God
rightfully wants
The immediate abolition of all things
Without a purpose and with no
beauty
Without a purpose
And no soundness

—Untitled, Dr. Radovan Karadzic,
PBS Online and WGHB, *Frontline*, 1998

It is the absolute right of the state to supervise the formation of public opinion.

—Paul Joseph Goebbels, 1923

One

Downtown Sarajevo was a parking lot.

I arrived in the capital at 6 P.M., the height of the rush hour. I came from the Zenica highway, which took me past the airport and deposited me at the end of Marshal Tito Boulevard—more commonly known as Sniper Alley. During the war, the run from the airport to the Holiday Inn downtown—past the morbid, spray-painted greeting "Welcome to Sarajevo" on the side of an exploded building—took anywhere from five to ten minutes, depending on how heavy the gunfire was and how quickly you felt you could drive without crashing into the burnt-out shells of other cars on the four-lane highway. There was little traffic in those days. Even in 1996, with the snipers in full retreat, people still drove at top speed and ignored red lights because after nearly four years of terror it was hard to believe that stopping at an intersection wouldn't get you killed.

In 1998, however, the streets were maddeningly jammed with traffic that would have made a Serb sniper go cross-eyed in joy at his choice of targets—had there been anyone in the hills to level such a deadly gaze.

The last time I had been in Sarajevo, the Holiday Inn had been covered with four years' worth of small-arms pinpricks and several artillery shell gashes, which had spilled rebar and bits of furniture onto the empty concrete plaza below. Though it was hit repeatedly, the Holiday Inn survived with far less damage than other buildings, even though it's easily visible from every hilltop. The hotel managed this feat by bribing the Serbs not to shoot at it. The deal worked out well for everyone: the Holiday Inn was the only hotel to take guests throughout the siege and the Serbs made a little money by turning their cannons elsewhere.[1] When I arrived in 1998, most of the bullet holes had been plastered over and the tank holes were being repaired. There was a pleasant outdoor café on the freshly swept plaza, less than 100 yards from a red-brick building that had flown the Jolly Roger in 1996 and that had sheltered Serb snipers who maintained the threat of death outside the hotel's front doors. The UNHCR all-weather plastic sheeting in the lobby had been replaced with ultraviolet ray–reflecting plate glass, and the whole building had gotten a new coat of paint. Sadly it was the same saffron-and-dirt tones it had been painted before. Rooms were 290 deutsche marks a night. Cash. I decided to look elsewhere for a hotel room.

Driving around present-day Sarajevo looking for a place to spend the night was a bizarre experience. Sarajevo's two realities were superimposed one on another, the Sarajevo its residents had known before the siege and the one everyone else had grown to know during the siege. On the ground, it was easy to imagine that you'd been sucked back in time to before April 1992 when Bosnian Serb radicals opened fire on a political demonstration from the roof of the Holiday Inn. Before those bullets started flying, things had been tense but fine, much like they are today. Traffic is dense and noisy, and pedestrians settle into every empty space like water poured into a jug of rocks. People are everywhere, streaming to and from open air cafés, en route home from the market carrying sacks of food purchased at a fair price (as much a novelty, I'm sure, as being able to walk out in the open at all), or kicking soccer balls in fields clear of unexploded ordnance.

Anyone who chose to sell paint and hardware supplies as a postwar career is undoubtedly thinking of early retirement. Whereas before you'd be frustrated trying to find a building without bullet or shrapnel damage, these days the difficulty is in locating a building where at least some reconstruction hasn't begun. In their fervor to erase the war damage, however, Sarajevans have given precious little thought to aesthetics, seeming to take their color selection cues from the offensive yellow-on-brown Holiday Inn: as a result, the whole city seems to have been overrun by Ken Kesey and his Merry Pranksters. Here's a new café with exterior colors of crayon purple and Day-Glo green, accented with pink neon; there's an office building with alternating red, blue, yellow, and brown checker squares; up the block is a house whose public-swimming-pool-aqua walls with canary-yellow trim must glow in the dark.

Of course, there are more sinister characteristics that have yet to be tackled. The Bosnian Parliament building, a granite-colored obelisk towering over Grbavica, whistles in the breeze thanks to dozens of powder-burned artillery shell holes and the huge chunks of concrete that have fallen off like picked scabs to expose the steel ribs inside. Next door is another high-rise as haunting as Coleridge's apparition in *The Rime of the Ancient Mariner*: "His bones were black with many a crack / All black and bare, I ween; / Jet-black and bare, save where with rust / Of mouldy damps and charnel crust / They're patch'd with purple and green."

On the street corners SFOR battle wagons aim long machine guns at the mountaintops, and beneath their treads, the corpses of feral hounds killed by speeding cars are consumed by other former pets. In a field north of town is something of a refugee camp, little clapboard shacks with crooked stovepipes where people coax weak food from the ragged ground. And among the throngs of people on the streets are those who stand out from the rest with a vague despair ... they move slower and seem rendered in black and white, not distracted by their reflection in unshattered plate glass or the novelty of working streetlights. While the body may be on the safe streets of the city, the mind is not; it's locked in a choking cellar listening to the barely audible zing of superpowered explosive-tipped bullets passing by outside and the crunching footsteps of falling shells.

When I had last seen the Grbavica market across the Miljacka River, a white mud-splattered UN armored personnel carrier had driven slowly past the smoke-blackened, glass-littered building, crushing a sheep skull under its tires. Piles of garbage five feet high had been smoldering on the sidewalk under a gray rain, and the only people around had peered deep from gutted rooms that had become caves, eyes twinkling darkly. Now, the smoke stains were still there and the grass was still dead, but the garbage had been bulldozed off and the market razed. A young man washed his Volkswagen Jetta on the sidewalk, and the children who chased one another through the still-empty ground-floor rooms shone with laughter and glee rather than pending insanity.

In 1996, the building with the Jolly Roger had come under IFOR siege when I alerted the soldiers to a suspected sniper sitting on the balcony with an assault rifle above our passing truck. The building had been on a dead end, the street in front of it covered in a high berm of earth, barbed wire, and land mines. More than anywhere else, that block looked like a nuclear aftermath, every apartment building in sight apparently the victim of a car bomb attack. Unlike simple village houses, modern buildings crumble like collapsed accordions, so superreenforced concrete slabs sagged onto each other like a giant stack of pancakes, scattering their inside contents to the street below for everyone to see. Metal frames barely identifiable as former cars and busses rusted on the sidewalks, which had been mostly dug up to make trenches and tunnels connecting the buildings. You literally had to walk staring at the ground to navigate the land mines and avoid falling into a rat-filled pit.

When I drove down there in 1998, I wasn't sure I was in the same place . . . there was no dead end, and cars drove straight through where the barricade had been, heading downtown. Most of the rubble had been cleared away, and a trench I had nearly fallen into last time was filled with black dirt, like the grave of an impossibly long snake. But the buildings were still a loss—in fact, without prior knowledge, it was almost impossible to tell that the eight-story piles of concrete slab and asphalt had been buildings. I spotted a straight-backed wooden chair on the very edge of a fourth-story apartment whose walls had been blown out, awash in instant déjà vu. That same chair had been there two years ago, on the same precipice, the same featureless picture teetering on the wall behind it. Both times I felt the urge to climb up there and explore, to maybe kick the chair off into the void. I didn't do it in 1996 for fear of mines and booby traps. This time, I didn't want to disturb the disquieting scene portrayed, one of everyday life violently interrupted. I wondered if whoever last sat in that chair was dead.

On Grbavica's other former front line is a destroyed sports stadium and the shell of the home where the Croat couple had managed to live throughout the siege. The machine gun bunker was still there, maybe even the land mines I had narrowly avoided stepping on. So were the fire scars, and the white bucket she'd carried around, vainly looking for water, was blown under a low scrub pine with melted plastic appliances. The Croat couple, however, was gone, as I expected them to be. Their former home was perfectly preserved in the horror of the Grbavica arsons.

But I could drive away from there this time, no need to pick through the mined cabbage garden. The sinkhole had been filled, allowing cars of people to drive past without looking.

I found Banjalucka Street where I'd left it, lording over the view of the Holiday Inn and the Unis Trade Corporation towers. My snapshot memory of it is of a smoke-filled corridor, the weak winter sun catching large lazy motes of swirling dust and white spark showers from exploding ammunition. The street had been full of holes and powdered brick and ghostly figures stumbling over the rock piles and flitting into tunnels and doorways. Now the corridor walls were being reenforced; every burned-out home had been rebuilt with fresh plaster and smart red bricks. Number 7 was wedged between two newly constructed homes, looking a little worse than it had when it was surrounded only by pebbles and charred beams. I stopped the car on the narrow street and looked up at the window. It hadn't changed, offering me a glimpse into the high-ceilinged living room, where I'm sure the same furniture and dusty doilies sat in their same locations. I thought about knocking on the door, to see if the residents were home . . . but I wasn't sure what I would say. We didn't speak each other's language. I contented myself with knowing that I was following the same course I had two years ago, just swinging by on the street to see if everything was all right. By outward appearances, everything was.

Two

I was reluctant to spend almost DM 300 on one night's sleep at the Holiday Inn. But the day was receding and I was running out of time; since I was in Grbavica, I sped over Mount Trebevic to Pale in Republika Srpska to see if I would have better luck there.

The light was fading as I crested the mountain and began the long smooth descent through the hills to the bowl that holds the village. The road was bordered by tall trees and raced over steep drops and rocky cliffs. Pale had once been a resort town; it's not hard to be reminded of how it must once have looked and the majesty it must once have projected, though bright new yellow Cyrillic—the preferred alphabet of the Bosnian Serbs—road signs told me that things were different here now. The old green road signs of a formerly unified Bosnia have been torn down and discarded.

There were very few cars on the roads, the result of international economic sanctions and the withholding of reconstruction aid because Srpska hadn't enthusiastically cooperated with the Dayton Accords. Therefore, the sight of a car was cause for every pedestrian on the road to turn his or her head, which made me nervous because, since my car was meant only to be driven in Croatia, it didn't have a new Bosnian license plate that made it impossible to tell the driver's ethnicity. I didn't want to be taken for a Croat in RS.

Pale and Sarajevo are worlds apart, even though from Pale you can see the city lights of the Bosnian capital turn the air around Mount Trebevic into a glowing halo at night. Where Sarajevo is dense with people and buildings, Pale seems largely empty of both. Sarajevo is loud with traffic and laughter; Pale is still and quiet. Sarajevans move with the distinct swiftness of those who live in an important metropolitan city; those in Pale trudge from place to place as if they had all the time in the world. And of course, Sarajevo is the capital of the Bosnian Federation. Pale had been the capital of Republika Srpska.

Technically, that's not true any longer. The new RS capital was relocated to Banja Luka in the wake of the 1997 regional elections, when Bosnian Serb moderate Biljana Plavsic became president of RS. Moving the capital was a symbolic gesture meant to convey to everyone—both Bosnian citizens and international observers—that the Bosnian Serb agenda had changed from that of aggression and intolerance to one of compliance with the Dayton Accords.

It was an unexpected coup that sent the international community into a spiraling swoon over the breakaway Serb who suddenly seemed capable of doing what they'd failed to do by not arresting war criminals like Karadzic: suck away his malignant power. All the more shocking is that Plavsic, a cofounder of Karadzic's political party, the SDS, and a former deputy to Karadzic, had been considered by many to be his hard-line lapdog. Bosnian Serb soldiers had even named tanks after her. But by positioning herself as a moderate, she had also moved toward the accomplishment of another goal that would be better served by Karadzic's trial at The Hague, the exoneration of the Serb people as a whole. By proving that there are sensible, peace-minded Serbs interested in complying with the Dayton Accords, Plavsic had gone a long way toward relieving her followers of the collective guilt of the war's atrocities.

There was a lot of work remaining on that front, however: I was still nervous driving into Republika Srpska. Simply stated, there were more wanted war criminals in Srpska than anywhere else in Bosnia, most of them loose and free in that little area, presumably running around stoking the same type of hatred and stupidity that started this whole thing in the first place and that was no longer the singular skill of career politicians. A veritable cottage industry of nationalistic passion throve in places like Pale and Foca . . . and Drvar and Brcko and Travnik and so on, like a virus that had been released into the air or the water. The current hosts had received their power and blessing from above, from people like Milosevic and Karadzic and Mladic, and they had taken it to the people, who whispered from bar stools that nothing was different, the guns had been silenced, but only temporarily . . . just smile at the UN, and then we can carry on our work when everyone goes home.

It'll be this way until everyone indicted for war crimes has been sent to The Hague in the back of an airless black van . . . and until that time, Pale will be the vortex of malignant Bosnian Serb nationalism regardless of what recently elected Serb party leaders and international monitors say.

Karadzic, the former political leader of the Bosnian Serbs, lives in Pale and is, along with his minion, General Ratko Mladic, one of the most wanted men on the planet, indicted by the International Criminal Tribunal for the former Yugoslavia (ICTY) for genocide and ethnic cleansing. Strangely enough, neither one is considered especially difficult to find, yet both seem to enjoy a level of freedom that has only increased since the Dayton Accords silenced the guns. For the first six months of the IFOR mission, NATO commanders were in regular contact with Mladic through the radio he kept in his car.[2] They reportedly spoke with him often to make sure he knew what was expected of him in terms of the Dayton Accords. It's unclear if they discussed that one of those things was the surrender of indicted war criminals, including him.

An organization called War Criminal Watch tracks wanted people and updates their latest known whereabouts on its website. According to information from mid-1998, Mladic is in Belgrade writing his memoirs, an eagerly anticipated work if only for his interpretation of the Srebrenica massacres.[3] He'll undoubtedly set the record straight about what happened that week in 1995, and in certain circles, there's good money bet on the official explanation. Will he explain that the prisoners suddenly attacked the troops with well-hidden weapons and that the only recourse was swift and savage action by the Serbs, who, after all, had been planning to set them free in exchange for Serbs held by the Bosnians? Perhaps he'll reveal that the dead Muslims trying to escape to Tuzla were members of an elite military unit and carried so few weapons because they were so deadly with their bare hands. Or will he suggest that they committed mass suicide to make the Serbs look bad, just as they had bombed their own market in Sarajevo during the siege? Or it could simply be that there was no massacre, despite convincing evidence to the contrary.[4] With Mladic any of the above explanations are possible. After all, when he entered Srebrenica after four days of shelling, he announced that "the time has come to take revenge on the Turks in this region," illustrating that his propensity for either sheer lunacy or bald-faced propaganda is apparently boundless.[5]

Karadzic is in Pale, something that no one disputes. In 1996, historian Charles Ingrao visited Pale with colleagues and, while waiting outside the local IPTF office, saw Karadzic drive past in a jeep with three other lightly armed men. When Ingrao mentioned this to the Swedish officers inside the station, they shrugged and said that he passed by there often, on his way to his headquarters at the Famos truck factory.[6] The factory is familiar to the international military peacekeepers. One monitor mentioned that the air over the factory must be worn out because of all the drone plane flights overhead snapping spy pictures. But Karadzic is as worried about spy planes as he is about getting arrested by his own security detail. He's gone through IFOR/SFOR checkpoints at least six times on his way to Banja Luka to tape a television show; he's been spotted less than 100 yards from an IFOR checkpoint in Brcko manned by American soldiers; and he was once in the same building as High Commissioner Carl Bildt, something military officials acknowledged they knew about at the time.[7]

In terms of a hideout, Pale isn't Argentina. I drove from one end to the other in two minutes and was stared at by probably everyone who lives there. I wasn't sure which mountainside house was Karadzic's, but the people who are said to know—intelligence commanders of the UN, the IPTF, and SFOR—are only a fifteen-minute drive away in Sarajevo. All three organizations have offices and bases in Pale.

I stopped at a new mountain motel with neon signs and a smart elevated outdoor patio that looked as if it belonged in Vail rather than Bosnia. I tried to park the car where the plates would be out of sight, but when I trudged up the steps to the deck, I was given a full treatment of the Balkan Stare nonetheless. The motel looked comfortable—rough-hewn wooden tables were topped with Heineken umbrellas and clustered with young men and women from an L.L. Bean catalog. But their faces stood out from the pleasant ambiance. I felt as if I'd stumbled into a den of bank robbers who were just then planning their next heist and were trying to gauge how much of the plan I'd heard coming up the stairs. It was the same feeling I'd had in the Croat bar outside Bosanski Petrovac.

Even though the Serbs are the undisputed champions in the world loathing contest thanks to a mountain of monstrous deeds during the war, they're obviously not all guilty. In fact, they're a fine and warm-hearted people in many circumstances, their only sin being suckered by hate-mongering propaganda. They had been told, as far back as 1986, when Milosevic began his rise to power, that they were in mortal danger of anyone other than fellow Serbs. "Remember that the Muslims are enemies of Serbs," they had been told by the state-run media. "They slaughtered us at Kosovo and then sowed seeds in Bosnian women that flourished into nothing less than the bastard offspring of our sworn foes. And don't forget the Croatian alliance with Germany in World War II, when 700,000 of our people were slaughtered like pigs at Jasanovac." (For the record, the Ustashe-run Jasanovac concentration camp was indisputedly horrible . . . even the

SS was appalled by the brutality of the slaughter.[8] But we'll probably never know the true number of Serbs who died there, along with thousands of Jews and Gypsies. Serbians say 700,000 of their countrymen perished; Croatians say "only" 60,000.[9])

Germany inadvertently fed this propaganda by strong-arming the European Community—as the EU was called at the time—into recognizing Croatia when it declared independence in 1991; the recognition lent credence to the nonsense from Belgrade. Things snowballed quickly when Serbs living in Croatia's Krajina region—thinking they were defending themselves while simultaneously creating a safe nation to live in (Milosevic's "Greater Serbia")—with the help of the JNA, began pillaging Croats and Muslims in east-central Croatia days after that country seceded from Yugoslavia.

The same type of brainwashing was happening in Bosnia. While Serb media inundated the population with terrifying news of atrocities being committed against the Serbs in Croatia—news that was almost always either false or grossly exaggerated—the JNA started handing out weapons and encouraging blue-collar Bosnian Serbs to form their own militias to protect themselves from their neighbors. And what better protection than to strike first? The Serbs had *almost all the firepower* in the country because they controlled the JNA from the start, a fact they took full advantage of, and one that was aided immensely by George Bush's misunderstanding of the situation when he imposed an arms embargo on all of Yugoslavia, a nation that was by then nothing but a memory. All the embargo served to do was ensure that the victims of Serb aggression would remain unarmed.[10]

Of course, not all the Serbs believed what they were being told by their Belgrade television stations. Many of them were living just fine with other ethnicities, some of whom were in their very own families. In Sarajevo, particularly, the whole notion of "ancient Balkan hostilities" was patently absurd. Sarajevans weren't morons . . . they were well-educated professionals living in a cosmopolitan city, working happily side by side with those they were supposedly in mortal danger of.

But in the smaller villages, such reason was hard to rely on when a garrison of heavily armed savages rolled into the town square and started rounding people up. Bosnian Serbs in that situation were faced with decidedly simple choices: end your life as you know it by standing up and denouncing the aggression, thereby identifying yourself as a traitor to "Greater Serbia" and earning a bullet through the ear or worse; or take the AK-47 being thrust at you and begin herding your neighbors into flatbed trucks, thinking only that you've spared yourself and your family the same type of horror. You may have to live with the knowledge that you sent innocent people to an early grave, but it's either that or living with sending your wife and daughters to a rape camp.

As war broke out all over the place, the original propaganda was self-fulfilling. Seeing the writing on the wall, Croats and Muslims decided not to wait for the inevitable and began first strikes on their Serb neighbors, even the bravest Serbs of them all, those who held out against the insanity welling up all around.

The media machine couldn't have been more pleased. "See?" it said. "We warned you that you couldn't live with those people." People suddenly started misremembering things they'd been taught in history class—that the Muslims were pawns of the Turks, who had slaughtered Serbs at Kosovo; that Croats had killed nearly a million Serbs only fifty years before; that the Serbs had always been imperialist barbarians who dared challenge the Byzantine Empire. Things quickly got out of hand. There were tortures, mass rape of teenage girls, concentration camps. The international community quickly declared it insanity.

By then it was, a fact that even some perpetrators later admitted. Ed Vulliamy, an award-winning journalist for the *Guardian* in London, had a singular conversation with Dr. Milan Kovacevic, the administrator of the Omarska concentration camp in northwest Bosnia, that illustrates all that needs to be said about the predominant mentality among the aggressors. The interview was published in *The Nation:*

> What about burning the Muslim houses along the road? Was that necessary, or a moment of madness? Kovacevic proceeds cautiously, accompanied by a second glass of brandy: "Both things. A necessary fight and a moment of madness. The houses were burned at the beginning, when people were losing control. People weren't behaving normally." This comes as a surprise. Was it all a terrible mistake? "To be sure, it was a terrible mistake." A third glass, and suddenly, unprompted: "We knew very well what happened at Auschwitz and Dachau, and we knew very well how it started and how it was done. What we did was not the same as Auschwitz or Dachau, but it was a mistake. It was planned to have a camp, but not a concentration camp."
>
> Usually it is only "enemies of the Serbian people" who invoke Auschwitz when talking about Omarska. But the anesthetist plows boldly on. He has never had this conversation before, he says. In fact,

no one in Bosnia has had this conversation before. "Omarska," he continues, "was planned as a camp, but was turned into something else because of this loss of control. I cannot explain the loss of control. You could call it collective madness."

Another glass of brandy to steel the spirit, and for reasons not hard to guess, his childhood in Jasanovac comes to mind. "Six hundred thousand were killed in Jasanovac," he muses. "I was taken there as a baby, by my aunt. My mother was in the mountains, hiding. We remember everything. History is made that way." But Jasanovac was run by Croats; why did the Serbs turn on the Muslims? Kovacevic straightens himself. "There is a direct connection between what happened to the Muslims in our camps and the fact that there had been some Muslim soldiers in the [pro-Nazi] Greater Croatia. They committed war crimes, and now it is the other way round."

In Omarska, he says, "there were not more than 100 killed, whereas Jasanovac was a killing factory." Only 100 killed at Omarska? He blushes. "I said there were 100 killed, not died." Then Kovacevic loses his way and throws off caution: "Oh, I don't know how many were killed in there; God knows. It's a wind tunnel, this part of the world, a hurricane blowing to and fro. . . . "

By now the cheaply paneled room is steaming with the exhaled fumes of fast-disappearing cigarettes, a fifth glass, and talk of death. So, Doctor, who planned this madness? "It all looks very well planned if your view is from New York," he says. He edges forward on his low chair, as if to whisper some personal advice. "But here, when everything is burning, and breaking apart inside people's heads—this was something for the psychiatrists. These people should all have been taken to the psychiatrist, but there wasn't enough time."

In 1992, Kovacevic did not hide his role in operating the camp, but now The Hague is becoming serious. Were you part of this insanity, Doctor? "If someone acquitted me, saying that I was not part of that collective madness, then I would admit that this was not true. . . . If things go wrong in the hospital, then I am guilty. If you have to do things by killing people, well—that is my personal secret. Now my hair is white. I don't sleep so well."

Three

The easiest way to explain the crisis, one that became the de facto truth only after the fighting started, was that these troubling ancient hostilities had boiled to the surface and now there was bloodshed. No one seemed to know what to do except let the thing run its course.

For the most part, the international community not only embraced this conventional wisdom but did little to correct it. That view made it easy to avoid getting involved, something the United States was especially wary of, given the hard-learned lesson of Somalia. Former Secretary of State Lawrence Eagleburger summed up the government's position when he said, "I've said this 38,000 times, and I have to say this to the people of this country as well. This tragedy is not something that can be settled from the outside and it's about damn well time that everybody understood that. Until the Bosnians, Serbs and Croats decide to stop killing each other, there is nothing the outside world can do about this."[11]

Of course, other people grasped the reality of the situation. Warren Zimmerman, former U.S. ambassador to Yugoslavia, wrote in his memoirs:

> The pièce de résistance of Milosevic's manipulation of the media, as of Tudjman's, was the manufacture of ethnic hatred. The outbreak of sporadic fighting in Croatia during the spring of 1991 aided their efforts. . . . It was nearly impossible for diplomats and journalists to sort out who was responsible for each instance of violence. Press reports of the same event in Belgrade and Zagreb were diametrically opposed.
>
> In one sense, it didn't matter, since both Milosevic and Tudjman wanted violence and did all they could to provoke it. Fresh corpses, laid out graphically on color television gave their hate campaigns— literally—new blood. The slogans—"Croatia's sovereignty in danger!" "Serbs threatened with genocide!"—bit deep as Serbian and Croatian television viewers were exposed to a nightly fare of defunct compatriots martyred for their nation. At times, Belgrade and Zagreb television shared corpses: the same television picture of stiffening bodies was shown in each capital, portrayed in the one case as heroic Serbs, in the other as patriotic Croats. . . .
>
> The nationalist media sought to terrify by evoking mass murderers of a bygone time. . . . People who think they're under ethnic threat tend to seek refuge in their ethnic group. Thus did the media's terror campaign establish ethnic solidarity on the basis of an enemy to be both feared and hated.[12]

What was unique was that the international community recognized this top-down nationalism, which flowed through the people like rainwater down a steep hill, but it continually refused to act against it. The hatreds were real ... but they had been buried by decades of communism that, in the words of Charles Ingrao, was like methadone to a heroin addiction.[13] Communism isn't an efficient form of government, it's agreed. But it's head and shoulders above the complete vacuum of governance that comes from ethnic cleansing and fervent nationalism. Milosevic, followed by Tudjman and Izetbegovic, jerked the Yugoslavs out of the methadone clinic to plunge a healthy dose of nationalism straight into their hearts. Until Tudjman's death late in 1999, all three of these leaders were still in power, along with many of their underlings who are wanted at The Hague, and to varying degrees all three keep pushing their ethnic agendas. Yet the international community still insists on leaving peace up to the voters, those lucky enough to have lived through the war.

Could something have been done to stop what turned into the wholesale slaughter of hundreds of thousands of people? Maybe. It's been proven that outside military intervention successfully stopped the Bosnian war, if not ethnic hatred. But a case can certainly be made for the United States having been reluctant to move in that direction. Not only had the war been baffling and confusing, but there had been other political issues that prevented a quick response. If the United States had started bombing Serb targets early in the aggression, the European Union would have screamed bloody murder that we were flexing our muscles so far from home without a tangible national interest at stake, making us appear arrogant and drawing criticism from all corners, including at home. The Russians would have flipped as well, interpreting the action as the United States taking the first post–cold war opportunity to bomb a dissolving Communist country with close Soviet ties.

The reasons for not getting involved early are clear ... but far less clear is why we didn't get started by the time war was in high gear from 1993 to mid-1995. The Europeans and the United Nations had wholly failed to do anything other than make themselves the laughingstocks of the world at best and patsies of genocide at worst.

The UN force that went to the Balkans at the beginning of the war in Croatia was called the United Nations Protection Force, or UNPROFOR. It quickly proved neither protective nor forceful. UNPROFOR personnel were an odd sight to the pillaged villagers of the country, not only because they drove ceramic-white vehicles and wore powder-blue helmets, but also because they didn't protect any-

one, not even themselves. UN soldiers were prohibited from inter-
vening in the fighting and weren't allowed to use their weapons unless, to paraphrase writer P. J. O'Rourke, they were under such a
heavy attack that they were probably already dead. When NATO
bombed Serbian targets in Spring 1995 because of their relentless
shelling of Sarajevo, the Serbs promptly took 350 French soldiers
hostage and chained them to bridges and radar installations as human
shields against further attacks. When the UN declared Srebrenica,
Zepa, and Gorazde "safe areas" (designations that came about from
Security Council resolutions that in retrospect seem hubristic and
doomed from the outset—there was no one in Bosnia, least of all the
United Nations, that could declare any place safe or dangerous except
the Serbs), the Serbs' laughter could all but be heard echoing across
the Atlantic. Safe areas fell and their people were butchered. Dutch
UN soldiers handed Srebrenica's Muslims over to Mladic's troops because they believed that they were going to be turned over in a prisoner exchange. Even if they didn't believe it, they certainly couldn't
fight. "Even if we'd wanted to," one observer who'd been in Srebrenica at the time told me, "we would have only been able to fight
for an hour before we would have been out of ammunition."[14]

During the worst period, France talked about pulling the UN out
of Bosnia altogether, the United States was worried because it had
committed troops to NATO to assist in such a withdrawal, Croatia
launched a new offensive to take back Krajina from the Serbs, and the
only people likely to be smiling were the ones who are still out there
today, feeling safe and warm in executive offices in the three capitals
or in mountain hideouts in places like Pale and Hans Pijasek.

Four

These thoughts zipped through my mind as I was standing there in
Pale on the deck of a Swiss Miss–style chalet, under the scrutiny of
two dozen Serbs who were sitting with their beers, slivovitz, and suspended conversations. Which group did these people fall into? The
brainwashed or the brainwashers? Was there any such distinction
anymore?

I sauntered as casually as possible inside and found someone who
spoke English.

"Yes, we have many rooms," he said, staring at my SFOR press
pass, smiling in a way that wasn't very reassuring. The entire bar was

listening to our conversation. "For one person, it's DM 60 for one night." That beat any price in Sarajevo . . . but I felt far from the safe lights of the city, there in the bottomless shadows of Republika Srpska, where, in spite of my best efforts, the work of the anti-Serb propaganda—including my own—convinced me that the people who lived there posed more danger to me than those who lived in Sarajevo.

Ten minutes later, I was creeping shamefully back over the mountain and checking into the Hotel Belvedere back in Sarajevo.

The Belvedere was something of an oasis within walking distance of the old Olympic stadium, where hundreds of graves stand up like goose bumps on the practice soccer field. It was one of the new places, done up in the kind of colors you'd see if Ronald McDonald were picking limes on the outskirts of a Grateful Dead concert. The lobby was a collision between a strip-mall antique store, K-Mart's garden aisle, and an Old West saloon. The whole thing was carpeted with Astro-Turf, over which was cluttered lawn furniture and used wooden tables whose only refurbishing had come from a bottle of Pledge. At the back of the room that served as registration area, café, and dining room stood a long wooden bar twinkling in the reflection of track lights aimed at the liquor bottles. The young woman in charge was about sixteen years old; she had the studied boredom of a cover-girl-in-training.

There was an air of newness to the hotel, overshadowed by a generous amount of almond perfume. Two days of road travel had greased me with a sheen of sweat that never seemed to go away, and I was coated in a fine layer of dust and grime. Trudging into the Belvedere with three oversized bags and baggy shorts that came to my knees, I fell quickly under the withering gaze of the innkeeper. She knew I was a journalist from the press card hanging around my neck, and her expression made it clear that I was as unwelcome a reminder of the "old Sarajevo" as the decimated buildings littering the skyline. In fact, her demeanor was so unpleasant as she processed the paperwork that I thought she'd start scolding me any minute: "You know, the war is over. We *won*. We don't need you people around to gawk at us and what we went through, you vultures who make your living on the corpses of the dead and dying. Well, we *didn't* die, just look around you. You no longer have a story to file about 'poor Sarajevo.'"

She didn't say anything, though, just handed me the key and pointed to the door leading to the stairs. But she may as well have given me the lecture; it was spoken in her every gesture. Such a reaction to the media is generally uncommon outside tense situations, but it's not unheard of—Sarajevans have an instilled pride that's well deserved, and they take any and all opportunities to remind you of it.

Sarajevo hadn't always been the capital of Bosnia. That designation went to Jajce, a village so small that I didn't even notice when I'd driven through it earlier in the day. Sarajevo was nothing more than a modest mining town when it fell into the hands of the Turks in 1464, but it soon became the seat of Muslim nobility and was blessed with the type of material and spiritual excesses common to the Turks. It was also the birthplace of a peculiar tenet of the Slavic character: a low-grade mutiny that would be familiar to anyone today frustrated by trying to get Dayton's signers to implement its provisions. Bosnians gave up to the Turks because they had no other choice—but they never forgot that this strange new tribe that had brought rare wealth and power into their city centers and villages was their enemy. As Rebecca West wrote, "There could be no two races more antipathetic than the Slavs, with their infinite capacity for inquiry and speculation, and the Turks, who had no word in their language to express the idea of being interested in anything, and who were therefore content in abandonment to the tropism of a militarist system."[15] So the Bosnians were subjects of the sultan and willing converts to the religion of Muhammad . . . but they were just insubordinate enough to forge something of an independent culture based in Sarajevo. The Turks had no option but to accept the Bosnians and try to live with their uncooperative minions. The Bosnians lived as they liked "according to a constitution they passed based on Slav law and custom and defied all interference," reported West, so much so that the Turks didn't even feel comfortable making Sarajevo their seat of government; for that, they chose to be exiled in miniature from their own conquered territory, operating from Travnik, fifty miles to the west. Such insolence gives some insight into the mentality of the people who came under siege five hundred years later. Though of course the Turks were long gone and businesspeople in Sarajevo were far more interested in international banking than in mining, they were still Slavs of the type who submit and go hungry because there is no other choice. But they never gave up hope on their city, one of the few places in Bosnia that was truly "multicultural" in every sense of the word.

The architecture of Sarajevo is a jangled mixture of Turkish, Austrian, Slavic, communist, and global multinational corporatism.

Minarets poke the air next to Stalinist apartment blocks, which teeter over the narrow maze of the ancient marketplace, whose cobble-stones date back to the time of Christ. The people are an equally eclectic mixture: Serb, Croat, Muslim, Jew, Gypsy, and practically every other nationality and religious identity imaginable, all of whom have intermixed and intermarried and are as ethnically indistinguish-able as the citizens of any typical American city.

For many people, Sarajevo *was* the Bosnian war. Any city under siege is a dramatic story, but a European city full of starving rich white people being bombed by bumpkins from the country was too unique for media bosses to believe. The city came under siege shortly after the shooters atop the Holiday Inn poured hot bullets into a crowd of people demonstrating for Bosnian unity in front of the Parliament building. Karadzic ordered artillery pieces placed atop the surrounding hills. The guns dropped an average of 4,000 shells into the city per day, targeting marketplaces and water lines. All roads leading in were cinched tight, and hundreds of Serbs fled the destruction to join the attackers in the hills, either because they believed in their cause or simply because they were tired of getting shelled themselves. Strangely, some of the people who left and took up arms against the city telephoned their friends who stayed trapped under their very guns, calling them to chitchat about their lives be-fore the war. The sound of shooting was a constant feature of the culture during those years, whether it was the hammering of a ma-chine gun, the flat crack of a sniper rifle, the whistle of an artillery shell, or the thud of a mortar. The city was eventually surrounded on all sides.

To understand how the siege of Sarajevo was allowed to go on for so long, it's only necessary to understand one thing about the UN's mission in Bosnia since 1991: the international peacekeepers were not there to see justice done, they were there to facilitate the end of the war. The easiest and quickest way to get that done was for the Bos-nian holdouts in Sarajevo to give up and allow the Serbs to roll vic-toriously down Sniper Alley. The longer the Bosnians refused to give up the fight, the longer the siege dragged on. And the more resentful UNPROFOR became. One aid worker remarked, "If the UN had been around in 1939, we'd all be speaking German."[16] During his only visit to Sarajevo in 1992, Boutros-Ghali admonished its citizens with a statement that explains a lot about the UN efforts in Bosnia: "I understand your frustration, but you have a situation which is better than ten other places all over the world. I can give you a list of ten places where you have more problems than Sarajevo."[17]

No one but journalists were actually interested in seeing such a list, however, and it's surprising Boutros-Ghali wasn't stoned to death before he could escape to the airport.

Five

I woke up at 5 and ate a nervous breakfast of fruit, yogurt, and coffee in the hotel lobby in Sarajevo. The wake-up call wasn't supposed to come until 6:30, but I was eager to get on the road. The day would be long and tense—five minutes after I left the comforting early morning buzz of the hotel, I would be back in Republika Srpska, where I couldn't read the Cyrillic road signs.

The route was easy and short—it would only take about an hour or two to get from Sarajevo to Foca, and from there, it's only another twenty-five miles or so to Scepan Polje, the border crossing, which—I prayed—had my Yugoslavian tourist visa waiting for me on some clipboard. Of course, regardless of the outcome of the border crossing, things wouldn't get any better. If I were turned back, I'd still be in Republika Srpska . . . if I was allowed to cross, I'd be in *Montenegro*, the other Yugoslavian republic besides Serbia, a land I knew very little about. Once I got through Montenegro, I would come to the end of the road at Kosovo.

By that time I had no sense at all whether my vague fears about traveling in Bosnian Serb lands were founded or not. Without the distraction of everyday conversation, I was left alone to ruminate on tales of war atrocities, death, and my own wisdom. The only voice other than my own was that of Mark Milstein, the shock-troop photographer who had warned me that driving a car that identified me as a Croat onto Serb land was like signing your own death certificate. Of course, hyperbole from full-time combat correspondents is the most shameless kind, something I knew well, but there were no voices telling me otherwise. The only people who approved my travel plans as anything less than suicidal—a waiter in Bihac and the hostess at the breakfast counter in Sarajevo—both knew nothing of actually doing it.

"Driving your car is no problem," said the young lady at the hotel. "People drive to Srpska all the time."

"Yeah, but cars from Croatia?" I asked. "Have you ever done it?"

She snorted at the thought. "To Srpska? I would not go there for one million dinars."

I felt guilty for being so nervous, especially in light of the emotionally inspired decision to stay in Sarajevo rather than Pale, a decision that had far more to do with my falling victim to propaganda than it did with anything in my experience with the Serbs. I was losing sight of the accuracy of my feelings—were they based on true dangers or imagined ones? Was driving a Croatian car in Serb areas as great a risk as I'd convinced myself?

I could no longer tell, but common sense told me that there was certainly some merit to my paranoia. I would have felt as uncomfortable coming from the other direction and having to drive through Drvar in a car rented in Belgrade.

So I packed my bags into the trunk, checked that the bullet-proof vest was sitting where it should in the passenger seat foot well, meandered through sunrise traffic down Sniper Alley to the exit for Foca, and decided to just drive quickly.

The road began in Dobrinja, running through a cluster of destroyed houses scrambled on the side of the road like crushed dinosaur bones. No one else took the exit to Foca behind me, and soon, mine was the only car on the road in either direction, save for the odd rhombus-shaped French SFOR jeeps that sped past from time to time.

It had rained shortly before sunrise, and everything was dripping and cloaked in a heavy fog. Complicating matters further, all the road signs were in Cyrillic, an alphabet as indecipherable to me as hieroglyphics. The map useless, I pointed the car down the narrow misty road overhung with weeping vegetation and floored it, trying to remind myself that "Serb" doesn't necessarily mean "war criminal."

When I got to Foca I had the same queasy feeling I'd had in Pale, only amplified, because in Pale the one known war criminal isn't accused of personally raping and torturing people. Here, however, in this grimy collection of faded concrete buildings straddling a sluggish river, were at least seven people running around who made the Marquis de Sade look like Richard Simmons.

Foca had fallen in April 1992. The conquering force consisted of regular army JNA troops and hardware, a hodgepodge of local militias that had by that time revived the label *Chetnick* from the lexicon of World War II, local police, and warriors from Montenegro. The prewar population consisted of about 20,000 Muslims who were quickly rounded up and sorted out on the road overlooking the Drina River.

It's hard to imagine that day in anything but a medieval context, especially sitting there looking on the village in a hot, gray mist. The buildings are ashen, the red roofs dull and depleted of color. On the hillsides, unchecked vegetation had obscured all but simple chimneys jutting into the sky, spilling oily cooking smoke that ran together in the desultory haze. The people themselves looked and moved like tree trunks, as if they were permanent parts of the town's physical structure, breaking away from buildings like amoebae, only to gravitate across the void of a street or a park and be absorbed into the background of a thousand different shades of gray.

But there's nothing to suggest that Foca was not a typical Bosnian village before the Serbs came—that is, one with satellite television and filled with people as painfully normal as those in any rural American city. So it's safe to assume, with some exceptions for the elderly, that the Muslims who were assembled and categorized as prisoners must have looked harrowingly modern, dressed in Levis, T-shirts, floral spring skirts, Nike sneakers.

The women, children, and elderly were separated from the men, who were either bussed off to concentration camps or crammed into the local prison. The women were sent to one of three detention centers: the hydroelectric dam compound, the Partizen sports hall, or the local high school. All three became recreational facilities for the Serbs and their Montenegrin counterparts; they became living hell for the women.

According to the indictments handed down by the ICTY, the women held in detention were raped so often that it's somewhat surprising that the soldiers occupying the town managed to get anything accomplished other than the complete mental and physical destruction of their female prisoners.

The hydroelectric dam facility was used as a barracks for 200 or so soldiers and as an interrogation center for captured prisoners from surrounding villages, some of whom had fought back at the Serbs and inflicted casualties. On July 3, 1992, about sixty Muslim girls and women were brought to the facility, lined up along the river, and warned not to resist or else they would be killed or raped. In turn, each one was brought before people who had overnight found themselves in positions of power as police and military commanders, including Janko Janjic, an unemployed Foca car mechanic; Dragan Zelenovic, an electrician from a nearby village; and Zoran

Vukovic, an ex-waiter from Montenegro, who suddenly found himself in charge of a squad of Chetnicks. All of these men—who were later indicted for crimes against humanity, breaches of the Geneva Convention, and violations of the laws or customs of war—were commanded by Gojko Jankovic, a former café owner who became the subcommander of the military police and main leader of the Chetnick units after Foca's defeat.

During the interrogation, the women were ordered to reveal the whereabouts of the men who had fired on the Serbs from the villages surrounding Foca and were warned that if they lied, they would be raped mercilessly before they were killed. One woman was gang-raped by at least ten men before losing consciousness. From there, the women were sent to either the school or the sports complex for detention and more rape.

On a typical evening, a unit of soldiers would go to the Partizan sports hall, for instance, a medium-sized building next door to the police station, and select three or four pretty young women to go with them. They were taken to apartments around town, the local soccer stadium, or other buildings where there were usually more soldiers eating and drinking and ready for a night of inhumanity. There, the women would be repeatedly raped by scores of men, sometimes for up to three hours. If they weren't whisked off somewhere else for torture by another gang of soldiers, they were returned to their group cell at the sports hall. Often, another group of troops would select the same women on the same night for more of the same horror. This happened every night for months. One fifteen-year-old girl was trucked around from one apartment to another night after night, being raped by different men in each location. She quickly became suicidal. Another, according to the tribunal indictment, was "sexually abused . . . in all possible ways. . . . For about three hours, [she] was gang-raped by at least fifteen soldiers (vaginal and anal penetration and fellatio). . . . The soldiers put their penises into her hands and ejaculated all over her. During the sexual assault, one soldier took out a knife and threatened to cut off her breast, but another soldier prevented him from doing so."

One woman reported the abusive treatment to Foca's police chief, Dragan Gagovic. He raped her and threatened to kill her if she ever told anyone what had happened. Afterward, she was raped so repeatedly that she can no longer bear children, Serbian or otherwise.

Finally, after five months of this incredible torture, the International Committee of the Red Cross managed to secure the release of most of the prisoners. But the Serbs stashed at least eight teenagers, and one girl who was twelve, away from the aid workers, enslaving them in a local house that they operated as a sort of brothel. For the next several months, the women were shuffled from house to house, forced to wash uniforms, cook, clean, and sexually please their captors. One woman was sold by one soldier to another for DM 200.[18]

The nine people who committed these acts are still on the loose, and blatantly so. Actually, to say they're on the loose presumes that they're being hunted; for the most part, they're not. Inexplicably, like riot control, refugee repatriation, and nearly everything else in the Dayton Accords outside suppressing military threat, arresting war criminals isn't SFOR's job.

Or so SFOR says.

5 The Problem with War Criminals

I was caught in the whirlpool of events . . . a merciless fate threw me into this maelstrom. . . . I wanted much. I began much, but the gale of the world carried away me and my work.

—Drazha Mihailovich, World War II
Serbian Chetnick commander, statement made shortly
before he was executed by Tito's partisans
for treason and murder, 1945

One

I was in no mood to hunt indicted war criminals—it certainly wasn't in *my* mandate—but I certainly could have if I felt like it, and I probably would have had some degree of success. Gagovic, the former police chief, had stayed in Foca and opened a bar.[1] Though the last thing on my mind was pulling up to cafés asking questions, people with weapons and UN Security Council clearance—SFOR—certainly could. Why they haven't is a question everyone is asking.

It's certainly not for lack of opportunity—most other war criminals are as easy as Karadzic for intelligence experts to find. Many have fallen into NATO hands only to be turned loose. Radovan Stankovic, for instance, one of the Foca Chetnicks indicted for running the slave brothels, works in and travels throughout Bosnia. He passes through SFOR checkpoints with complete impunity; he was even so bold as to go into an IPTF station to file a complaint stating that Bosnian police had fired on his car, and he took the opportunity to commend the international officers on the fine job they were doing. According to the latest available reports, as of July 1997, Stankovic still held his position as police officer in Foca. Gagovic told a reporter from the *Guardian* that he regularly drank with UN officers at his bar. Jankovic, the former café owner cum alleged rapist, was spotted by another British reporter sauntering into a café with his bodyguards. He ordered a drink feet from French SFOR soldiers who were also there.

These encounters haven't been restricted to indicted war criminals from Foca: Simo Zaric, indicted for sending Muslims to concentration camps in 1992, bragged to a human rights worker that he'd gone through hundreds of NATO checkpoints without incident. U.S. soldiers had even checked his ID. Milan Martic, a Croatian Serb leader (indicted for cluster bomb attacks on Zagreb, killing at least seven), was seen at a press conference in northwestern Bosnia by an IFOR officer whose only action was a sly shuffling of positions so that he wouldn't be caught on camera with Martic, a situation that would have been embarrassing. Martic is apparently used to close proximity to international peacekeepers, reportedly living less than 100 meters from an SFOR base in Banja Luka.[2] Stevan Todorovic, a police officer from Bosnanski Samac in northeastern Bosnia, was indicted for murdering civilians; yet a year into the Dayton Accords, he was still driving past a large U.S. Army base every day on his way to work.[3]

As for many of the others, the ICTY provided IFOR with wanted posters of the men under indictment, complete with their home addresses and telephone numbers. IFOR could have either called them on the phone to arrange for their surrender or driven to their houses and knocked on the door, as a number of journalists have done. Reporters found twelve indictees in four weeks in 1996 using the posters and discovered that most of them were working as government employees or police officers, in flagrant violation of the Dayton Accords. As Colin Soloway wrote in *U.S. News and World Report* in December 1996, "IFOR's first response to embarrassing questions about the demonstrable ease of finding war criminals was to reprint the wanted posters—without the street addresses. ICTY protested and insisted that its logo be removed as well. IFOR commanders then decided not to print any new posters."[4]

The obvious question is this: Why, after nearly $10 billion and three years invested in the peace mission,[5] with the United States' military and diplomatic reputation at stake—not to mention NATO's—and the lingering possibility of renewed warfare if and when SFOR pulls out, are U.S. military leaders not instructing their troops to do the one thing that could actually give Dayton the opportunity to become the peace it was meant to become?

It seems that the only person interested in having IFOR/SFOR arrest war criminals was Richard Holbrooke, who led a small band of hawkish diplomats in a doomed effort to win the Joint Chiefs of Staff and the Pentagon over to their way of thinking. Having worked closely with all three warring leaders and knowing well the evil influence of people like Karadzic and Mladic, Holbrooke argued that "after IFOR carried out its primary missions in Bosnia it should undertake additional tasks in support of peace—including keeping roads open, assisting in the election process and arresting war criminals. Without the backing of IFOR, the civilian part of the agreement—the test of true peace—could not be carried out."[6]

But it was a battle Holbrooke was destined to lose. First of all, as he pointed out in his memoirs, the military wasn't very keen on taking orders from a civilian. Second of all, and more important, nearly everyone he was arguing with was a Vietnam veteran. The veteran who would have the most influence in deciding the role of IFOR was General John Shalikashvili, whose emotions about Vietnam were as clear as his uniform. As chairman of the Joint Chiefs of Staff, he was entitled to wear the insignia of any military unit he wished. He chose to display the symbols of the since-decommissioned Military Assistance Command Vietnam, a long-defunct unit, as a tribute to the men and women who died in that conflict.[7]

Vietnam was no small matter when it came to deciding on the military's role in Bosnia—even though most of the field-grade soldiers who would end up being stationed there weren't old enough to even watch Vietnam on television, their military leaders in Washington remembered all too well the half-hearted, dubious reasons many of their colleagues had died. They were determined not to make the same command-level mistakes as their predecessors.

The other factor was Somalia, an imbroglio that was fresher in everyone's mind, especially that of the public. It was an unqualified disaster for America's foreign policy. We emerged from the rubble-strewn streets of Mogadishu looking like cowards and weaklings, with little or no direction and less resolve about what it was our military forces should be doing overseas. As a result of both these crises, the Dayton military policy was driven by one overriding concern: not to risk American casualties. By not *obligating* IFOR/SFOR to do the things Holbrooke suggested but instead *authorizing* them to do such things if they chose, the Dayton drafters doomed themselves. And the decision to put the safety of the soldiers first, though commendable, was no help to the military commanders who pushed so hard for such a low-profile role. The less the military assists in such "civilian tasks"—which would inherently raise risks for the troops—the longer their mission will become. When announcing the agreement to the American people on the completion of the Dayton negotiations, Clinton promised that American soldiers would be in Bosnia for only one year. That, more than anything, should have been a clear indication that our commander in chief was as interested in protecting the image abroad of the United States as a helpful, powerful international partner as he was in reassuring critics at home by providing a solid "exit date" and promising low casualty figures. Ever sensitive to the polls, Clinton knew all too well that nearly 70 percent of the public didn't agree with sending American troops to Bosnia;[8] but if America was to save face internationally, it couldn't decide not to. The only thing missing from Clinton's consideration seems to have been ensuring that the Dayton Accords, celebrated so strongly as a major American foreign policy breakthrough, would actually have an opportunity to succeed.

The one-year deadline passed as everyone suspected it would. IFOR was downsized to 33,000 international troops and renamed SFOR. The new date for troop withdrawal was June 1998. While I was in Foca, NATO voted to further extend SFOR's mission.

Two

There is a lot of debate regarding the "military versus civilian" provisions of the Dayton agreement. The document itself says very little about the military doing anything other than destroying ammunition dumps, separating the forces, and so forth. The only mention of civilian implementation as it regards IFOR comes in vague phrases stating that the military force "shall have the right to fulfill its supporting tasks, within the limits of its assigned principal tasks and available resources, and on request." Those supporting tasks—which apparently must be asked for nicely and will be done only if IFOR has the time and the inclination—do not specifically include arresting war criminals, at least not in so many words. Instead, the language is a masterpiece of vacuity: if it feels like it, IFOR may "help create secure conditions for the conduct of others of other tasks associated with the peace settlement."[9]

Technically, this falls shy of a "mandate" to arrest war criminals. According to the agreement, that responsibility is up to the signing parties, Croatia, Bosnia, and Serbia (which signed for Republika Srpska because war criminals themselves weren't allowed to negotiate on the peace agreement). Bosnians turned over all three of their war criminals immediately. Croatia produced some low-level suspects. The Serbs haven't delivered a single person on their own. This, say SFOR commanders, is a failure of the "civilian provision" and is none of its concern.

But in truth, all the provisions have a military component, thanks to the last-minute inclusion of a "silver bullet" clause allowing the military great autonomy. It reads, "The Parties understand and agree that the IFOR Commander shall have the authority, without interference or permission of any Party, to do all the Commander judges necessary and proper. . . . The violating Party shall be subject to military action by the IFOR, including the use of necessary force to ensure compliance with the Annex."[10] Since this clause is so broadly worded that it can be interpreted any number of ways, it became supremely important that the IFOR commander be a responsible person who understood well the importance of military intervention in ensuring peace, and who was not afraid to rely on that clause to make sure Dayton's provisions were being followed.

Unfortunately, that wasn't the case. The job fell to U.S. Admiral Leighton Smith, a seemingly qualified career naval officer who had almost 300 combat missions in Vietnam, was the commander in chief of all U.S. naval forces in Europe, and was the commander of NATO's southern forces. Smith had been in charge of the NATO air strikes in August and September against the Serbs, the action most responsible for their agreeing to the cease-fire that culminated in the peace talks in Dayton. But Smith may well have single-handedly doomed the entire mission from the outset because of his reluctance to fully involve the military in the peacekeeping mission beyond what was "mandated." As IFOR commander, he became a caricature of the West's reluctance to involve its military personnel in potentially risky endeavors despite their importance to making peace stick. Smith looked at the silver bullet clause and decided that it meant he had to do nothing at all other than what was strictly military. Whether he didn't want to risk lives or whether he thought helping civilian implementation was beneath him, is beside the point. But obviously, no one explained to him the consequences of adopting an UNPROFOR approach to peace . . . all of which were readily apparent in Grbavica in March 1996, a microcosm of what was to come if IFOR didn't take its job more seriously. Admiral Smith's attitude was reflected in every IFOR/SFOR spokesperson in Bosnia who stated that riot control, arresting war criminals, and providing security for refugees were not the military's job.

When that attitude was combined with the utter flaccidity of High Commissioner Carl Bildt, who had oversight of the implementation of Dayton's "civilian provisions," and the inherent weakness of IPTF, it's somewhat baffling Dayton has seen the degree of success it has.

In many ways, Smith's appointment as IFOR commander is indicative of the trouble the world has had from the very beginning in responding to the Bosnian crisis. In an era that focuses on consensus building, international alliances, and global security cooperation, almost every decision has to be reached after careful efforts not to offend any other countries. In many cases in Bosnia, concessions had to be made that would jeopardize the peace, which was already on shaky ground to begin with. In the case of Smith, NATO's Supreme Allied Commander in Europe, George Joulwan, wanted a four-star general with experience in ground combat to lead IFOR, but the French insisted that if the United States were to appoint a new person as IFOR commander, he had to be French.

France is the one country in Europe that could get away with making such a demand. France arguably did more for Bosnia than any other nation and therefore suffered the most casualties. French president Jacques Chirac was instrumental in spurring the United States to get involved in the crisis. Also, the French military would be in charge of the sector that included Sarajevo, where IFOR headquarters would be located. Therefore, it felt a certain sense of entitlement to having its people in key leadership positions, insisting on French leaders in both IFOR and the OSCE. American advisers managed to talk the French out of the OSCE position and avoided the situation with IFOR by keeping Smith in place and changing his title from NATO commander to IFOR commander.

Militarily, Smith took his role seriously. When I first arrived in Tuzla, I was stunned by the speed (less than three months) with which the U.S. Army had produced an entire military village in the woods next to the airfield. There was a control tower hunkered in the trees, a complex of barracks and PX stores, and exercise facilities. The roads and forest had been mostly de-mined, pathways had been constructed, and the front entrance already looked as if it had been there for years. Shortly before I arrived, Smith had sent a team of commandos into the hills, where they arrested eleven mujahideen freedom fighters and, in what would come to be a bold anomaly to the rest of the IFOR/SFOR mission, stormed a jail in Sarajevo where two Serbs were being held for questioning by the ICTY. Because the Serbs hadn't been formally indicted, their capture by Bosnian forces was an early threat to the stability of the Dayton Accords that Smith's forces defused by transferring them to the Netherlands rather than letting them stay in Sarajevo.[11] With expected military precision, IFOR met every one of its Dayton deadlines. The strong show of force early in the implementation process impressed everyone, and establishing the Zone of Separation happened with less strife and resistance than expected. Most reassured were the noncombatants living near Tuzla, who saw the sudden appearance of disciplined international troops as a sign that things were suddenly going to start turning around. To express his gratitude—and earn a buck—one enterprising businessman even opened a bar-brothel called the American Club in Tuzla at what must have been great expense. It reportedly had a jukebox full of Conway Twitty songs and a cooler full of imported American beer, but by the time I got there, it had gone out of business; the owner hadn't realized that the American soldiers wouldn't be allowed to leave the base.[12]

On the civilian side, things were far more bleak. Smith's civilian counterpart was Carl Bildt, a skinny Swede who didn't even have enough of a budget to afford an office in Sarajevo or a telephone.[13] He ran the entire show from his personal cellular phone and quickly fell so far behind schedule that observers became worried that he might never catch up. Like the IPTF, Bildt's Office of the High Representative was independent of IFOR at the insistence of Joulwan, who didn't want any civilian interference in the military chain of command.

Three

Under such a structure, Dayton became little more than a means of partitioning the country, something everyone had tried to avoid. While IFOR kept both entities apart and confiscated weapons when necessary, because the civilian components were so far behind schedule there was plenty of time for the local warlords—including war criminals—to establish de facto control in their regions of influence. IFOR had strict rules not to arrest any people indicted for war crimes (PIFWCs for short, pronounced "PIF-wix") unless they literally bumped into them in the course of their daily duties. This was Smith's version of a compromise. Checkpoint commanders were to be given pictures of the wanted men in case they stumbled across them, but months after this announcement, Charles Ingrao found that "nobody had any pictures of anyone."[14]

The tales of how far IFOR was willing to go not to run into PIFWCs are legendary—and ludicrous. Human Rights Watch reported, "NATO peacekeepers admitted to spotting a man they believed to be indicted war crimes suspect Pero Skopljak in downtown Vitez, but after driving back to their base—where they confirmed from a poster that it was indeed Skopljak—they did not go back, 'because that would have amounted to a manhunt.'"[15] In another situation, when checking for illegal weapons around Mladic's hideout near the mountain village of Hans Pijesak, IFOR officers demanded access to the command bunker. The Serbs said OK, but that the international troops were sure to see Mladic if they went inside. That meant they would have "bumped into him" and would be obligated to arrest him. The soldiers reconsidered and left the bunker alone.[16]

Under mounting criticism from human rights groups and the citizens of Bosnia themselves, a litany of excuses has flowed from SFOR headquarters. The earliest one—lack of information on suspects' whereabouts—was soundly deflated by the media and remains intact for only the most elusive. Some argue that arresting PIFWCs will cause a violent backlash that could disrupt the peace. This argument is, of course, ridiculous because it's their continued presence and influence that are the greatest threat to peace. Many war crimes suspects continue to be in positions of power—either official or unofficial—and it's not likely that they've changed their beliefs since the signing of the Dayton Accords. A similar excuse is that arresting war criminals would cause a violent backlash aimed at NATO forces and would therefore jeopardize one of the Holy Tenets, which is not to risk casualties. Although this is a consideration, it's the people they would be arresting who are most likely to orchestrate a retaliation. The risk will be transferred to the people of Bosnia if war crimes suspects are left to roam the countryside unhindered. And it's a risk that has yet to emerge in light of recent arrests.

The latest excuse is that the military commanders aren't sure some indictments will hold up at The Hague and are therefore unwilling to risk lives to capture a criminal they believe will eventually be set free. Robert Gelbard, the president's implementation czar, addressed the U.S. Institute of Peace symposium on "Bosnia in the Balkans" on February 25, 1998, by teleconference. SFOR, he said, will arrest war criminals if possible, but "a significant number of the indictments will not stand up in court. We will not risk the lives of any soldiers . . . to try to apprehend indicted war criminals if we believe their case is weak."[17] This is the ultimate in hypocrisy. The military has rejected assisting its civilian counterparts at every juncture, falling back on the explanation that it doesn't want civilians to interfere with its chain of command. But when it's convenient, there's apparently no compunction about interfering in civilian affairs by questioning the legitimacy of ICTY's indictments. With this attitude, SFOR has become the judge, jury, and executioner, trumping the tribunal's authority to press charges.

In fact, some see this as the ultimate way to dodge responsibility and not risk casualties. Like everything else relating to the Dayton Accords, the ICTY has no enforcement mechanism other than SFOR if the signing parties don't voluntarily surrender war criminals. And it began suffering from severe funding and staffing shortages as far back as December 1996, leading many to believe that it will eventually dry up and die of neglect if it's forced to wait for SFOR to take action. Michael Stiener, Bildt's deputy, responded to this scenario in an interview with *U.S. News and World Report:* "I don't see that you can have an exit strategy for peacekeeping troops as long as [indicted war criminals] remain free. There are some countries that want to avoid the issue. But they will pay the price later."[18] That price is renewed warfare, which not only would be catastrophic for the people of Bosnia but would be a failure of the first major military test of

NATO, a failure that would substantially weaken the organization's effectiveness in future situations that are bound to emerge.

Four

Thankfully, SFOR seems to have changed its traditional position of avoiding war criminals. Perhaps realizing that the future of NATO was at stake—or perhaps finally discounting their own rhetoric that the political gains in RS would lead to peace sometime in the distant future—SFOR has begun to step up to its responsibilities. In June 1997, British soldiers surprised nearly everyone by actually capturing Milan Kovacevic, the administrator of the Omarska concentration camp who told Ed Vulliamy that he didn't sleep well at night and that his hair had gone white. More surprising, the soldiers had gone out of their way to encounter him—he was arrested at his office in the Prijedor hospital without incident. At the same time, another "arranged encounter" was taking place near the village of Gradina, where SFOR helicopters swooped over former police chief Simo Drjlaca while he was fishing at a little lake. Determined not to be taken alive, Drjlaca raced to his red BMW and grabbed a pistol just as a group of commandos hit the ground. He shot one of them in the leg before being gunned down.[19]

These incidents left the press wondering aloud what had changed in the official policy of giving war criminals a wide berth. Officially, the Clinton administration said that nothing at all had changed: the allied troops had always been serious about arresting war criminals. But the real reasons probably have more to do with a key change in personnel at the top: General Eric Shinseki had taken over as commander of SFOR, and General Wesley Clark was now NATO's Allied Supreme Commander in Europe. Under their leadership, it seems that SFOR has finally emerged from its slumber. Even though critics gripe that the arrests that have been made amount to little—they argue that the suspects are "little fish" who mostly worked in the concentration camps and will therefore be easier to indict than those charged with more vague crimes like genocide—Shinseki and Clark began capitalizing on a broad intelligence effort that, once again, was initiated by the French on the very night the Dayton Accords were being formally signed in the Elysée Palace in Paris on December 10, 1995. While Milosevic, Izetbegovic, and Tudjman toasted their agreement under crystal chandeliers, Clinton and Chirac were huddling in Chirac's private office, according to a report in *Time* magazine. The topic of conversation: the arrest of Karadzic and Mladic.[20]

The French have always vowed to see both men either dead or dying slowly in a foreign dungeon, as much for the crimes they've been indicted for as for the personal suffering they've caused French peacekeepers and soldiers. In addition to the human-shield incident during NATO air strikes, two French pilots were captured by Mladic and tortured in custody. Mladic reportedly told the men, "You are my prisoners and you will be treated as criminals."[21] They were eventually released, but the French death toll still stood at over sixty over the course of the war. Chirac argued forcefully that those responsible must be either captured or killed if the peace agreement being celebrated in the ballrooms on the floor below was to succeed.

It was an argument that Clinton was familiar with; he'd heard it enough times from Holbrooke and his maximalist cronies. But Clinton was still highly influenced by his military advisers, who prophesied heavy casualties if IFOR/SFOR moved to snatch either man. Nevertheless, the two leaders agreed to join forces in a secret Franco-American intelligence operation designed to closely track the movements of Karadzic and Mladic, with the eventual goal of capturing them. Killing them outright was out of the question: assassination is illegal for the United States. Even though it's not for France, France would not act alone in such a measure, in part because such an action might jeopardize American relations and also because of concerns about retaliation on the French troops who patrol regions of Republika Srpska. In fact, *Time* magazine reported that both Mladic and Karadzic have been in the crosshairs of French commandos but that they were allowed to escape the bullet because final approval for their deaths was never issued.

The resulting cooperative intelligence effort was code-named Operation Amber Star and eventually included Great Britain and Germany in the planning process. By April 1997, a plan had been formulated to kidnap Karadzic in Pale, but it wasn't until Clark and Shinseki had stepped into their new positions that the plan gained momentum. According to *Time*'s sources, French and American special operations forces would raid Karadzic's villa. Helicopter gunships would neutralize the Serb leader's forces—a small army in itself, estimated at between thirty and sixty men with armored vehicles and an arsenal of weapons—while a ground unit would storm the residence and capture the suspect. However, the plan was never carried out, for two reasons.

The first was, again, purely political . . . by the time the operation was ready to proceed, NATO had made the historic step of inviting Poland, the Czech Republic, and Hungary into its ranks. Simultaneously, to ease Russia's fears about NATO expansion, the organization signed the NATO-Russia Founding Act, "which formalized Russia's role in the security architecture of post–cold war Europe," in Holbrooke's words.[22] With the ink on that agreement still drying, and reassurances about Russia's place in global security affairs still fresh in Boris Yeltsin's ears, he would have to be made aware of Amber Star, especially since it was designed to nab a Serb. Russia and Serbia have always had close ties. And since the operation was to take place in a sector that was also patrolled by Italian soldiers, Italy would also have to be informed. Chirac didn't like the odds of the plan's remaining secret. "If we tell the Russians and the Italians," *Time* quoted him as saying, "we might as well hold a press conference." The decision to proceed was postponed, but actions by the French themselves, ironically, caused the whole plan to be scrapped entirely not long afterward.

While Amber Star was being formulated, there was a parallel effort to get Karadzic to surrender. This effort coincided with an open international alliance with the Serb moderates who eventually wrested formal political control from Karadzic and moved party headquarters to Banja Luka. Many believe that the diplomatic approach was having an effect on its target: Karadzic's money and power base were slowly but progressively dwindling, and officials were conducting negotiations with him, discussing the terms of a hypothetical surrender, the type of legal representation he might have, and so on. But one French officer was accused by the United States of having gotten a little too chummy while pursuing this course: Major Herve Gourmelon had not only hinted to the most wanted man in the world that a plan was under way to kidnap him but may also have handed over the plans, U.S. officials claimed. French officials immediately denied that this was the case, noting that they weren't even sure Gourmelon had access to the plans—but he was jerked out of Pale like a rotten tooth nonetheless. Eventually, the French admitted that the officer had overstepped his authority in a moment of "carelessness," and the arrest plan was abandoned.[23]

So were secret alliances with other countries. After that failure, the United States jettisoned its efforts to involve other nations in the hunt for Karadzic, opting instead to trust only its own internal snoop network rather than those of other countries (for his part, Mladic has reportedly eluded intelligence trackers and fled to Yugoslavia). As a result, elite counterterrorism commandos from the U.S. Navy's SEAL Team 6 had to be smuggled into Bosnia in eight-foot-tall oil drums that kept them from the eyes of untrustworthy allied soldiers, according to a July 1998 article in *U.S. News and World Report*. The commandos were on a mission to apprehend five PIFWCs in northwestern Bosnia, sent there at the behest of one of the most massive U.S. intelligence efforts since Vietnam, one that involved the Central Intelligence Agency, the National Security Council, the State Department, the U.S. Army's prized Detachment Delta unit, and the U.S. Army's supersecret, ultraelite spy unit, Torn Victor. The plan cost up to $50 million and involved more than 300 people. It operated beyond the normal channels of NATO and was overseen directly by Clark.[24]

Such a large operation is difficult to keep quiet, even under the best of circumstances. Only hours before getting the green light to hit their targets, the SEALs were called off—a Bosnian Serb official told a U.S. soldier that he knew of the plan.

But there were other operations in the works, most of them centered on Pale, which is apparently overrun by spies gathering information on Karadzic. Not only were many of the information-gathering operations done without the knowledge of the French, but some were also directed *at* the French. *U.S. News and World Report* quoted an anonymous source stating that U.S. commandos had bugged a French officer's car and telephone when they suspected that she was having unauthorized conversations with top Serb officials close to Karadzic. But on the day she was scheduled to meet his associates, she took a different car, and it's unconfirmed whether or not the meeting ever took place. Other security aspects involved monitoring Italian communications to make sure the Italians weren't leaking sensitive information to the Serbs. No incriminating conversations were ever heard.[25]

In the meantime, under this quilt of overlapping code names, paranoid operatives, tangled and tapped phone lines, high-altitude drone flights, and backroom back stabbing and double-crossing sat the tar-get, a tall, shaggy man who more or less started this whole mess in the first place, seemingly concerned with little more than spoiling his newborn grandson. And the funny thing is that, by birth, he's not even a Serb. He's a Montenegrin.

6 The Land of the Lost

In skating over thin ice, our safety is in our speed.

—Ralph Waldo Emerson

One

Beyond Foca was the road leading to Montenegro and the Yugoslavian border, a road I wouldn't have attempted even in a bullet-proof Jeep if there had been any choice. But there wasn't. Without a legitimate travel visa issued by the Yugoslavian embassy in Washington, there were only two choices if I wanted to get to Kosovo: either sneak into Yugoslavia illegally, which would have gotten me arrested at the first police roadblock, or slink in across the border of Montenegro. The choice was obvious, but the road gave me pause; after Foca, it got progressively worse. At first, it was the same pitted, crumbling blacktop of every other road in Bosnia. But then it degenerated to chip-seal macadam with a rough washboard texture. And then, around a slight bend where the road squeezed through a gateway of embracing overhead limbs, it ended altogether. There was nothing ahead but a thin dirt goat path.

I stopped the car and got out. Surely this isn't right, I thought, staring down the trail. It wound up the side of a smooth mountain and vanished over the horizon, leaving a deep valley and the vista of olive humps that marched into the distance. I looked at the map. There was only one road to Scepan Polje, and in Foca, less than two miles back, I had triple-checked the road sign (an older one that hadn't been replaced by a Cyrillic counterpart), so that there wouldn't be any mistake.

I was completely alone, sweating in the dust, wondering what to do. There was only one thing *to* do, but that didn't make it any easier. There were Serb police down there guarding the border, and I'd have to deal with them. And there was no telling who was in the trees, opting to live in these parched hills for their own reasons. On top of that, there didn't seem to be any place to turn around if I had to: the path was barely as wide as the car. Once at the border, I would be completely at the mercy of a foreign bureaucrat I'd never met, relying on one late-night phone call that had assured me there would indeed be a legal document permitting my entry somewhere at the end of that road. I had mixed feelings about that promise. If things worked out, I'd have wangled my way into a country that was all but shut off from the world . . . but several hours later, I'd be in a region where the bloodshed was occurring at that very moment, where the Serbs were battling guerrillas of the ethnic Albanian Kosovo Liberation Army. Unlike in Bosnia, there wouldn't be the threat of violence, just actual violence. I drove on.

I had the windows down to capture any breeze that might wander up from the valley below, but the only thing that came through was a swarm of strange black flies and a shrieking chorus of summer locusts. I drove slowly, not daring to risk a flat tire here. The "road" was nothing more than a gutted dirt lane that obviously didn't see a lot of traffic, filled with deep holes and ruts that scraped the underframe. From time to time, I passed the hollow shell of a car that had been shoved off the road, peppered with rusting bullet holes. And then I passed a woman's bra hoisted onto a stick like a victory flag. Given the history of Foca just behind me, it was an ominous sight. The route had most likely been a main thoroughfare for soldiers and weapons between Bosnia and Serbia during the war.

The road crested at the top of the hill and ran like kite string down the other side and up another at least ten miles across the brown valley formed by the Drina River. Nothing to do but keep going, although I wasn't even sure if I was headed in the right direction.

Finally, after what seemed like forty miles but was probably no more than fifteen, I crept around a curve in the deep cleavage of two unusually close mountains. Two Serb cops stood in the dirt next to a plywood shed and a red-painted iron gate, arms folded.

Two

It was exactly as one would expect. The two guards were direct from a Grade B espionage film, complete with heavily starched sky blue uniforms, the type of icy glare perfected by the KGB, and the air of people who are fully in charge of a situation and plan to make the most of it. The car was searched, of course; they rifled through my duffel bags, my camera bag, and my shoulder bag; questioned me about the flak jacket; and scoured the map for margin notations (I'd been careful to keep it perfectly unmarked, having been warned that circled villages or highlighted routes are a common excuse for calling someone a spy). One of the guards circled the car slowly, hands behind his back, as if he were considering buying it from me. The other stood two feet away and stared at my head.

The fellow completed his inspection and called me to the trunk with his index finger . . . which he slowly pointed at the license plate. He raised his eyebrows and smiled slightly as if to ask, "And what have we here?"

Suddenly I had the answer to my question: apparently it *was* foolish to drive in Serb lands in a Croatian car. Fortunately, the two soldiers knew I was American; there's no telling what would have happened next if I had been Croatian. Maybe nothing. Maybe I would have been arrested.

Maybe it would have been worse than that.

Staring at the guards, though, I found it inconceivable that either of them was capable of doing evil. I was face to face—literally—with the Bosnian conundrum that's plagued Western observers: here were two very nice-looking, although stern, fellows. Both looked to be in their midtwenties. The one who wouldn't stop staring at me wore his blond hair tightly cropped, but otherwise he looked for all the world like Matt Damon in *Good Will Hunting*. The other one looked about the same age but had a sallow complexion and sharp, slightly too-big facial features. He looked as if he would have a tough time finding a date if everyone else in his unit looked like his partner. Of course, I knew nothing about them. They might be perfectly well-trained IPTF success stories. But intuition told me that those rare cases probably weren't guarding an obscure border crossing deep in the wooded cleft of two mountains at the end of a perilous dirt road. They could just as easily have gotten their instruction from Dragan

Gagovic, the Foca bar owner-war criminal-rapist-etc., who, much to the international community's chagrin, had somehow made it into the ranks as a police trainer.[1]

These thoughts moved with electrical speed. Realizing the tense position I was in, I didn't waste time gawking. Instead, I shrugged and pointed to my chest. "American. U.S.A.," I said, then pointed to the car. "Auto Hrvatska, da. Me—American." It was all I *could* say.

The thin one pursed his lips and shook his head. My excuse wasn't good enough. Although I'd established that I didn't understand Serbian, he nevertheless began a lengthy, bitter fulmination on, I suppose, my gall in driving such a vehicle to his border post. He pointed wildly at the car, at me, at the hills, and at his pistol, finishing his entire tirade with a huge, gluey spitball hurled emphatically at the car. It hit the rear windshield and rolled lazily down toward the license plate.

Reflecting on the confrontation later, I realized I should have been terrified. But it was his tone—though vitriolic and condescending, it also was tinged with the type of quality usually heard only from loudmouth foremen far from the ears of the shift manager. It was all bluster. He was telling me that he ought to shoot me for being so confoundingly inconsiderate, and that he would do just that if it were up to him, but the rules said there should be freedom of movement, and he had to go by the rules. But by god, he didn't have to like them.

Thus martyred, he stalked off to the shed, where I heard the yelp of rusting bedsprings. I wasn't sure what to do. Would he change his mind and come out for more yelling, maybe giving into the urge to let me taste his rifle butt?

No, but I wasn't getting off the hook either.

"Doo hun-ret deutsche mark," said Matt Damon in afflicted English, pointing at the car and then at the road on the other side of the barricade.

"What!?" I said, stunned that my penance was to be measured in money rather than blood—and suddenly pissed at the price. "Two *hundred* marks? What for?"

My outburst must have surprised him as much as it did me. He shuffled back a step and, for the first time, broke eye contact. But a second later, he remembered that he was the one with the assault rifle and stood his ground, holding up two fingers.

"Doo hun-ret. Because Hrvatska," he said, pointing to the plates again. I sensed an unexpected opportunity presenting itself. I had the sudden lunatic urge to shove a finger into his chest and begin shouting maniacally, to see if he would back down. But it was only a fleeting urge. His partner was within earshot, and I didn't think he'd need much of an excuse to fill me with holes.

Instead, I rolled my eyes. Two hundred deutsche marks was a substantial investment at that point, but I clearly wasn't in a position to bargain. So much for freedom of movement. Grudgingly, I fished a pair of bills from my wallet, and I was waved through.

Forty yards later, I came to another shack, another barricade, and another gang of law enforcement misfits who'd fouled up enough in their regular responsibilities to earn a tour of duty out in the middle of nowhere. It was the gateway to Montenegro.

Three

There's not much for a language-impaired foreigner in a war-torn country to do at police checkpoints except submit to whatever happens. By the time I got to Montenegro, I'd been stopped by three different police forces more than a dozen times in two days. Nothing so dramatic as a car with flashing lights appears from a shady alley; the stops are more like U.S. sobriety checkpoints, usually manned by anywhere from two to ten cops standing next to a plywood cube with a bunk, a desk, and a telephone. Normally, you pull up and nod firmly to the officer, asking if he or she speaks English. They never do, but it gives you the needed excuse to shrug and act dumb. You get out of the car and hand over the "papers," a collection of documents that differs from place to place but that always includes your passport. Regardless of the language barrier, you're asked a million questions in up to three or four languages, each one at a higher volume as if shouting can make you understand. Failing to get an answer from you, the cop will make you open the trunk and all your bags, maybe even the first-aid box from the Budget company. Normally, you're given your things back and waved on . . . if they want to make things hard, they'll retreat to the shack with your passport and read everything over the phone, arguing with the person on the other end in a way that I always thought meant bad trouble before I realized this behavior was unique to cops in former Yugoslavia.

But at each of those other stops, I'd never been going anywhere so ominous. Things might be vaguely menacing in Bosnia and even downright violent at times, but they were nothing compared to Serbia that summer. Just over the mountains of Montenegro, no more than five or six hours' drive away, ethnic cleansing was not a thing of the past but a goal of the present. Though Montenegro has managed to stay out of the Balkan wars for the most part, it's still Yugoslavia; many Montenegrin soldiers aided the Bosnian Serbs during the war, acting at least as brutally as their comrades. And the country has always been shrouded in mystery; most people draw a perfect blank at the mention of its name. Few people even know where it is. Even fewer know more than that. One quickly gets the impression that the Montenegrins like it that way.

The border guard wasn't about to let his country's secrets pass easily to one like me. Never before have I seen a face so expressive; it spoke better English than his mouth did Serbian. In a full saunter that could have been learned only from reruns of the *Andy Griffith Show*, he seemed to take a month to cross the fifteen feet from the shed to the car. He was all shins.

Barney Fife lost his swagger, however, when he found I had a direct connection to his boss. He immediately supplicated and, through a translator, apologized for the fact that I might have to wait for a few minutes while they made contact with the home office. I pulled the car to the side and drank a Coke from the trunk.

A couple minutes turned into forty-five, and I spent the time watching an amazing spectacle. About ten minutes after I arrived, a massive Toyota Land Rover festooned with European Community Monitor stickers, CB antennae and wire mesh, had pulled up in the dust, disgorging two salt-and-pepper-haired Brits dressed for eighteen holes at St. Andrew's. They regarded me as a ruffian, offering a curt nod and a flash of empathy that I had to sit there stranded in the heat because of some unfortunate bureaucratic red tape that they were confident of avoiding.

Their first mistake with the cops seemed to have been patronizing them. Neither spoke Serbian very well, but they had tried to communicate in the native tongue nonetheless for a fruitless five minutes, all the while waving off the offer of free translation services from a guy who seemed to work for the UN in some capacity. The Brits wore their importance like a generous splash of Old Spice, and the cops were having thin patience with it. Finally, they broke down and spoke in English, by then exasperated that they'd been delayed as long as they already had.

"We're going to *Kosovo*," said the driver, the more vocal of the two, as if he were speaking to brain-damaged children.

"Yes, but where did you come from?" asked the translator, who seemed to be speaking as much for himself as for the cops. He seemed eager to get back to his work in a UN truck parked nearby, in which, I'd learned while sitting there, he was installing a new JVC CD changer in the back.

"We came from Tirana, in Albania; then we went to Sarajevo; and now we're going to Pec before going back to Tirana," explained the Brit, repeating what he'd obviously stated several times in his flawed Serbian.

"Excuse me." The translator cut him off with a curt slash of the hand. "*Tirana* is over there, on the *other* side of Montenegro," he said, frustrated and eager to establish who was really in control. "Sarajevo is in *Bosnia*, which is on this side of Montenegro." Then, like a game show host asking the bonus-winning question. "*How* did you get from *there* to *there* without coming through *here*?"

This went on for some time, the driver of the EC truck becoming increasingly upset by people he saw as bumpkins with guns haggling over minutiae . . . he may have had a bullet-proof car, reams of official business, and a finer understanding of Balkan blood wars than many, but he didn't have the right papers, and it made his blood boil.

Ending the conversation abruptly, the translator turned back to his task with a brisk order: "You'll just have to wait and see what happens."

The driver started to argue, probably because no one moved to make anything happen. But his companion touched his elbow and whispered in his ear, making him think better of it. They slunk back to the truck and glowered . . . until the main guard delivered the coup de grâce, ordering them to move their vehicle so that a formless hatchback filled with dirt-poor Gypsies could go through the gate with a cheerful wave.

The amusement provided by the arrogance of internationals is never-ending. Clearly, these men were of some importance, a fact that they knew well. They were here to help someone, to try to prevent people like the ones at the border station from being killed by other people just like them. And surely, as their expressions and demeanor revealed, they were just now wondering why the hell they were bothering. Ungrateful savages . . .

But this was the gateway to Montenegro, home to one of the most hardy, heroic, and vainglorious people on earth. They didn't need help from anyone . . . especially the descendants of imperialists the likes of which they'd spent their entire existence successfully battling. No one orders a Montenegrin to do anything.

Which may be one reason why keeping quietly to myself off on the side, sitting on a log in the shade of the forest, may have paid off. With great fanfare, the cop hung up the phone in his shack and gathered everyone in sight to join him in welcoming me to Yugoslavia, handing over a small cardboard slip as if it were a diploma. I'm not sure how much of this ceremonial delivery was for the sake of the Brits standing ten feet away, but I smiled broadly and shook hands all around as if I'd never doubted the outcome.

"You have been very patient, and for this we thank you," said the translator. "It is typical rules, just like in any country. Enjoy your stay in Yugoslavia."

And like a fun house barker twitching back the purple velvet curtain that leads to fortune-tellers and mysticism, he raised the gate and waved me through, giving me a look hinting that if I found anything to enjoy, I deserved everything that was coming to me.

Four

If there's a town associated with Scepan Polje, I missed it. Instead, the road continued to follow the Drina and emptied with it into a stunning lake-gorge system forty miles long. The road twisted along a narrow cutout. Above was nothing but hundreds of feet of sheer golden rock cliffs; below, a straight 200-foot plunge into a pool of turquoise water. The opposing walls of the canyon were no more than 500 feet apart at points, their honey hues dabbed with explosions of purple-and-white wildflowers growing on outcroppings. A steady, cleansing wind rode through the canyon, bringing with it the scent of water, hay, and pine, the raw smells of nature.

But it was dangerous in its shocking beauty—the very geography made the thought of auto travel seem unlikely, and the gorge resisted it with convincing inflexibility. The road here was thoroughly deadly—since there was nowhere to park construction trucks, it had been allowed to degenerate with the seasons, crumbling to the river below in places, impacted and littered with rockfall in others. Worse, the iron hull of the earth had proved impervious to all but the most destructive means of roadmanship in some places, and tunnels into its stone heart had had to be blasted out with dynamite. These aren't like civilized tunnels: the ones in the gorge had no lights in them and often twisted to the left or the right within feet of the mouth. And they turned out to be a favorite place for lost livestock to wait out the heat of the summer day. The final obstacle was the sun, which was right overhead and turned my unwashed windshield into a solid golden screen of bug corpses, impossible to see through at all when I was approaching a wall of shadows leading into a tunnel and maybe a cow. The road required an even higher degree of attention than the others I'd been on, and therefore I was like Odysseus tempted by the songs of Sirens . . . if I indulged in more than a quick glance at the scenery, I might end up a permanent part of it.

The scenery of Montenegro is certainly something to behold, unlike that of any other region anywhere, composed of razor-honed chrome ridges and bottomless valleys filled with fires of green foliage, mad outbreaks of the purest floral yellows and pinks, and an air that's as clean and sharp as a hospital knife. The scenery rises and falls to exaggerated extremes, the petrified waves of a child's stormy sea. Everything has a just-disinfected feel to it, including the people, who, though covered in the same sheen of dust and grim as anywhere else in former Yugoslavia, radiate an undefeated beauty that would be hard on the eyes if they were naked and freshly bathed. Inland Montenegro is several thousand feet in elevation higher than its neighbors, producing a hard climate and a people of undue strength and clarity. Montenegro has never been successfully conquered.

An old tale points to why. It's said that a traveler once asked a Montenegrin, "How many of your people are there?" The man replied, "With Russia, 180 million." Sensing a fudging of the data, the traveler asked how many there were, not counting the Russians. The Montenegrin answered, "We will never desert the Russians."[2]

Good news for the Russians because anyone with enemies would do well to have people from Montenegro on their side. Throughout the Turkish occupation of Bosnia, Serbia, and Albania on all sides, the Montenegrins stoked the last coals of Eastern Orthodoxy in the region for centuries, turning it into less of a religion than a weapon, a bottomless vat of divine power from which they had received the order, and the power, to crush their attackers. While the Turks were advancing on Hungary and Vienna, the Montenegrins continually fought, and continually defeated, the Muslim invaders, with the aid of Serbs who scattered into their high hills after the Kosovo loss. A high-school textbook map of the Ottoman Empire at its apex would show a tiny pocket of Christianity in an otherwise vast ocean of Islam—that's Montenegro.

These victories were never easy . . . the attacks were unrelenting, regardless of the enemy. Montenegro has a very valuable seaport that was coveted by both the Byzantines and the Austro-Hungarians long before the Turks ever tried laying hands on it. So each generation spawned warriors who spent their time either engaging in or resting up for one battle or another. As a result, nothing Montenegrin is at all subtle: the heat is unfettered, the stones are hard as iron, and traditions have never been preserved because very little has come along in centuries to make the "traditions" need preserving. Roaring into Montenegro in a fuel-injected 1998 car with dual airbags and an AVS braking system is as close to time travel as I'll ever come, a realization that became more and more acute after breezing through the doddering city of Niksic and heading even higher into the barren tundra along a road that could have been built in the twelfth century. I was heading toward Savnik, listed by the ICTY as the boyhood home of Radovan Karadzic. It was pure coincidence—I was trying to take a shortcut through the mountains rather than stick to the more circuitous route that circumnavigated them. Climbing through altitude-stunted scrub pines jutting from white limestone outcroppings, I was running on nothing but pure instinct, the land apparently too remote and desolate for the makers of my map to do anything other than provide rudimentary indications of roads and distances. I could hardly blame them; the country is so vertically crooked one would think that God crammed all His leftover mountains into Montenegro once He had finished creating the rest of the world. I was forced to pilot the car between whole ranges, many of which were too steep for roads, and the route I traveled zigzagged like a manic-depressive profit-and-loss graph.

There were no road signs at all; obviously no one traveled these highways without knowing where he or she was heading. Branching off the main artery were countless forks and tracks, disappearing in the maze of the thorny bone-bare arms of millions of hardy shrubs that couldn't grow high enough to obscure the horizon but were tall enough to hide the course of the road. I tried to stick to whichever option looked like the most often used although it was sometimes impossible to tell; all roads seemed to be the one less traveled. For all I knew I was getting hopelessly lost in the loneliest land under the heavens.

Homesteads appeared as often as they seemed to have been touched by modern life, which is to say not very frequently. Glass seemed to be the most current contemporary invention to have made it this far inland. Farm machinery consisted of muscles and a scythe. Raked rooftops were shingled in hand-carved pine so old it looked like slate. Even the wheels on some carts were made of wood.

So it was a shock indeed when I stopped to let a cow cross the road and happened to glance to the left to see a little kid sitting on the hill with his head in his hands. He was wearing jeans and a yellow Adidas T-shirt . . . and next to him on a tree stump sat a carefully displayed collection of American cigarettes, chocolate bars, and beer bottles. The cairn of goods seemed as out of place as a shopping mall. Just as shocking, he spoke English.

"Hi there," he said.

"What are you doing out here?" I asked.

"Selling things."

"To who?"

"People like you," he said. "People who drive past."

I was about to ask sarcastically how business was, as I seemed to be the only person "like me" to have come along in decades, when my attention was attracted to one of the bottles sitting on the stump. Staring at it through the shimmering heat haze jetting from the ground like rocket exhaust, I suddenly realized how thirsty I was. I could barely believe I was still living in the same day that had begun in my hotel room in Sarajevo and that it was only noon. I was sure I'd been in Montenegro for at least fifteen years.

"You got beer there, huh? Pivo?"

"Yes. One mark." Seventy-five cents . . . too good to be true. But it was. I followed him up the hill (leaving the engine on and the car in the middle of the road—I wasn't concerned about traffic). He pulled a yellow Coleman cooler from the shade of a tree, and when he pried open the lid, I felt as if I were in a beer commercial. Floating in melting shaved ice were dozens of huge beer bottles.

"I'll take five."

The kid, acting as if he were heading for early retirement, insisted on carrying the bottles to my car, like an armful of bowling pins.

"You're English?" he asked.

"American," I said.

"I never met an American."

"Until today, I never met a Montenegrin," I said, gingerly stacking the drooling bottles in the trunk.

"You like Montenegro, yes?"

Like? Actually, I hadn't thought about it. In truth the emotion was as close to a mixture of love and loathing as one can get. But I frowned and said, "Sure," tossing him a five-mark coin and getting in the car.

The question bothered me—what *did* I think about this place? I pulled over into a meadow about a mile away to lounge in the long, hard grass and think about it over one of the beers. I neither liked Montenegro nor disliked it, though there were strong tinges of both . . . it was strange, as if I'd landed on another planet and was intrigued by its alien beauty but feared that it was emanating some sort of radiation that was making me sick and afraid. My feeling had little to do with the people, who, despite their ancestry, were more-or-less similar to everyone else I had encountered. It had to do with the landscape, but it's not something that can be gleaned from a picture. Its beauty was almost too intense, like an overbearing friend who is too willing to please. You're left wondering what your part of the bargain entails. The fields were a little too green, the mountains too white. The air was rarefied but seemed chlorinated. The perfect anachronism of the place was more of an assault than a pleasure, like a theme park whose underlying emotion is paranoia rather than joy. The houses were stunning in their simplicity and the impression they gave of coming from nature as naturally as a tree . . . but I did not want to be invited inside. The people in Bosnia read newspapers and watched CNN. The people here, well . . . they really were different from me. If the ancient Balkan hostilities apply to anyone in former Yugoslavia, it's the Montenegrins. Not because they're more prone to spill blood than anyone else—in fact, the opposite seems to be true— but because they live in this stark setting, an eternally unconquered people who've never known anything but having to defend themselves against an outside world intent on crushing them. And since they've been so successful in their defense, they've never had to huddle together in cities but instead have maintained their distant homesteads high in the hinterland, where neither clocks nor calendars seem to work and the same legends that were told in the time of the Turks are repeated today as bedtime tales. Like the pastures and the wildflowers, Montenegrins burn with the full intensity of what they are.

Five

Karadzic was a result of this strange sanctuary, by all indications a complete lunatic. Many people will say that Karadzic's only thought was that of evil, a man who was born wrong and just got worse. It's easy to think that way, looking down on Sarajevo from the hill in Grbavica, where his madness was written with artillery and machine gun shells on a once beautiful canvas. Karadzic is one of the most perplexing people of our time: a literary aspirant, a psychiatrist, an anti-Communist revolutionary, a self-described "bourgeois Serb," an indicted war criminal . . . and by most accounts a frighteningly affable person.[3]

When *Washington Post* reporter Peter Maass interviewed Karadzic during the war, he found what everyone else has found: an enigmatic, likable man whose only obvious flaw happens to be that he orchestrated and carried out genocide. Maass wrote in his book *Love Thy Neighbor:*

> When Karadzic arrives in a room, you notice his presence immediately, as though six trumpeters in red coats blared their horns to proclaim his presence. He is a bear of a man, six foot four, wide as an oak tree, who loves being the center of attention, loves to talk and boast, eat and drink, tell jokes and recite poetry. If it were possible to put the matter of the war aside, I would say that he is quite enjoyable to be around.

Karadzic's particular skill is his ability to tell lies, wrote Maass, "not little lies, white lies or deceptions, but whopping lies, lies that were so big and so incredible that you wanted to laugh, to say, in response, Hold on, Radovan, you expect me to believe this?"[4]

His favorite lie was the one about the Muslims in Sarajevo bombing themselves in order to make the Serbs look bad, one he repeated in April 1997 after giving a rare postwar interview to Dutch reporter Rob Siebelink (at the same time Clinton and Chirac were diddling and fretting over how to get close to him). Asked to justify the bombing of the Sarajevo marketplace and the bread line that resulted in international horror, Karadzic replied:

> It is very clear what happened there. The Muslims have done that themselves to show the world how the Serbs slaughtered innocent citizens.

They have done that several times. What happened when the pope paid a visit to Sarajevo recently? Along the road the Pope-Mobile was supposed to go, 25 anti-tank mines were discovered. Of course the Serbs were blamed. But how on earth could the Serbs get a truck with 25 anti-tank mines into a city that is dominated by the Muslim army? The Muslims were able to detonate the mines within 20 minutes. I assure you: our experts would have needed at least two hours to do the same. It was a set-up. A game they have played over and over again and the world believes it. When they needed their no-fly zone, they shot an Italian helicopter down. It was deep in Muslim territory, but the Serbs got blamed and they got their no-fly zone.[5]

Perhaps the most astounding thing is that Karadzic actually got enough people to believe him—or at least question the Muslims' victim image—so that he was able to continually get away with murder. Literally. The Western governments were gullible enough to believe that the Muslims had bombed their own people that they ordered a "crater analysis" every time a shell killed someone during the siege of Sarajevo. Crater analysis is the practice of determining what type of explosive caused a shell crater and which direction it came from. It was generally easy enough to determine both, but as a science, crater analysis fell short of providing iron-clad evidence of which individual weapon a shell had come from. Therefore no one could ever say with 100 percent certainty that the Muslims hadn't bombed themselves, even though the argument is patently absurd to most.[6]

But, as Maass pointed out, Karadzic wasn't interested in proving that the Muslims had done the things he said they had done; he just wanted to instill enough doubt in those who might intervene so that he could buy more time to finish his work. Which was the complete destruction of Sarajevo.

It was a perplexing goal, for Karadzic is as much a product of that city as he is of Montenegro, probably more so. When he was fifteen, he moved to Sarajevo from the mountains, a country boy with a single grimy sweater woven from wool from his village who got credit at the local pastry shops just for being likable.[7] Although he was from Montenegro, he told Siebelink that he's always considered himself a Serb living in Bosnia. Karadzic aligned with the Serbs, he said, because he supported keeping the country of Yugoslavia together.

Karadzic married and went to the University of Sarajevo, and he continued his education in Belgrade and Zagreb. Though by profession he was a psychiatrist—he once attempted to put the entire Sarajevo soccer team under mass hypnosis to pull them out of a losing streak—he was also something of a Yugoslavian version of a beat poet, hanging out with anti-Communist dissidents, political rabble-rousers, and Sarajevo's literary illuminati. He wrote well enough to penetrate the fringes of this latter group, but his poems were never taken seriously, nor were they very good by any other than the most generous standards. By all indications, he was far more affected by the political elements among his friends—who spanned all ethnic backgrounds—than by those whose highest passion was literature. He spent eleven months in jail for fraud in 1985, and in 1990, he formed the Serbian Democratic Party (SDS) in response to what he called fierce campaigning by Tudjman and Izetbegovic to drum up nationalism against the Serbs.[8] The party was meant as a vehicle, he explained, to promote the cohesiveness of Yugoslavia—and to protect the interests of its Serbs. At first, there was more of the former than the latter in the party's rhetoric . . . but two years later, he left Sarajevo for the last time, moving to Pale, where he orchestrated Sarajevo's violent demise.[9]

After the war, as a consequence of the Dayton Accords, Karadzic was forced out of public life and banned from holding official office. But that didn't matter very much to those who still looked to him as their leader. After the Dayton agreement was signed, Karadzic continued to wield incredible influence on the Bosnian Serbs he had directed so brutally during the war, using a cadre of "secret police" to intimidate any Serb who was publicly or tacitly supporting the peace measures. His first target was the Serb mayor of Banja Luka, an open Dayton supporter who was prevented by Karadzic's forces from attending a meeting with Clinton in Tuzla in January soon after IFOR had been deployed.[10] Barred from actually participating in the elections as a candidate, Karadzic immediately set about disrupting them to the point where Robert Frowick, the American head of the OSCE (the international organization overseeing the elections), and Richard Holbrooke discussed disqualifying Karadzic's entire party from the elections. It was the right thing to do, many believed, because Karadzic was openly violating the Dayton Accords on almost every level except militarily. In a document tellingly titled "A Failure in the Making; Human Rights and the Dayton Agreement," Human Rights Watch didn't mince words describing why the elections should have been postponed:

Blindly ignoring the mounting evidence that the Bosnian parties to the Dayton peace accord have failed to create the conditions for free and fair elections, U.S. Secretary of State Warren Christopher stated on June 2 [1996] that the elections would go ahead this year. Christopher's statement was part of a growing campaign by the Clinton administration to ensure that the election in Bosnia take place this September, always arguing that, although the elections will not be perfect, they are still in the best interests of the Bosnian people. But they are wrong. While holding elections in Bosnia may be in the best interest of Mr. Clinton's own re-election campaign, it is certainly not in the best interest of those who believe in a Bosnia that is not partitioned along ethnic lines, where the ethnic slaughter of thousands is not simply forgotten in an effort by foreign governments not to upset their own domestic political agendas.

Mr. Christopher seems to believe that elections, regardless of how flawed, will "give all the people of Bosnia a chance to shape their future." It will be difficult indeed for many of the Bosnian people even to participate in the elections given that there is limited freedom of movement throughout the territory, the press is severely restricted along ethnic and political lines, refugees and displaced persons have not been able to return to their homes and indicted war criminals—in particular Bosnian Serb political leader Radovan Karadzic and military commander Ratko Mladic—maintain predominant political and military control. If the elections go forward under these conditions, the international community will become an accomplice to a lie. The message will be sent that compliance with the Dayton agreement is not necessary or even expected, and it is likely that interference and intimidation by hard-liners will result in a corrupt election, serving to undermine the entire peace process and to increase the likelihood of renewed conflict.

What is more, elections that are held under current conditions—where persons indicted for war crimes monopolize the media, using it for their own nationalistic goal; and those who would voice an alternative, multiethnic view of Bosnia and Hercegovina are silenced—will only consolidate the power of the extremists.[11]

That's pretty much what happened, despite an eleventh-hour negotiation with Milosevic that resulted in the complete removal of Karadzic from official power. After the election, the seats of the co-presidency—the odd office created by the Dayton Accords that gives one seat to each of the three ethnic groups, with the person getting the most votes acting as chairman—went to Croat Kresimir Zubak, Izetbegovic (who also won the chairmanship), and Momocilo Krajisnik, a grumpy-looking hard-line Serb who is a close friend of Karadzic's and looks like a mad scientist or a gargoyle. Christopher called the elections a success, but the more astute observation came from the man who knows the Balkan political scene better than anyone, Holbrooke, who confirmed Human Rights Watch's doomsday prediction: "The election strengthened the very separatists who had started the war."[12]

The only good thing to come from the elections—in which voters also selected second-tier presidents with authority over the nation's two separate entities—was the election of Biljana Plavsic as president of Republika Srpska. Eight months after taking office, she publicly denounced Karadzic and moved party headquarters to Banja Luka.

But Karadzic was hardly dead in the water. Just because he's no longer president does not mean that he's out of power. Indeed, a huge number of Serbs continue to see him as their savior, the man who watched out for their interests. The driver who took Siebelink to his singular interview told him, "Karadzic is still my president, he helped us through the war." The resulting interview, and others like it, was published all over Europe and represented Karadzic's reemergence onto the political scene. Even in the Bosnia of 1998, small stickers with Karadzic's face plaster the railway underpasses and highway road signs in Pale, Foca, and other small towns in RS, in subliminal preparation for the 1998 elections.

The continuing influence of hard-line separatists and the glacial pace of implementing key Dayton provisions are hardly the only obstacles to smooth and democratic elections. Another hurdle is the labyrinthine complexities of the political system itself. In addition to the three-person presidency and the regional presidents, voters must choose national and regional parliaments. As can be expected in a country recovering from three and a half years of war, there are as many political parties, coalitions, and splinter groups as there are opinions in Bosnia. The ballot for the 1998 election contained eighty-three candidates and enough political acronyms for a tub of alphabet soup. Engineer Munevera Ljutovic told reporters that she didn't even understand her country's political infrastructure. "It's the country's [Bosnia's] setup," she said. "I didn't understand from the very beginning how this [country] is composed and which parliament is which."[13]

Not only is the process complicated—this will be the third election in three years; an earlier election for local posts was postponed because of blatant corruption and was conducted on a separate schedule—but its effectiveness is also being questioned by the people who count most in any election cycle: the voters. So far this decade, hardly anything has been accomplished democratically—everything has been done at the point of a gun, including holding elections in the first place. Christopher Bennett, head of the Bosnian branch of the International Crisis Group, an independent group monitoring the peace process, said, "Everything achieved so far in this country was achieved by cheating on democracy . . . by undemocratic means. Elections are needed only to ratify the new reality."[14]

Six

After Savnik—a lonely, insignificant-looking village—the road I was taking escaped human influence and came under that of sheer nature. Why there was a road at all from Savnik to Mijoska, the next major intersection, is open to speculation. Obviously no one traveled that way unless it was on foot or horseback. The road started out mildly decomposed and eventually became nonexistent. I was literally driving the car—which I'd promised to return unmolested after my "trip to Dubrovnik"—along scree fields and talus slopes, the proper course being a judgment call as to what section of passage looked the most level and the least likely to collapse under the weight of the car. I was perfectly sure that every bend would present me with a washed-out chasm or an insurmountable landslide and that I would then be doomed, utterly stranded in the middle of Montenegro, halfway up a mountain that even experienced four-wheelers would have thought twice about tackling. Turning around was out of the question: two feet to the right was a drop of several hundred feet through pine and beech-wood forests; on the left was a solid cliff I could reach out and touch, one that kept spitting pebbles off into the void. Only the fear of retracing my steps in reverse over delicately fixed rocks that threatened to dislodge without the proper application of force and weight kept me inching forward. By this time, the heat had crested at well over 100 degrees. I drove with my shirt off, desperately keeping an eye on the dashboard temperature gauge that flirted with redline readings. I couldn't have known in advance what I was rapidly discovering at the moment: You *can't* get to Kosovo this way.

•   •   •

Beyond the mountains, the land cascades downward, to the east, to the Kosovo basin and then Asia Minor: Istanbul and the land of Ghengis Khan. It's sprinkled with villages that had by then lost their foreign quaintness for me—red bricks and sloppy mortar work slapped around a frame of thick timber, same as everywhere else. Descending into the lowlands, I passed a well-built man out for an early-evening jog. He flashed me the three-fingered Serb salute as I streamed by.

In fading amber daylight, I tooled around the last Montenegrin village on the safe side of the Kosovo border, Rozaje, looking for a hotel. What I found instead was a pleasant roadside park on the outskirts of town with a chuckling stream bouncing through the towering evergreen forest. The park served as a community bath, recreation facility, day care center, and sports complex: it was as packed with people as Coney Island on Labor Day. Scruffy children raced after flat soccer balls in the full grip of World Cup fever even way out here; teenagers in bikinis and shorts lounged in the swirling pools of the creek, flirting; parents drank beer out of their car trunks and stood in wide circles, jabbering and shouting in animated conversations. I drove across the overgrown lawn and parked near the stream. When the engine died, it was like a conductor dramatically dropping his hands to bring a bizarre symphony to a long-awaited end. I was too tired to applaud, however, exhausted from a full day of anxiety and heat fatigue. I was rather astounded that after traveling several hundred miles through dangerous territory on unmarked roads across some of the most challenging physical terrain I'd ever applied a car to, I'd made it there, to that little park on the edge of Kosovo, my final destination of Pristina no farther than a quick three-hour drive over flat roads.

I held no illusions, however, that the final push to Kosovo's provincial capital would be in any way easy; in fact, it would probably be the most dangerous section of the entire journey. I planned to follow the road to an intersection at Pec, the province's second largest city, where I would pick up the final highway across the scorched earth of Kosovo, through embattled Serb military checkpoints, and under hills that held snipers and guerrillas of the KLA.

7 Kosovo

Can you picture what we'll be
So limitless and free
Desperately in need of some
Stranger's hand
In a desperate land

— The Doors, "The End"

One

Pristina, the provincial capitol of Kosovo, is not a sight for sore eyes. Until I crested a brown hill and saw it sprawled on the plain below like a gray tumor, I'd held onto visions of a city not unlike Zagreb, but smaller, one that I expected to be run-down but that, for some reason, I thought might be quaint in some ways. What I found instead was a filthy ghetto that smelled like a burning landfill, a jumbled collection of geometric apartment blocks and office buildings lost in the haze of a rancid smog. The events of the morning leading me to that place had made me forget Robert Kaplan's description of the city, which surely would have lowered my expectations: "Defeat is more than just a writer's historical metaphor. It is an overpowering reality written in streaks of tar, cinder blocks and corrugated metal, easily visible from the hill overlooking the famous battle [of Kosovo]. Defeat even has a name: Pristina."[1]

It also has a smell, one that can make you queasy anywhere within a five-mile radius. It's an unhealthy combination of coal smoke from

147

a nearby power plant, fuming roadside garbage, and rotting meat. It's pungent and sulfuric, and it clings to the inside of your nose. It's the smell of something recently dead, one that's appropriate to a place like Pristina, which has swollen like a gangrenous arm with zombified Albanian refugees from the countryside. They stagger the streets and the trash heaps looking for food while their children loiter on the street corners with squeegees and rags waiting for a red light to dash out and scrub a windshield.

Thanks to them, windshields are the only things that seem to be clean. The public greens are either brown because the grass has died or hectically overgrown and littered with broken bottles. The buildings are made of cracked cement and barely seem to remain upright under their own weight, teetering like crooked teeth. Even the newer shops seem shattered and warped. Homes on the hill are arranged with all the randomness of salt cubes under a microscope. Garbage blows through the streets like pollen.

Two

The only thing that makes Kosovo notable is the blood that's been spilled into its soil. As a landscape, it leaves much to be desired; it's composed mostly of lumpy tan hills and bumpy plains divided into uneven squares of farmland. The predominant color is brown, and it's found in shades that run the gamut from cardboard to well-done steak. The sky is white and vast, bled of color by the sun, perfectly cloudless except for the jet streams of Serbian fighter planes flying too high and fast to see with the naked eye. The people below walk painfully over the scorched ground like ants under a broiler. Everything seems barely out of focus. The most depressing thing is that so many people have died—and continue to die—over such a barren and unmajestic scrap of land.

The Kosovars, as they're called, are Albanian, ragged folks who've taken the Balkan Stare to new heights, crouching by the side of the road as if spring-loaded, waiting to be accosted by Serb police, boring holes through the skulls of anyone driving by. Their paranoia was well founded. The Serbian government's hunt for radicalized Albanians was on.

It was a course of events as sure as the annual arrival of Christmas. As far back as 1992, Holbrooke and others had urged world leaders to deploy troops to Kosovo's Macedonian border to keep the Bosnian war from spreading. The Clinton administration wisely followed this advice, sending 500 U.S. soldiers to a UN-directed peace-keeping force to prevent trouble. It was an astute move: Macedonia was as explosive as Bosnia in those days, being an unarmed nation with a diverse portfolio of serious problems, any one of which could lead to warfare between neighboring states, some of whom are in NATO together. To the south is Greece and to the north is Serbia—both of which consider Macedonia part of their traditional nations. Greece hates Macedonia because it named itself after a northern Greek territory and stole an ancient symbol found on the tomb of Alexander the Great for the Macedonian flag, leading Athens officials to fear that the Macedonians would co-opt Greek culture, history, and, eventually, their land. Serbia hated the little nation because it had supported international economic sanctions levied against Serbia. To the east, Bulgaria coveted it and busied itself with creating anthropological arguments as to why the Macedonians were really Bulgarians. And approximately 30 percent of the population were ethnic Albanians, who, like their brothers in Kosovo, wanted nothing more than to join together as a free and self-ruled people.[2] If the Macedonian Albanians headed for the door, Macedonia's neighbors would leap at the opportunity to claim a piece of it for themselves. The potential for trouble was contained with the deployment of the troops, but Macedonia's volatility would figure prominently in the international community's response to the violence destined to break out in Kosovo.

The actual number of Albanians in Kosovo is disputed. Serbia says there are 1.6 million; the Kosovars claim 2 million. Either way, both sides agree that whatever the number, Albanians account for about 90 percent of Kosovo's population.[3] And almost all of the Albanians are in the mood for revolution.

It's a mood that's been a very long time coming and has its roots in the fact that both the Serbs and the Albanians claim Kosovo as the cradle of their national identities. Unlike the Bosnian war, the conflict in Kosovo really is about ancient hostilities and will therefore be more difficult to stop. When you look at the history of this forlorn plain, it's a wonder violence took this long to erupt.

It was June, and the heat must have been oppressive, especially under woven gold-encrusted chain mail and the weight of maces and battle axes. Prince Lazar's knights were ready but jittery, facing the Turkish army alone on the empty field that would one day cradle the slums of Pristina and the power plant. Though the Serbs outnumbered their Muslim foes, they were plagued by disunity and premonitions of defeat. The Turks, on the other hand, were so confident of success that long before the first blow was struck, they ordered their men not to destroy any nearby villages in the wake of the battle so as not to unduly alienate their newly conquered subjects. The battle lasted all day, but the Serbs were no match for the sultan's men mounted on indefatigable Mongolian ponies. Under the cornflower sky, sweat and blood moistened the ground, and the din of battle must have carried for miles. Realizing that the Serbs were losing, Lazar's brother-in-law, a Serb nobleman, defected to the Turks and was brought before Sultan Murad, the Turkish commander. The night before the battle, Lazar, in a fit of paranoid hysteria because of the pending battle, had openly accused his relative of treason; perhaps in an attempt to prove himself in the ultimate fashion, the brother-in-law, in a final kamikaze attempt to turn the tide, whipped out a hidden dagger and plunged it into Murad so deeply that it emerged from his back, killing him. But the battle was too far along for Murad's death to have any military effect. Another of Lazar's brothers-in-law (one who *should* have been accused of treason) inexplicably withdrew from the battle the 12,000 men under his command. Things shifted immediately, and the sultan's heir, "The Thunderer," crushed the remaining Serbs and captured and executed Lazar. Flocks of large scavenger birds descended to eat the dead, forever earning the desolate plain the moniker Field of Blackbirds.[4]

Over the course of the next four and a half centuries, there were three more major battles on Kosovo's plains, ones few people discuss. The Serbs were defeated again in the first two, but in 1831, they finally managed a victory against the Turks, which put the bodies of their enemies into the same soil that was the tomb of their culture and identity. But the victory came 400 years too late to matter; the course of history had been established. The first battle had robbed the Serbs of the greatness they believed they deserved, turning them into a people of slavery and defeat.

Shortly after winning at Kosovo, the Turks hit Albania, to the south. Albania was yet another beleaguered nation that had seen centuries of invasions by Goths, Huns, Bulgars, Slavs, and any other wandering tribe that felt like taking a shot at it. Like the Serbs, the Albanians were Christians and, faced with the prospect of assimilation into the Islamic faith, backed steadily up toward the Adriatic and Ionian Seas. Because of the rugged topography of the country, which is not dissimilar from that of Montenegro, the Albanians held off the

Turks until 1468. Most Albanians converted to Islam after they were overrun that year.

The Turks had about as much luck controlling the Albanians as they had controlling the Bosnians; that is, not much. While the Albanians never lived as freely as the Bosnians in Sarajevo, for instance, they nevertheless maintained a thirst for independence that manifested itself in Kosovo shortly after the Serbs had routed the Turks from Serbia. Sensing the demise of the Ottoman Empire, in 1878, Albanians from all regions met in Prizren, Kosovo, a small city about forty-five miles southwest of Pristina, to establish the Albanian League, a group dedicated to ensuring that all Albanians in the region would one day be able to live together in one united, autonomous country.[5] The Albanian League bore little fruit, however, because all of its leaders were shortly captured or killed by the Turks ... but it provided the same thing for the Albanians that the 1389 Field of Blackbirds battle had provided the Serbs—an inspiration based in Kosovo that would eventually germinate into full-blown nationalism.

Three

After the Balkan Wars, which finally punted Turkey out of the region once and for all, Albania got the short end of the stick. The Great Powers that decided where the new nations' borders would be drew one around Albania that many thought was unfair—40 percent of the ethnic Albanian population was suddenly living outside their own country, scattered across Serbia, Montenegro, and Macedonia. The real borders of Albania, the Albanians argued, included Kosovo and western portions of Macedonia. It made sense: unlike the Serbs and the Croats, for instance, the Albanians are not of Slavic descent, and they spoke a different language from their northern neighbors. It seemed only natural that any international border would include all the contiguous land where Albanians lived. It would hardly have been a voluminous concession; Kosovo is about the size of Connecticut. But the Serbs had better ties to the West and were therefore able to make their case that Kosovo belonged in Serbia. Albanians have never gotten over this unfairness and have fostered an underdog mentality throughout the years, seeing themselves as surrounded by marauding enemy nations intent on crushing their culture and stealing their land. The modern Albanian national agenda has never strayed very far from the dual goals of moving from communism to democracy and uniting all Albanians into a single contiguous country, one that would include Kosovo.

Naturally, this goal clashes with the Serbians' determination to defend their culture and territorial integrity, even though the Serbs have almost always been outnumbered in the region. Modern clashes between the two groups in Kosovo go all the way back to the early 1960s, when the Serbs saw their influence weakening with the rising number of Albanians holding positions of power in the province. This fact was exacerbated by the unusually high Albanian birthrate, which threatened to make the ethnic gap in the region even wider and eventually to turn Serbia into a bilingual country. "The Albanians, you know, want to conquer the world by outbreeding us," griped a Serbian nun to Kaplan in the late 1980s.[6] Large-scale student demonstrations in 1968 convinced Belgrade to grant the province a substantial degree of autonomy. In 1974, Tito revamped Yugoslavia's constitution to make Kosovo and Vojvodina (Serbia's other province, which is north of Belgrade) constitutional federal units with their own provincial governments. But this wasn't good enough for the Albanians, who wanted the status of "republic," which came with the theoretical right to secede.[7] Only a year after Tito's death in 1980, the Yugoslavian National Army swooped into Kosovo to squash more protests, which verged on a revolution. When Milosevic came to power in 1986, he brought with him a renewed Serbian nationalism that was soon to prove deadly in Bosnia. One of his first acts as a future dictator was to travel to Kosovo Polje, the little village near Pristina that's the actual site of the famous 1389 battle. In what has since become a legendary appearance, Milosevic stood on a balcony over a nearly rioting crowd of Serbs, pointed to the Field of Blackbirds, and announced, "Nobody, either now or in the future, has the right to beat you."[8]

As a battle cry, it falls short of "Remember the Alamo!" but those present needed no interpretation. It meant that defeat was a thing of the past, that the glory denied to the Serbian people for so long would finally, in this generation, be realized. But long before Bosnia ever became a household word, Milosevic first turned his sights on Kosovo.

In 1989, he jerked the province's autonomy out from under it and placed it under martial law. Immediately, parliamentary Albanian leaders declared Kosovo an independent republic within Yugoslavia. In response, Milosevic suspended Kosovo's parliament and its government, fired Albanians holding influential political posts and purged them from the police force, shut down Albanian-language media, closed all Albanian educational institutions, and banned Albanians from being treated in state-run medical establishments. By 1990, the complete political absorption of Kosovo into Serbia was complete and had had its desired effect: large numbers of Albanians fled Kosovo. The Serb-dominated police force fueled the migration through brutality, violence, and torture aimed at the Albanian majority.[9] But the Serbian crackdown didn't quell the Kosovars' desires for autonomy; it simply upped their demands: now, instead of wanting just intra-Yugoslavian freedom, they were demanding full independence as a new nation.

Technically, the situation of Kosovo was like that of Slovenia, Croatia, or Bosnia, which all decided to secede within the next two years. One substantial difference was that Kosovo didn't have the political or military clout to force the issue, since it was still a "province" rather than a "republic." Recognition of Kosovo as an independent entity was denied by the EC on those very grounds.

Another major factor that had kept Kosovo out of the bloodshed until now was the election of Ibrahim Rugova as president of Kosovo's shadow government in 1992. Rugova, a small, wiry man with thinning but wild hair, was known for little but his literary criticism, yet he rose to the top of a group of Kosovar intellectuals who'd formed the Democratic League of Kosovo, the first non-Communist political party to be formed in the region since World War II. Unlike other leaders in Bosnia and Croatia, Rugova is an avowed pacifist who urged his constituents to sit tight and wait for the international community, led by Richard Holbrooke and his group of negotiators, to come to the rescue.

They never came.

In retrospect, Kosovo's revived autonomy should have been included in the Dayton Accords as a necessary provision for peace in Bosnia. No one negotiating the agreement had any illusions about the region's stability . . . but in fairness, there were more pressing matters at the time, like the wholesale slaughter of Bosnians. And the Dayton Accord negotiations were so contentious that inclusion of Kosovo would have complicated the process further and a peace deal may never have been made.[10] According to Holbrooke's memoirs, he pressed Milosevic time and time again at Dayton to restore Kosovo's status to defuse the situation, but the demands were never put into writing, and in Holbrooke's words, "the long feared crisis in Kosovo was postponed, not avoided."[11]

The Kosovars were not pleased that they had been summarily ex-
cluded from the Dayton Accords. To them, this exclusion was nothing less than tacit approval of Milosevic's goals in the region, as the
only pressure apparently applied before people started dying was
half-hearted efforts by Holbrooke. In fact, from the Kosovars' perspective, it seemed almost as if the United States was in cahoots with
Belgrade, coddling it endlessly and turning a blind eye to human
rights violations in efforts to win compliance with the Dayton Accords, rewarding Belgrade with international financial aid when it did
comply. This perception became radically less theoretical because of
the imbecilic actions of Robert Gelbard, the U.S. implementation
czar. According to a wire service article in March 1998, "Last month,
U.S. special envoy Robert Gelbard visited Belgrade, praised Milosevic for his new cooperation in Bosnia and branded the Kosovo Liberation Army 'without question a terrorist group.'"[12] Predictably,
Milosevic felt no pressure at all to sway from the course he'd set for
Serbia in Kosovo—which was no less than the complete destruction
of the Albanian will to secede through brute force. And the Kosovars, in turn, felt little obligation to continue listening to Rugova or
to special envoys from the United States. (Gelbard later recanted,
saying that he had meant only to condemn terrorist actions in general, not to characterize the KLA as a terrorist group.)

For Rugova, it was only a matter of time; as a politician who had
demanded full independence from Serbia yet had advocated nonvio-
lence while praying for intervention from a country whose representative just called his people terrorists, he did nothing either to make
the Serbian leadership take his demands seriously or to convince his
followers that he knew what he was doing.

And even without the "terrorist" comment, the West was not in a
much more influential position. Once the results of Dayton became
clear—that without aggressive interpretation of the military aspects
of the agreement, the country had been de facto partitioned and ethnic cleansing had been validated—the Kosovars saw the writing on
the wall. Even if the West intervened, the people of the region could
count on little more than what had settled over Bosnia, a semi-
autonomous limbo that would leave its citizens in a strange no-
man's-land that tried to accommodate competing nationalistic identities and agendas. If the Kosovars wanted independence, they were
going to have to get it themselves.

Even the Serbs knew the door was shutting on Kosovo's desire to
free itself from Serbia in the wake of the signing of the Dayton Ac-

cords. The head of the Serbian Academy of Arts and Sciences, Aleksandar Despic, had spoken of partitioning Kosovo only eight months after the Dayton Accords had been agreed upon, an ominous proposal. As Elez Biberaj wrote in *Albania in Transition,* "The problem with this solution is that partitioning Kosovo, where the Serbs are scattered and account for only about 8 percent of the total population, is likely to lead to war and massive sufferings. It is also likely that the Serbs would want to retain the largest, mineral-rich parts of Kosova [*sic*] which would involve the forcible resettlement, or ethnic cleansing, of more than a million Albanians."[13]

Indeed, modern arguments about the Serbs' sentimentality toward Kosovo have as much to do with history as with money; the Stari Tng mine north of Pristina is a treasure trove of minerals like iron and zinc, an important resource to have in a country permanently under economic sanctions. The mine's resources are estimated at several billion dollars.

The Kosovars were stuck. Albania was frightened of fully supporting Kosovo in its bid for independence because its armed forces were no match for those of Serbia. The international powers viewed the simmering trouble as little more than an ongoing low-intensity conflict that paled by comparison to other trouble spots around the globe. The United States needed Milosevic compliant and friendly if the Dayton agreement was ever going to get off the ground, so it wasn't about to pressure him into backing off from what it saw as a police action within Serbia's own borders. And Rugova had proved himself to be all bark and no bite—his conflicting statements espousing both independence and pacifism sounded stale at best, impotent at worse.

Things couldn't founder like this forever, and they didn't. In February 1998, in response to yet another government crackdown on suspected dissidents in Kosovo, the KLA, a hitherto-unheard-of group with no affiliation with any known political party, roared from the hills with machine guns blazing, forcing the issue into international headlines. Milosevic reacted to the KLA threat as one might have expected he would: the blood began to flow.

Four

I remember little about the road from Rozaje to Pristina because I was intent on nothing more than moving fast while keeping a low profile. I whistled nervously through three military checkpoints without being stopped. These were tense affairs, and I sensed that the others on the road were as jittery as I was, passing small clusters of buildings that had been co-opted by blue-and-purple-garbed men standing in the dirt with their rifles jacked onto their hips, faces as inviting as those of cemetery statues. I was stared at intently . . . but I kept my eyes straight ahead and tried not to give in to the urge to stand on the accelerator.

By the time I got to Pristina, I was soaking wet with sweat, both from the heat and from the stress . . . and instead of sanctuary, I got a gutted, grimy hotel that was the headquarters for the international press.

The Grand Hotel was nothing of the sort. It was an eight- or nine-story tomb in the heart of the downtown slum that was slowly decomposing, just like every other structure in sight. In fact, the only thing that made the Grand stand out was the herd of armored Land Rovers parked in a madcap tangle in the turnaround where valets would have parked cars if the hotel had had any. All the trucks were white, and all were marked distinctively with duct tape spelling *TV* on the sides. There didn't seem to be an entrance to this makeshift parking lot, so I just drove across the sidewalk and left the car between a few empty planters.

The hotel had been a gift to Kosovo from Tito's communist government in the tradition of communist governments everywhere; that is, it had been constructed with the intention of replacing ethnic unrest with the inspired awe that would result from building something grandiose. Albanians hate the Serbs, the reasoning went, so let's build them a massive hotel with three dining rooms, each with its own orchestra and a vast outdoor plaza for relaxing and drinking champagne! With such wonderful things to enjoy and be proud of, hatred will surely evaporate.[14]

Surely not, especially in the case of the Grand Hotel. If anyone had given me something so gruesome and ill constructed, my hatred would only flare. The outside staircase leading to the plaza—formed from the same lumpy concrete as the hotel itself—is sinking into its foundation, cracked down the middle as if from earthquake damage. The black marble lobby is filled with cigarette smoke, and gangly waiters in threadbare monkey suits know all the guests, but not out of professional courtesy . . . they want to be the first to offer strangers the opportunity to be ripped off when changing deutsche marks into Serbian dinars. The carpet in the hallways is difficult to look at, the color of old pea soup, except in the numerous places where it's been stained by vomited stomach juices. Vacant-faced charwomen lurk in the breezeways like ghosts, and for reasons that will never be clear, my private bathroom was painted matte black and lit with a fluorescent yellow light.

But it was sanctuary for the moment. I showered, dressed in fresh clothes, and headed down to the government-run media center on the second floor to get my bearings.

Five

"Never trust these guys for anything other than figuring out where the fighting happened," advised a television producer with a respected European news agency. Over beers in the media center, he was giving me a situation report. It was his day off, he explained, and he intended to drink it away. But a remote-controlled bomb had exploded in Pristina at daybreak, and he'd been forced into service. The unexpected event, however, had not curtailed his day-off activities, and he waved for another round. "These bastards are usually full of shit."

The media center was a combination lounge, spin control center, war room, communications nexus, and sports bar. I imagine that it had once been intended for use as a conference room, but the media had made it theirs: a wall of satellite-fed televisions, each tuned to a different frequency, glittered at one end. Interspersed throughout were overstuffed lounge chairs and low tables guarded by a lackluster servant, who brought beers and coffee to the correspondents from the small bar in the corner. In an adjoining room were long tables cluttered with laptop computers and recording equipment. A bank of fax machines and telephones stood ready to connect you to foreign bosses. Near the badly cut glass doors sat the people the producer had been referring to: the government media agents who reported their version of the day's events on badly reproduced, grammatically impaired press releases stacked on a table in the corner. The press release reporting on the explosion read, "This morning, at 6:15, strong explosion blew out a few cars and windows on the buildings in Dardanija, Kralja Petra I Oslobodioca street, in Pristina. There were no casualties. The police is carrying our [sic] the investigation."

Other than the painful composition, there didn't seem to be anything overtly sinister about the release, but I was assured that the entire purpose of the media center was to promote the perspective of the Serbian secretary of information, who saw all Albanian casualties as the death of "terrorists."

"And don't trust the Kosovars, either," my companion slurred. "Every police action they report is always conducted with 'excessive force,' even if they [the police] are retreating."

I expected as much. Every news report up to that point had contained information that the news services emphasized couldn't be "independently confirmed." The Serbs weren't allowing reporters or international monitors to go anywhere without an official escort. Therefore, most of the information up to that point had come from refugees who'd stumbled across the mountains into Albania. And after being forced from their villages to wander through the summer heat, such sources can hardly be considered objective. But the very fact that there were refugees at all made it obvious that something was indeed happening . . . practically the only thing that was known for sure was that there was full-blown warfare between the KLA and the Serbs that was resulting in a massive displacement of Albanians and a body count that had exceeded 300 by the time I arrived.

The international community, more-or-less represented by U.S. Secretary of State Madeleine Albright, had moved with uncharacteristic swiftness to condemn the combat as ethnic cleansing. There's little doubt that the criticism heaped on world leaders for their inaction in the Bosnian crisis was still stinging like an open wound, something made obvious by the U.S. State Department's strong statements that it wouldn't stand by and allow Kosovo to become "another Bosnia."

To that end, NATO scrambled warplanes in a coordinated show of force called Operation Determined Eagle. The sorties had been nothing more than saber rattling, however, and the fighting hadn't even paused.

By the time I pulled into Pristina, a few hours after the car bomb "blew out a few cars and windows," things were heating up in the countryside. Milosevic goose-stepped over every line Albright drew in the sand, an act of defiance that produced nothing but another line for him to march toward. The attitude of everyone was that another Bosnia was happening at that very moment.

The question that remained was what the international community was going to do about it.

8   The KLA Reserve

All diplomacy is a continuation of war by other means.

—Chou En-Lai

One

I stayed at the Grand Hotel only long enough to get my bearings and a good night's sleep. Even though it was fitfully spent on sticky sheets, with strange footsteps crossing in front of the door all night and Serbian jets splitting the sound barrier on a flight path that seemed to take them right past my window—which wouldn't shut properly and kept blowing open on a wave of stench that woke me up almost hourly—it was relaxing in the sense that I knew I didn't have to drive anywhere once morning arrived. But it was clear that I had to leave for saner environs . . . the hotel made me nervous. First of all, it was an information vacuum of black-hole proportions; not only did the government carefully parse the news it was willing to release, but the secretary of information insisted that all journalists register with the state before attempting to cover anything. This registration included listing where you could be found if anyone started looking for you . . . which might be the case if you wrote anything too controversial. One of the media center's "services" included compiling a stack of stories filed by registered correspondents from the Internet into a daily information package. Though this was undoubtedly helpful, I never shook the conviction that its real purpose was letting the reporters know that the government was watching their coverage closely. Although I wouldn't be filing any stories until I was long gone, this subtle form of oversight made me nervous.

On top of that, I didn't like the idea of living in a hotel while reporting on people who were in fear of losing their houses. There was very little chance of the hotel being bombed while the Serbian media made its headquarters there, unless the KLA did it, but the KLA seemed to know better than to alienate the only outlet it had to the rest of the world by blowing up the international media's base camp. Those living in Pristina and the surrounding villages had no such guarantee. With a steady stream of refugees making its way through the mountains toward the Albanian border, most of the other Albanians in Kosovo were wondering when their homes were going to be in a Serbian tank's crosshairs. It was somehow dishonest to speak with such people about their fears of losing their lives and their homes and then retreating to the relative safety of a hotel that, in all likelihood, would remain standing if war ever erupted in the city. I decided I had to spend a week or two living with an Albanian family in order to get the best perspective on their situation as possible.

Which is how I found myself in the company of local Albanian journalists later that day, sitting around a low table near the headquarters of the International Committee of the Red Cross. Local journalists differed vastly from the foreign reporters. They had no sex appeal at all, looking like just-released prisoners of war. They worked with the type of equipment that would be found in a low-end Sunset Boulevard pawnshop. They were also without pretension; to them, the conflict in the field was personal, not just another job. All of them had been born in Kosovo.

By contrast, the foreign reporters staying at the Grand Hotel were indeed just doing a job. . . . As well meaning as many of them were, and as seriously as they took the plight of the Albanians in Kosovo, very few, if any, would have been there if there hadn't been a war to report on. Foreign combat reporters, by definition, have a high stake in the stories they cover because, whenever they go out on an assignment, there's always the chance that they'll get injured or killed. To have chosen their line of work in the first place, they're undoubtedly a special breed of person, but they drive into villages being shelled for altogether different reasons than Albanian journalists do: the foreigners need video footage to feed to a satellite, which in turn is seen in faraway countries by people who are in no direct danger of the violence being portrayed. Again, it's their job. And retreating to the hotel each night is the equivalent of returning home from the office after a more typical day's work.

Local Albanian reporters, however, never really leave a story. They know they'll not be reassigned to another war zone once the violence in Kosovo comes to an end in one way or another. They know all too well that the people they see through the lenses of their cameras are no different than themselves and their families. The reporters are paid woefully by combat correspondent standards, and to say their equipment is subpar by those same standards is a generous description. Yet the men I sat with near the Red Cross office all had far more horrific tales of personal danger than any I'd heard from those who had lounged in the media center at the Grand after their day's work. One Albanian reporter drove through the night with his headlights off— through government-controlled regions, where he was an enemy by virtue of his ethnicity—to investigate rumored massacres and to report the stories of people who'd lost their homes during Serbian shelling attacks. Another had stayed in a village overnight, even though a Serbian assault force was threatening to overrun the KLA unit that strove to protect the little town. A government helicopter strafed the trench he was sitting in, using tracer bullets that ate up the ground, amazingly hitting no one.

The local reporters, like the visiting international reporters, took their risks because it was their job . . . but for them, the stakes were far higher. The audience they reported to fully expected the same things they read about happening to other people to happen to them in the near future. And again, to these reporters, Kosovo was home and their home was burning to the ground. They were there not just to film it and capture the details but to try to extinguish the blaze.

One of the men was a heroin addict, I found out later, which explained the caved-in eyes, the profuse sweat running from his upper lip, and the sewing-machine action of his legs under the small table. Another was a talented photographer whose work had appeared in a number of international journals, but looking at him, you'd never guess. He obviously hadn't bathed or shaved in a week, and dental hygiene wasn't high on his list of daily habits. And the third was more-or-less KLA. He also turned out to be my de facto tour guide and host, after agreeing to put me up for twenty-five dollars a night. The deal was perfect—I would be given a comfortable room in a quiet house on the edge of town, breakfast prepared by his mother, a key to the front door . . . and a full immersion in the culture of the underground "KLA Reserve."

Two

For obvious reasons related to his personal safety, I'll call him Josip. We adjourned to a restaurant specializing in watery spaghetti. It was typical of most newer places in Pristina, freshly painted in bright pastels and with a fondness for chrome furniture. It was intimate to the point of claustrophobia, perhaps eight feet wide by forty feet long, crammed with angular tables filled with hip young people straight from *Beverly Hills 90210*. When the waiter came, I did my best to fit in.

"Dobro veche," I said. Josip ordered for us and immediately turned to me, as if to whisper some personal advice.

"Listen," he said. "Don't speak that foreign language in here."

"What are you talking about?"

"You spoke Serbian to him. He is Albanian."

"Oh."

"If you speak Serbian to the wrong people, you might get in trouble. If you speak Albanian to other people, you'll get in trouble, too. Just speak English. Is best."

We had connected through a friend of mine who'd been to Kosovo a month or so ahead of me. I made the mistake of asking if his newspaper was sympathetic to the KLA. Coming on the heels of speaking Serbian to the Albanian waiter, the question made him think I was stupid.

"You've never been here before, have you?" Everyone, he said, was sympathetic to the KLA. Well, except for the Serbs, who were responsible for the KLA's popularity among Albanians in the first place. "We wouldn't need KLA if the Serbs let us live," he said.

For the rest of the afternoon, we stood out in the rain in front of the Albanian shadow government's headquarters with forty other reporters waiting for a progress report on the peace negotiations. Holbrooke and Christopher Hill, U.S. ambassador to Macedonia, were inside with Rugova, trying to figure out a way to stop the bloodshed. No one was very confident that they would: the KLA didn't like Rugova very much, and it roundly ignored his constant pleas for peace and dis-

cussion. Rugova had brought this dislike on himself; in his zeal to negotiate a cease-fire and end the violence, he had met with Milosevic
without international observers along, an act that seemed treasonous to
some. Ever since then, Rugova had steadily lost credibility, his con-
stituency had abandoned him, and he'd been rendered powerless to
speak on behalf of the rebels—whom he refused to recognize anyway
as a legitimate political force until they calmed down and started talking about peace. The only reason any of the negotiators seemed to be
speaking with him at all, despite his obvious lack of power over the
KLA, was that he was the only Albanian leader in sight advocating negotiation over retaliation. Meanwhile, the press corps huddled under
thin branches outside, trying to keep our cigarettes dry in the torrent.

It was a typical media circus: the barest movement from the front
door would send everyone into a pack lunge for the gates in case Holbrooke came out to announce something. Tall bald guards would
hustle out and beat us back until we stood in a dense cluster between
the negotiators' getaway cars and their only point of escape, through
the front door. We were hip to hip, banging each other's heads with
boom microphones, minicams, and motor drives until someone
would come out and tell us it would be another half hour before anything happened. Then everyone would disperse to talk on cell
phones. "I'm still out here waiting for this thing to happen!" yelled
one reporter into his phone. "We're not going to get anything today.
They're saying they might not make an announcement until tomorrow. So much for my day off . . . "

Then, unannounced, Holbrooke and his team of suits bolted from
the building and leapt into waiting Chevy Suburbans, which spun
mud and rocks on everyone as they sped away, blasting people out of
their path with bursts from their air horns. For the media pack, this
had the same effect as someone throwing firecrackers into a crowd of
jittery greyhounds. Everyone scattered and ran straight into one another trying to find their drivers, tripping over audio cords and
stepladders. A huge cloud of dust rose from beneath the mud as cars
churned out of the parking lot in hot pursuit through the skinny
streets. The whole thing ended only eight blocks away, at the American Information Center, a quasi embassy without the U.S. Marines
or the right to grant asylum. The small street it was on wasn't wide
enough to accommodate all the press cars, so people just stopped
wherever they got stuck and dashed out to see what was going on.
Which, of course, was nothing.

This happened several times over the course of the day, to and from party headquarters and the information center. We weren't around to participate, however. Josip's deadline had passed without his getting a photo, and I'd seen as much shuttle diplomacy as I needed to see to know what it was like.

No one was expecting very much of note to emerge from the political effort. Kosovo was quite different from Bosnia even though in many ways it was also quite similar. For one thing, unlike the previous aggression with its support in Belgrade, these acts of alleged ethnic cleansing weren't happening in what had become a foreign country. With Kosovo, the international community was faced with the touchy situation of condemning a nation's sovereign right to suppress a rebel uprising on its own soil. Also contrasting with Bosnia was the swiftness with which the United States and the European Union reacted to reports of violence in Kosovo—it had taken the internationals only five months to get to the negotiating phase, as opposed to three years. This relative speed was undoubtedly born of shame, for no one let the United States forget its role in failing Bosnia through inaction. The press had been uncharacteristically livid about this failure, and a slew of books based on that very topic had flowed from the presses like blood from an open wound. During the siege of Sarajevo, Christiane Amanpour, CNN's Bosnia correspondent, blasted President Clinton on live television on the issue of U.S. reluctance to commit to Bosnia.

The United States hadn't done anything, however, until it was too late to reverse the tide of death that had drowned so many people. One of the reasons the Dayton Accords are on such shaky ground is that the Serbs were allowed to conquer and consolidate so much land before real peace measures were pursued, ones that could be backed up with outside military force if necessary. Sure, the United Nations had been working on peace practically since the beginning of the fighting—but the moment it became obvious that the peacekeeping soldiers weren't going to use the weapons they carried, their presence didn't matter at all. It was the power of the United States—and its influence in using that power through NATO—that brought the killing to a stop. But by then, there was little to do except recognize the conquered towns and villages as Serb territory, a fact that continues to hinder refugees in their desire to return to their prewar homes.

Because the international community had committed itself to preventing "future Bosnias," diplomatic efforts were undertaken in Kosovo far more swiftly, although it still takes death and the threat of wider escalation to spur diplomatic measures; not everything can be prevented. Fortunately, far less death was required this time.

But the most critical difference was the one that made most efforts to secure a cease-fire seem doomed regardless of how early they had been started. The Albanians were not the Bosnian Muslims, a distinction that was the result as much of Albanian willpower as it was of the international community's lackluster response to the warfare in Bosnia. After sitting for three and a half years watching another Serb-oppressed minority slowly vanish into mass graves, the Albanians would have to have been harebrained to think that independence would come with the help of the United Nations or NATO. They were prepared to fight the battle on their own regardless of what outsiders said or did.

About NATO, they've been right, though for reasons that had less to do with hand-wringing vacillation than with hard political lessons learned from Bosnia that would be better avoided in Kosovo. By the time things were critical enough for Croatia and Slovenia to secede, there was little that could be done to stop the war. It would have taken a clairvoyant negotiator with all the best traits of Holbrooke and Winston Churchill being fully immersed in Yugoslavian politics as early as 1986 to ensure that the breakup of the country would be accomplished with minimal bloodshed. And even then, there wouldn't have been any guarantees. But by the time things had reached the crisis stage, everyone but Germany was terrified of recognizing the first two breakaway republics. Doing that, they rightly posited, would give other nations like Bosnia the courage to do the same, and given the hypernationalism of both the Serbs and the Croats, the result would be an explosion. That's just what happened, but everyone tried to avoid it nonetheless. This was the reason for Bush's ill-advised arms embargo on all of Yugoslavia—unfortunately, by that time "Yugoslavia" as the world had known it existed only on maps that were suddenly outdated, and the embargo did nothing but help the Serbs.

It would have been foolish to expect people to know these things in advance of their happening . . . but they know them now, and they're determined not to repeat their mistakes. If Kosovo is allowed to secede as an independent nation with blessings from the international community, its secession will have the same domino effect as Croatia's did, only this time with higher stakes. No one doubts that the moment Kosovo dives from the Serbian nest with the full approval of the outside world, Macedonia will go off like an

atom bomb. Its roughly 400,000 Albanians will rally for their independence, and within minutes, Greece, Serbia, and Bulgaria will send
troops into Macedonia like water from a bursting dam. Since Macedonia effectively has no army, it will simply become a killing field as
the three nations battle it out. This battle could drag in reluctant Albania, at least peripherally, since the Macedonian Albanians will have
no one to turn to but their historical compatriots and the Kosovars.
Albania's entry would heighten Greece's involvement as it strove to
fight off what it would see as an Albanian attempt to expand its borders into what Athens considers traditional Greek territory. Bulgaria
is friends with Turkey, which would need little encouragement to start
shooting missiles at Greece, as the two countries have fought from
what seems like the beginning of recorded time over the island of
Cyprus and other maritime issues. That would quickly lead to naval
conflict between Turkey and Greece, and because they're both members of NATO, that organization would go down the tubes as quickly
as respect for human rights. Then, without NATO, who would be in
charge of SFOR? The answer is no one, something the war criminals
it has steadfastly refused to arrest would seize on immediately, declar-
ing Republika Srpska an independent country, boycotting the tri-
presidency, and routing non-Serbs once again from the land Serbs
have claimed for themselves. Once the Dayton Accords are officially
rent in two, it won't be long at all—probably the same day—before
Bosnian Croats start calling their land Hercog-Bosna in public and
both sides begin moving again on Sarajevo. Rumor has it that the Bosnian Muslims are prepared for this course of events, having strengthened ties with Islamic nations such as Iran and Afghanistan in the
years since the beginning of the Dayton cease-fire, and have been
training in the hills north of the small town of Zenica with mujahideen
freedom fighters who are schooling them in the time-honored traditions of people like Osama bin Laden.[1]

That's the doomsday scenario, one that would take roughly three
to five weeks to engulf the region from Zagreb to Ankara, according
to bullpen estimates from the bar at the media center. It's a theory
that no one wants tested, and I was assured by a member of the negotiating team who asked to remain anonymous that if NATO gets
involved at all, "it certainly isn't going to be the [KLA] air force,"
meaning that an independent Kosovo is the last thing international
negotiators want to see.[2]

●   ●   ●

It's unclear whether the KLA had given this possible chain of events much thought by the time I got to Pristina. In fact, no one had officially heard from the KLA at all because it didn't seem to have a leader or a solid military structure. The closest thing it had to a political wing was Rugova's party, but only because of wishful thinking on the part of the negotiators, as the rebels continually failed to heed his pleas for a cease-fire. After a decade of repression, they seemed interested in nothing but fighting, and they weren't even doing that very well. The tales from the field gave little encouragement about their prospects for military success.

A case in point: in something of a freelance operation that didn't seem to be coordinated or authorized by any central command, a KLA unit "captured" the Belacevac open-pit coal mine a few miles from Pristina, a valuable strategic target that feeds Kosovo's power plant, which in turn provides electricity to nearly one-third of all Yugoslavia. You'd think that such an important piece of real estate would be gained through careful military maneuvers, but on close examination, the capture wasn't astutely executed. A band of KLA militants simply walked into the largely Albanian town near the mine, dug a few trenches, and called it theirs. A few days later, the Serbs lobbed some mortars at them, and most of the KLA soldiers stripped off their uniforms and retreated into the woods. Thus, the coal mine again became Serb property after only the lightest of skirmishing. Not the most dramatic confrontation, nor the most forceful attempt to gain important ground.[3]

But such actions didn't deter people from joining the rebels—in fact, by July 1998, the KLA had been called the fastest-growing guerrilla army in the world. People whose only military experience came from fantasizing about one day rising up to kill their Serb overlords began flooding the organization's ranks when the villages began to come under attack in February 1998. Women, children, and the elderly were shuffled over the mountains along thin rocky paths leading to Albania, where they passed rockets and rifles brought by mule train to the men who stayed to fight. The process of "joining" the KLA was something of a mystery because there didn't seem to be any real chain of command and only a handful of regional training camps. In many cases, it seemed joining the KLA was nothing more elaborate than gathering a posse of neighbors, collecting all the weapons in sight, and heading into the hills to take potshots at the roadblocks. No one's even sure how formal the KLA was prior to the February

1998 crackdown: though Milosevic had torched villages and blown up mosques with the excuse of hunting for terrorists, few people believed there was an organized revolution in the works, though it was certainly not out of the question given the extremes of Albanian unrest. But without a doubt, because of the government's military actions, it didn't take long for a legitimate opposing force to emerge, composed of everyday folks who had reached the breaking point and decided that it was now or never for taking up arms for Kosovo's independence.

Because of the KLA's secretive structure—or thorough lack thereof—and its unbridled passion for confrontation, NATO is in a bit of a bind. After stoking the Albanians into a revolutionary frenzy, Milosevic eased off somewhat once the international community reacted to the violence, and he retreated with the excuse that he had simply been defending his country's territory. By then it was true, regardless of the fact that Milosevic himself had been responsible for creating the very thing he was defending against. Nevertheless, for NATO to get UN Security Council clearance to bomb Serbian targets under such circumstances was a long shot at best. Such action would also inspire the Kosovars to continue their battle to wrest their land from Serbian control. The best option would be to quell the uprising, it seemed, or at least to discourage it. To that end, the Balkan Contact Group, a team of international diplomats (including representatives of the United States, France, Germany, Russia, Britain, and Italy) with oversight of Balkan affairs, publicly forbade outside financial assistance to the KLA, issuing the statement from Bonn, which is coincidentally also the location of another Kosovar government-in-exile. But there was serious talk floating around Pristina about the possibility of more drastic measures: NATO bombing KLA positions to get them to come to the negotiating table to discuss an alternative to independence, such as a return of the autonomy Kosovo lost in 1989, something the rebels have shown no inclination to consider. This course of events would be tragic in its irony—NATO jets flying missions on behalf of a man Lawrence Eagleburger suggested should have been indicted for Bosnian war crimes.

Potential long-term solutions aren't much more comforting; shortly after I eventually left Kosovo, U.S. Navy Admiral Joseph Lopez, current commander of NATO forces in southern Europe, suggested that if the government and the guerrillas agreed to NATO ground-troop deployment à la the Dayton Accords, a "ballpark" figure of necessary personnel was 50,000. Carlos Westendorp, Carl Bildt's Spanish successor as High Representative, was "alarmed" by the idea, telling Reuters, "I believe that governments are going to find it very difficult to have an additional 50,000 troops together with the 30,000 that we have here [in SFOR]—it makes 80,000 troops and this is a bit too much, so I think this is going to be very, very difficult, if not impossible."

Three

Josip and I were talking about these very things as we drove through the trash-filled streets looking for a bar in which we could get into some deep discussions and speak with some locals. It wasn't a difficult endeavor. There was nothing to talk about except the war. For the most part Albanians either don't believe NATO won't help them secede or they don't care.

"NATO is welcome to help," said Josip. "But they're not needed. We can do this ourselves."

By "we," he meant the KLA; he's a member of the unofficial reserve forces. The only reason he was not out fighting in the field, he said, was that the KLA planned to move to take Pristina from the Serbs sometime in the future and they needed operatives in the city. He had come into the ranks the same way as most of the other new recruits: by being confronted with the atrocities of the Serbs. A few months before I met him, he had headed out into the night to investigate rumors of a nighttime attack on supposed terrorists in the small village of Lubeniq. Risking his life as an Albanian traveling in Serb territory at night, he had abandoned his car halfway to the village and walked the remaining miles through the dark forest, stumbling across a scene that had welded him forever to the Albanian cause.

In the front yard of a farmhouse lay six or seven bodies. Most were in their underwear or pajamas; they had been sleeping soundly until Serb police stormed their homes and forced them outside, where they were shot and left where they had fallen. Josip showed me the photos as he told the story.

A corpse lies somehow flatter than a living person, limbs bent in a slightly awkward position that indicates the subject isn't merely sleeping off a rough night with a bottle. I counted eight or nine bullet holes in the chest of one man, who lay on his back in the dirt, eyes

wide open. Another, an old, overweight man in tight brief underwear had been shot in the back of the head at point-blank range. The
force of the bullet had elongated the shape of his head so that it
looked like a huge egg, the top of which had been blown completely
off in a twelve-inch exit wound that had spilled his pink-white brain
onto the hay. The blow had sprung both his eyeballs out of their
sockets; one was staring straight ahead in everlasting horror; the
other had been severed from the optic nerve and twisted gruesomely
upward, as if looking at his wound. His mouth was wide in a silent
scream, showing a single brown tooth.

More disturbing was a picture of a young pregnant woman who
hadn't even made it out of bed, much less out onto the lawn. The bullet that had killed her took her whole face away except for a small
rubbery portion of the chin and lower lip. Her head was nothing but
sopping brain matter framed with long black hair. The wall behind
her was still wet with meat and blood running down behind the mattress.

"I didn't sleep for a month after that," Josip said.

But the absolute worst picture was one that didn't have any blood
in it at all . . . Josip had found the photo in the dirt near a fresh grave-
yard. It was a picture of a little boy, about six years old, obviously
taken during a school picture session. It looked as if he'd had to be
prodded into smiling, looking as shy and unsure as anyone that age
shoveled in front of a camera manned by a bored photographer. I
don't know if he was wearing his best clothes, but I'm sure from
their careful coordination that his mother or father selected them
with a diligence reserved only for parents on picture day. He was in
black corduroy overalls, a blue knit sweater, and a flannel hunter's
shirt. He looked the way I imagine my two-year-old son might look
at his age.

"Look at those eyes," Josip said. "They're like a little angel." On
the back of the picture was the boy's name, Fidan. He's in a grave
now, in a narrow hole in the ground that's no stranger to the blood of
the martyred. Josip said he was shot through the head at point-blank
range.

There were more stories like that, told throughout the night, including one in which he helped exhume and rebury the victims of one
of the earliest ethnic cleansing episodes near Prekaz. The undertakers
finished their grim task before the midday heat had crested. Covered
in a dusting of Kosovo earth that made them all look jaundiced, the

unique stench of rotten corpses lingering on their clothing, they retreated to a clapboard shack that served as a makeshift pub.

"No one talked," Josip said, staring at the tablecloth while re-
counting the tale. "What could we say?"

What indeed? The men were trying to dilute their horror with alcohol across the street from a field with fifty fresh graves. Suspected
of being "terrorist sympathizers," those buried in the narrow holes
had been killed in a midnight shelling blitzkrieg and a subsequent
house-to-house mop-up by special forces. Many hadn't yet been
identified. They'd been tumbled into crude coffins and placed in open
trenches by Serb police, who ordered the Albanians to bury the dead
immediately or they'd do it for them. But there was one more chore
to complete before anyone, living or dead, could find peace: the Serbs
had intentionally placed the Albanians—who were Muslim—in their
graves with their heads to the west, away from Mecca. Their compatriots had assembled in the growing heat to lift the corpses out of the
earth again, to twist their souls toward the salvation that had been so
hard to find. After shooting only one roll of film, Josip had found
himself in the graves as well, able to move the coffins of children
without any help. "They weighed almost nothing," he said.

Perhaps it was morbid curiosity or a need to understand what had
happened to those they were burying . . . regardless of the reason, one
of the coffins was pried open. Josip remembered that the villagers had
had to force him to take a picture of its contents, so that the world
would know what was happening to them. He was reluctant, feeling
like a lecherous fiend for photographing someone so stripped of dig-
nity and humanity.

He hadn't even offered such pictures to his paper for publication.
Instead, they come out from time to time during conversations with
foreign correspondents, and always with the appropriate amount of
respect and gravity. The photo from Prekaz was taken looking down
into the grave, two men holding up a coffin whose lid hung stiffly
open like the cover of a new book. Everything encircling it seemed to
be wilting under the white-hot blaze of the summer day . . . but the
coffin's contents were as black as an eclipsed sun. She'd been burned,
her torso nothing more than coal ash, a charred arm jutting from
what had been her shoulder. But it hadn't been the fire that killed her;
a bullet had removed her face and the top of her head. Nothing remained but a rubbery dislocated jaw, which hung in a jack-o'-lantern
grimace, framed with long blond hair singed and shortened by the

flames that had partially consumed the corpse. There were no eyes, but she seemed to stare nonetheless, gawking from the grave in dead surprise, a rubble of cindery bones and mottled yellow-and-black flesh.

Josip pulled the picture to the safety of his photo-vest pocket. "You shouldn't look at it too long," he said. "It's not good to look at such things too long."

When the macabre task had been completed and after he had started on his third bottle of lukewarm beer in ten minutes in the slap-wood shack, he had turned to the man sitting next to him, a sweaty, powerful Albanian dressed in German camouflage fatigues. He had placed his hand over a Kalashnikov assault rifle lying on the table as if placing it on a Bible.

"I'm ready to fight now," he had told the man.

But they didn't want him then. He was told to wait underground with others like him, of whom there seem to be plenty—average people with day jobs as waiters and computer programmers who walk by the Serbs guarding the street corners everyday, invisible guerrillas in waiting. They spent their days blending into the background and their nights fueling their resolve with strong talk and stronger drink in the city's local bars and pubs. These places were Spartan affairs, each one seemingly smaller than the one before, giving the fitting impression of a bandit's hideout. They were always stuffed in the most unlikely locations—in the basements of abandoned apartment buildings, under highway overpasses, at the ends of dark, intricate tunnel systems. The odd locations weren't to protect the nightclubs from mortar attack or Serb spies; they were the result of a thorough lack of urban planning. Entrepreneurs in Kosovo locate wherever space is available.

"Here?" I asked Josip when he took me to meet his colleagues. We'd driven through a parking lot packed with dusty Renaults and Yugos, over a curb, through what seemed to be a pedestrian breezeway, and onto a narrow sidewalk that we somehow squeezed the car through. It was a dead end . . . broken brick wall on the left, slumped hurricane fence on the right, and a field of brown hay straight ahead.

He killed the engine. "This is the place. This is a very good place," he said. Sure enough, through a mostly hidden doorway was a small clean room, maybe ten feet by twenty, filled with typical cigarette smoke, four or five tiny tables, and a narrow wooden bar. A portable stereo played bad American rap music. The whole thing was lit with a few bare bulbs overhead. The place was crowded with the kind of Albanian men typical of every such place we visited, the younger ones wearing Tommy Hilfiger shirts and Levis, the older ones in threadbare suit pants held up by safety pins where there should have been suspenders and zippers. And typically, we were greeted by piercing, unwavering stares and a lengthy suspension of conversation.

We ordered drinks, the first round of what would come to be many. The local firewater is called *lovavacka*, some oily derivative of the grape that tastes like ouzo and gasoline. It's 50 percent alcohol, the type of drink that you can feel bending your mind with each sip. It's drunk all day, for breakfast, lunch, and dinner; we dubbed it "white tea" because of its frequent consumption. White tea shots were chased with big bottles of beer.

There was an endless flow of people to the table; folks were constantly wandering in and out of the place, stopping only to chat and down a quick white tea before heading back out into the night. Everyone seemed to know Josip. And everyone seemed to share his views, though the willingness to engage the Serbs varied.

Vagan, for instance, a twenty-five-year-old unemployed mechanic with a small son and another child on the way, was considered the local hothead. He had a fresh moon-shaped scar on his hand from where, in a drunken rage, he had put his fist through several dishes and a glass-topped table, then sprung for the door shouting about bloodletting before anyone could get hold of him. His other friends, including Josip, had been equally drunk, and it had taken a minute to mount a pursuit. They had found Vagan standing in the parking lot of the apartment complex shouting anti-Serb obscenities and daring the cops to come and arrest him. Fortunately for everyone, there had been no cops around, and they had managed to wrestle him into a car for delivery to the hospital, where his hand was stitched closed.

He hadn't gone to a regular hospital, he said now, but a "home hospital." He shrugged, explaining it. "When our autonomy was gone, all hospitals and schools are for Serbs only. No Albanians." The home schools and hospitals operated from wherever they could, in basements, crude derelict buildings, or people's living rooms. Books, medicine, and training all came from the black market, he said. "That is why we are so angry and ready to fight. Serbs shit on us for nine years."

"Do you think the war will come to Pristina?" It was a naive question, I knew ... with heavily armed Serb police on all the street corners, the Albanians considered Pristina occupied by the enemy already.

"Yes, of course."

"What will you do when the fighting starts?"

The look Vagan had given me quickly came to be familiar in everyone I asked the question: a fleeting glimpse of dread instantly washed away with a glassy mask of pride. The right arm jerked up with a closed fist, the solidarity salute of the KLA.

"I will fight. I am (KLA)."

I asked him if he'd tried to join the KLA like Josip, and he lowered his eyes. No, he said, mumbling something about his wife not letting him. But, he said, "we will all fight when the time comes."

Over the course of a week with Josip, I'd had so many of these conversations that they all tend to blend together. Only the people I talked to were different, vastly different. One's a student, a thin man with crooked teeth and a Sid Vicious haircut; another's a grandfather who used to be in the Yugoslavian National Army before the war in Bosnia, a sturdy man who looks a lot like a burly Sean Connery; another is a twenty-one-year-old piano teacher on break from studying in Skopje, Macedonia, on a Soros Institute scholarship, a stunningly beautiful young woman bathed in vanilla perfume who would surprise me if she could lift a heavy AK-47 to her shoulder.

None of these were planned encounters; that is, I was never told, "You should speak with her, she has a good story." Instead, the conversations had come up in the course of the days with Josip: at work with his coworkers, at home with neighbors, at night with his girlfriend, Jetta, who housed four refugees in her home.

When we met the refugees at Jetta's apartment, a relatively nice flat with a balcony looking off onto the scrub flats leading to the power plant, I was hard-pressed to identify the women as refugees—they were all beautiful and dressed as if for dinner with their boyfriends' parents. They were sitting outside on the patio playing cards under the blue glow of a bug lamp and a half-moon.

For the most part, their stories were no different from anything else I'd heard up to that point from others, except that those on the patio were lucky to be alive.

"I will kill Serbs if they try to take Pristina away from me," said a twenty-year-old law student named Adrianna matter-of-factly.

"All of you could kill Serbs?" I asked. Everyone spoke English, so the conversation was smooth.

"No," laughed Josip's girlfriend. "All of us *will* kill Serbs."

Everyone nodded casually, as if I'd asked if the weather had been nice. Only one person stared at the table, a young girl about thirteen years old. "How about you?" I asked.

"Yes," she said shyly. "I will run no further than Pristina. I can kill Serbs because it's easy to kill animals. If I had a gun, I would kill one tomorrow."

"I had a Serb girlfriend once," Josip said. There was low groan of disapproval at the table. "But if I saw her today, I would set her on fire."

Such talk is easy to make in the security of night, under the cold witchlight of the stars, reassured with a sack of beer in the company of friends. Their resolve, of course, remained to be seen, but of the people I'd met who recited such rhetoric, these folks had the most reason to seek revenge. The refugees had come from Decani, a village about fifty miles west of the city and the site of one of the earliest massacres of the current violence. "We lived in our house all our life," said the thirteen-year-old. "Our neighbors were a Serb family. One night we heard rockets and shouting and bullets hitting the walls. All the Albanian houses in the town were burning, and people were running through the dark, to get away from the explosions."

The family, a mother and her three daughters, left that night, certain that their house was next to go. They joined a caravan of refugees that was just then catching the world's attention, gathering only the belongings that they could carry, and fleeing into the night. They passed through orchards and fields and at one point were forced to crawl past a Serb armored vehicle lighting up the hamlet with streams of bright orange tracer shells that streaked from the muzzle of a machine gun like strangely propelled strings of Christmas lights. They hid in the basement of an abandoned house during the day and moved again once night fell. But the women didn't head to Albania or Montenegro; instead, they headed for Pristina to regroup and join the resistance. Fifty people died in Decani that night, a loss that nearly everyone I spoke with seems to think will be avenged.

Sooner or later, everyone seemed to believe, the KLA would decide to move, to take the city from the Serbs. It was the time Josip and all his friends were preparing for. Tactically, of course, it would be suicide until the rebels improved their fighting skills. The Serb police headquarters is in Pristina and a fully manned military base is just outside city limits. Any move by the KLA to claim Pristina as their own would have scorched-earth consequences, something at least some Albanians seem to understand.

"The KLA haven't moved to Pristina because they don't want to destroy the city," said the owner of the next café we migrated to. He had a slight paunch, thick black hair, and a jovial, Rodney Danger-field disposition. He was more than happy to host an American jour-nalist at his bar, which was beneath a highway overpass and faced an abandoned construction project across the street.

His English was spotty, and I wanted to make sure I understood him. "KLA doesn't want Pristina to become like Sarajevo, yes?"

He dismissed the comparison. "Not Sarajevo. Pristina will look like Vukovar," he said, referring to the Croatian city that was shelled into apocalyptic rubble by Serbs in 1991. Sarajevo got off easy com-pared to Vukovar.

"Really? Do you think so?" I asked.

He poured another round. "Vukovar, Sarajevo, Pristina. All same enemy: Milosevic."

Later, Josip told me that his friend was being melodramatic. "He's scared because he has children. KLA is strong enough to take Pristina."

Not everyone seemed to agree, including Josip's best friend Fitim. The two were inseparable, having known one another since child-hood. They were both twenty-eight, and until the last few years, they had led nearly parallel lives. But it was obvious, even without knowing the details, that Fitim held a more fatalistic view of their im-pending doom than Josip. While Josip talked of the KLA in terms re-flecting his dogmatic pride, a perfect icon of propagandist national-ism, Fitim seemed to consider the rebel force and its escalating engagement an inevitable cataclysm that was more something to be survived than treasured.

Along with thousands of student protesters, the two had taken to the streets of Pristina to demonstrate against Kosovo's lost autonomy in 1989. It never takes long for such things to erupt into full-blown violence in the Balkans, and this situation was no different. Serb po-lice had an armored personnel carrier on the street to meet the dissidents and turned a water cannon on them, a weapon made all the more painful because it was the middle of winter.

"I must have swallowed forty liters of water," Josip said. "They got me right in the face."

But the fervor that consumes him today was evident then, too. He simply closed his eyes, held his breath, and fought to hold his ground against the pounding torrent. He was arrested, along with Fitim and others who were throwing rocks at the APC. They were put in the same cell, given a thin blanket, and interrogated relentlessly.

"For two months," said Fitim, eyes fluttering at having to vocalize the memory, "we were beaten three times a day, every day. After meals."

Josip laughed with the casual ease of someone who has catalogued the memory as something that will, without a doubt, be avenged. "We would start to tell the guards, 'No thank you; we're not hungry.' Of course, they beat us anyway."

"Him worse than me," Fitim added, pointing a finger at his friend.

Josip just laughed harder. "Yes, because he is such a baby. All night long he would cry in the cell. I tell him, 'I will never get arrested with you again because you cry all the time.'"

"But I did get beat worse. It was my fault."

The laughter faded, the smile of humor replaced with one that was equal parts pain and menace. "I would try to resist, to show them that they couldn't hurt me. Fitim would fall to the ground as soon as the beating started, and they usually left him alone after a little while. I kept getting up."

Fitim nodded, putting a hand on Josip's shoulder, a sign of casual affection typical among Albanians, "There was this one guard; he had this ring he had taken the stone out of—the only thing left was a prong of metal . . . "

"He's still a cop," Josip said. "He works in Lodja. I was there a month ago, but I didn't see him. When we join KLA, we'll find him."

He looked to Fitim with a confident nod, for acknowledgment, commitment. It was a half beat slow in coming—only the most subtle of body language, but it didn't go unnoticed. The flash on Josip's face wasn't one of quick anger at his friend's reluctance, however; it was shame.

Later, in the car, heading toward home, he explained why.

"Fitim is a good father," he said. "He is afraid to fight because he thinks he will get killed. If he gets killed, it will be my fault because I talk all the time about joining KLA." One needn't be a psychologist to know that Josip is exerting serious pressure on his friend to join him, even though Fitim has a wife and two little girls. We had picked them up earlier in the night from their "home school," an austere building constructed in the parking lot of several rancid apartment blocks.

After their experience in jail, Fitim and Josip followed different paths, though they remained as close as ever. Josip began working for a local newspaper as a photographer, hoarding money for the time when he'll put down his camera for a rifle, money he'll use to send his mother to live with relatives in Turkey. He's got it all planned out; the route she'll take (which he reviews almost daily against information about Serb troop movement) has been memorized by both of them, and a small, easy-to-carry suitcase filled with little more than bare essentials is in the basement ready to go. His mother doesn't want to leave; Josip and his father built the house themselves a decade ago, and she's seen enough of her son's pictures to know what's to become of it. And she knows her son will probably die.

But she has little say in the matter. That Josip will change his mind and flee with her is impossible. In his time as a photographer, he's seen enough horror and death inflicted on Albanians so that turning away now would be like the pope renouncing his faith on his deathbed. Josip's course is set.

Fitim, on the other hand, has done all he could to make his life a normal one. He married his girlfriend, and together they have two cherubic daughters. His life is far from easy—he works three jobs, seven days a week—but he has a warm apartment and the love of his family. At the moment, he has immediate things to deal with, problems that are nearly immobilizingly normal. The three-year-old lost her Coke-bottom glasses on the playground and can barely see; the five-year-old recently broke her arm doing gymnastics, and she has an itch in her cast that's making her cry with frustration.

Though he'll rarely admit it in front of his friends, Fitim wants to leave the country, and it doesn't matter where he goes as long as his family will be safe. But as much as he loves them and wants to flee with them, he's worried about the implications of deserting his country in a time of such need . . . and he's worried about Josip. "I can't send him off to die alone," he said, awkwardly trying to pass it off as a joke. "I told him we should go to Croatia, the women there are much more beautiful than Kosovo."

It's a tragic dynamic that can't end happily. If they both escape, Josip will be haunted forever by the unavenged woman in the pine box and the KLA will lose part of what it needs most, dedicated warriors committed to a free Kosovo; if they both go to war, they may die or at least suffer psychic injuries that will last until physical death. If they go their separate ways, they will have lost one another, probably forever, an option neither is advocating.

"Maybe NATO will do something," Fitim said feebly.

9 Defenders of the Homeland

The war in Bosnia will look like a tea party if Serbian nationalism runs wild in Kosovo.

> —U.S. Representative Eliot Engel, on
> "Conflict Prevention" at the Institute of
> Peace symposium, "Bosnia in the Balkans,"
> Washington, D.C., February 25, 1998

One

The diplomats finally had something to report, though it wasn't
much. Starting in a few days, Holbrooke and Rugova announced in
front of party headquarters, where we'd gathered for another day of
waiting, that ambassadors from the Balkan Contact Group nations
would conduct observer missions in which they would drive around
Kosovo and see what was going on.

There was a moment of disappointed silence from the crowd of reporters.

"And what will the point of these observer missions be?" someone
finally shouted. To gather information, they responded. More precisely, for the "objectification" of information, so that they can see
accurately what's happening in the field. The press would be invited
to come along for the ride during the first mission, which would be
largely symbolic, they said. Rugova finished the press conference

with his typical coda, by thanking the international community for taking this step, but begging for deeper involvement, like NATO ground deployment.

This was good news for me: I'd been trying for days to bum a ride out into the field, starting each morning with a pilgrimage to the media center to see if there had been notable fighting the night before. At the time, most of the action was centered around Pec. Outlying villages were shelled every night, and even the reports from the government sounded dramatic. But I hadn't quite drummed up the courage to try driving there in my car, which, in journalism lingo, was "soft," capable of fending off a ball of lead traveling through the air at several thousand feet per second only slightly better than melting butter. I was extremely grateful that the damned thing hadn't suffered so much as a scratch in spite of what I'd put it through, and it wouldn't do at all to return it to the man from Budget full of machine-gun holes. Every morning, the Grand was crowded with photographers and correspondents who work for agencies that aren't wealthy enough to invest in "hard" cars, the bullet-proof ones. It was like a game of musical chairs as we dashed around looking for a ride in a network vehicle. That's always a tough gig; those of us with soft vehicles are constantly put in the position of the class geek forced to ask every member of the high school cheerleading squad out to the prom. Most TV people react like most cheerleaders would: rejections range from polite-but-no-way to downright rude. The people from ITN, a British television agency, took the cake in the latter category. When I asked politely if they were planning on heading to Pec, the producer didn't even look up. "No, but even if we were, you couldn't come with us."

After a week of this, the situation had gotten to the point where I began seriously considering forging out on my own and taking my chances.

In truth, I had a standing invitation to head out into the field, albeit not in a hard car, with a group of international human rights workers who were also staying at Josip's house. They ranged out every morning to speak with refugees from recently destroyed villages, trying to piece together events in their own effort to "objectify" information.

But I never took them up on the invitation for the simple reason that I didn't trust any of them enough to stay out of danger. For one thing, they all acted strangely toward one another; their group dynamics seemed all wrong. Their team was composed of a former Austrian priest who was defrocked for alleged homosexual proclivities; a beautiful Serbian translator who looked like Susan Sarandon; and a fortyish ex-Navy SEAL with a girlfriend in Russia and an unusually detailed knowledge of the range of specific artillery weapons. I was convinced he was a CIA agent. Josip called him "negative face" because he never smiled.

These three were led by a twenty-something American woman with frizzy hair who lived in Prague, collected prints of teddy bears, named her cat Romeo, and dedicated her life to human rights.

They were a strange mix to begin with, and none of them had ever worked together before. And now that they were, it didn't seem to be going very well. Negative Face would complain daily, in private, about the team leader. After one stressful mission, he told me that he nearly had to restrain her physically from taking their only vehicle to investigate a destroyed mosque they'd heard of, while the rest of them conducted refugee interviews. They could still hear sporadic gunfire nearby, and Negative Face didn't want to be stranded in a combat zone if something should have happened to her. The disagreement turned into an arguing match in front of a group of baffled refugees, who undoubtedly had more important things on their minds, like the fact that they were suddenly homeless. The Serbian translator seemed to like no one in the group, preferring, ironically, to socialize with Josip's Albanian family. The former priest avoided the whole crowd, retreating to the back balcony to read at every opportunity.

The friction came to a head once their mission was over and we'd all gathered on the outside patio for dinner. The conversation was about what we'd all done on the Fourth of July, but before we could get too deeply into it, the frizzy-haired team leader announced that she never celebrated the holiday because she thought the United States was the worst country on earth. "Democracy is a farce," she said. "I never felt free in the United States."

"You feel free in the Czech Republic?" Negative Face asked.

She snapped at him: "You don't know what I went through in the United States. I lived in a town that was run by drug lords, and I couldn't even decide who I wanted to marry—my parents chose who they wanted me to marry."

"Why didn't you move?" I asked.

"I did!" she said. "It was even worse."

Negative Face had a few beers under his belt and his mission was in the bag. Apparently, he decided that it was now or never to tell his boss how he felt about her. He held nothing back. "Ever since I met you," he began, "I thought you were the most annoying, snobbish bitch I'd ever met in my entire life. What does anything that's wrong with your life have to do with democracy? At least in the United States you have the freedom to make choices—it's your fault you made bad ones."

This was followed by a lengthy diatribe about the beauty of democracy that should have been recorded for use at a GOP indoctrination ceremony. Even I was having trouble stomaching it, but it was far too much for the Serb translator. "You Americans are so self-righteous, so arrogant," she spat. "You come here to my country and don't even have the courtesy to learn my language, so you have to hire me. But you are talking too fast for me to understand; you've done this all week, even though I told you to slow down! I took the time to learn your language to learn about your culture. Doesn't your democracy teach you something about tolerance and respect for other cultures?"

"Oh, great," Negative Face replied. "A Serb is going to teach me about tolerance and respect for other cultures."

It got worse, but that was the overall gist. Josip and I just sat back as if we were watching a microcosm of international failure in the Balkans in action. We had the bomb-'em-and-let-God-sort-'em-out type in Negative Face, who looked on any country that wasn't a democracy as something to be pitied; we had the American expatriate who laid all of the world's suffering at the feet of the United States, whether it was intercity crime or ethnic cleansing; we had the useless European who did nothing but watch and fret; and we had the poor Serb, who roundly summed up nearly everyone in the Balkans. She was frustrated, proud, sad, mildly brainwashed, yet friendly toward even Albanians when placed in the same room with them.

We found out later that the minidrama wasn't reserved to just these four . . . when their Belgrade-based boss discovered that the translator had gone to visit a colony of Krajina Serb refugees from the Bosnian war—on her own time on a day off—he refused to pay her, because she had made an unauthorized excursion. The whole episode was funny until you remembered that they're in charge of creating reports that sometimes affect international policy. If their ability to investigate human rights abuses was as crippled as their interpersonal skills, the Kosovar refugees didn't stand a chance.

Two

I put my plans to drive alone into the countryside on hold with the announcement that the press could travel with the observers. I knew that the chances of seeing any fighting were nil—the government had approved the route and the checkpoints would be open; all the stops had been planned in advance, and the soldiers knew we were coming—but it was better than nothing.

A few days after the announcement, the observers were ready to roll. So was the press, clogging the streets on all sides of the American Information Center, waiting for a brace of hollow statements from the participants that would send us off as if we were going on the Cannonball Run. We loitered in the gated courtyard out back, drinking little glasses of carbonated juice poured by a tuxedoed servant. There were more than 100 of us, with at least forty vehicles lined up for the trip, all garishly identified with duct tape spelling *TV* or *PRESS* large enough for snipers to see through binoculars. I did the same to my car, figuring that announcing my profession in big blue letters took attention away from the Croatian license plates.

After a round of comments that are typical in modern diplomacy—that is, everyone involved from different countries must make a statement so that it can be broadcast on television back home—we all charged out to our cars as if the starter gun for a desert race had been fired.

It actually *was* a race, in every sense of the word. Once we all filed out of the city to the highway, the object became to get as close as possible to the two Chevrolet Suburbans leading the pack so that when we stopped at a checkpoint, we could be among the first on the scene. My car was packed with reporters from Josip's newspaper; I'd abdicated driving responsibilities to Dukajgin, Josip's editor, since he knew the terrain better than I did.

The long flat highway from Pristina to the turn at Mitrovica became Kosovo's version of the Nevada salt flats. Every questionable opening in oncoming traffic saw at least a half dozen media cars swerve out wildly to pass one another. Horns blared, fingers flew, empty Coke cans were lobbed. It was like a college road trip. Dukajgin found my tape of old Beatles songs, and the volume was turned all the way up, everyone singing at the top of their lungs. "Why do you see it your way? There's a chance that we might fall apart before too long! We can work it out! We can work it out!"

People on the side of the road just stood and gaped at the spectacle: two silver Chevys flying small American flags, a clutch of Mercedes limousines with the colors of other nations streaming in the wind, more than a dozen identical Land Rovers, a motley collection of civilian vehicles, and one taxi. We roared through the city's northern checkpoint at eighty-five or ninety miles per hour, the Serb police resting their weapons on their hips, indulging the diplomats.

"Hey," I shouted over the screaming wind and the stereo. "Is this going to do any good? This whole observer thing?"

"Of course not," answered Dukajgin. "This is bullshit. We just have to be there to witness it."

As cynical as we were, for international observers to witness anything was something of a coup, since not even international officials had been allowed to go out and see what was happening. The only reports had come from the government, the KLA-sympathetic Kosovo Information Center, or refugees. Precious few reports had been obtained by journalists themselves because of the high degree of personal danger. For one thing there were bullets and flying shrapnel. Combatants aren't supposed to shoot journalists . . . but they're not supposed to ethnically cleanse people either, so it's a moot point. You're a fair target if you're out where you shouldn't be. But equally threatening are the people who don't want you there to report the truth. Each of the reporters in the car was full of tales from the field, of times they had braved death in the middle of the night to document on film victims of Serb raids, of times when they had been beaten and arrested for getting caught taking photos of sensitive scenes. Josip told the sorry story of the newspaper's video photographer. They had used the tape as documentation for the articles they wrote. The videographer had been out on the streets during a recent student anti-Serb demonstration and got caught filming the police beating a man with wooden truncheons. The cops had chased the photographer through the streets. Unfortunately, his judgment perhaps clouded by panic, the photographer had run into the newspaper's office, with the Serbs in hot pursuit. Trapped on the second floor with nowhere to go, he launched himself out the front window.

"He would have made it," Josip said, "if he had only seen the flag-pole socket." As it was, he had caught the small metal prong with his rear end on the way down . . . and it had spun him in midair, so that he landed on his face on the stone staircase below. He broke his facial bones in three places, his wrist, and two ribs. The cops got the camera and the tape, but before they left, they tracked down the managing editor and beat him to a pulp in his own office. Josip said they no longer use video.

When we got to the first observer stop, there was pandemonium. Press vehicles scattered in all directions on both sides of a lonely brown road, spilling reporters and cameramen, who bolted for the front of the line, tripping over curbs and dropping charge packs that exploded batteries in all directions. Everyone crowded around Wilford-Brimly-look-alike Richard Miles, U.S. chargé d'affaires, and followed him like a pack of belligerent guardian angels as he walked slowly up a desolate hill to the sandbagged command bunker manned by Serb soldiers who somehow managed to keep a straight face at the spectacle. I could barely do it myself. I elbowed my way to the innermost concentric circle of reporters because I couldn't imagine what type of conversation Miles was going to have with the outpost commander.

The Serb in charge was an imposing figure, standing at least six feet six inches tall. He was an older man, but sinewy and lean, pure muscle. His head was buzzed in standard Marine fashion, and an eight-inch combat knife hung at his waist, threatening a painful death. A large two-way radio crackled and bleeped in his hand. His eyes were hidden by Oakley sunglasses, so it was hard to gauge his emotions, but I was pretty certain "impressed" wasn't among them. He stood perfectly still as the roving mass of bodies and cameras surrounded him. Everyone made sure not to accidentally bump into him.

Except for the constant clicking of cameras, all was quiet for a moment as Miles shook hands with the commander. "So," he said, rocking back on his heels, hands clasped in front of him. "How are things here?"

"Everything here is fine," the commander responded.

"Have you seen much fighting?"

"Not much." There were bullet casings covering the ground like spent confetti.

More awkward silence.

"OK, thank you," Miles said.

If I hadn't seen it myself, I wouldn't have believed it. "You've got to be kidding me," I said to someone nearby. "That's it?"

Apparently, it was. We spent some time gawking at the soldiers as if they—rather than we—were from an unlikely sideshow. I crawled into the bunker where one man reclined on a few milk crates watching a television that was crammed among the ammunition boxes and shrink-wrapped cases of bottled water. He nodded and smiled at me as I looked around. There were shell casings in there, too.

A bit further down the road was an ancient bus, which couldn't get past any of the press cars, so it was stopped off to the side, bleeding oily smoke into the air. It was filled with ragged civilians who stared vacantly at the media mob. I trudged over and motioned for the driver to open the door so I could climb onboard. The air inside the vehicle was gravid with body odor and seeping humidity.

"Anybody speak English?" I asked the dazed passengers. No one did, but that didn't stop them from erupting into hysterics all at once, trying to tell me something. I grabbed a passing reporter from my contingent and asked him to translate.

"They say the shooting just stopped a few hours ago," he said. "The driver says the Serbs rocketed his house last night. He says he will take us to it so we can see. All these people are running away from here."

But there was no time to see the bus driver's blown up home; the diplomats were moving again, off to get more objective information. We had to dash back to our cars to avoid being stranded, leaving the people on the bus hoping that they could manage to get out of the Serbs' sight by the time all the press vehicles vanished.

There weren't any soldiers at the next stop, the former compound of the extended Jashari family, which was next door to an ammunition factory. The collection of low farmhouses was widely thought to be the site of one of the first battles back in February. No one lives there now but ghosts and phantoms. Josip pointed out into the parched dusty fields toward the site of the dead he had helped place in the ground.

The thin dirt road leading to the compound was quickly clogged with cars and a long column of reporters slogging toward the destroyed buildings, eerily quiet except for an American reporter going berserk at the pair of Serb secret police who had infiltrated our caravan. They'd tried to run him over, he shouted.

But nearly everyone ignored him because there was nothing anyone could do about it . . . and also because the Jashari compound, a spectral museum commemorating the reemergence of ethnic cleansing, made such complaints seem petty. There were several buildings at the end of the road, each one identical to those in Bosnia that had suffered the same fate. The outer walls were speckled with bullet holes, blown out from tank shells, or imprinted forever with the rose-petaled design of mortar rounds. The half-decomposed corpse of a horse lay shackled to the earth, its gray spinal column jutting into the sky from fly-covered flesh. Inside the rooms was the type of destruction one expects from a tornado: furniture was smashed, pots and pans lay in the ashes, children's shoes were scattered like spilled marbles. On a hook in the kitchen was a blue windbreaker, left where it was hung before the bullets tore the rest of the house to shreds.

Other buildings held similar evidence of the deadly interruption of the compound's daily life. A motorcycle that had been partially taken apart stood skeletally mute, never to be repaired. A ceramic mug half full of molding coffee sat forgotten on a windowsill. Gangs of reporters peered through the shell holes as if they were looking into a shadow box or some grim work of art, staring at mattresses where people had once made love or slept soundly but that were now up-ended and shredded. Sunlight streamed in from gaping holes in the ceiling. The only sounds were the far-off chatter of blackbirds and the hollow patter of people stumbling over piles of shattered cinder blocks.

Even though the destruction was exactly the same as that of the villages I'd driven through in Bosnia, there was an unsettling difference in this. This had happened just a few months before. The clothes scattered on the ground like autumn leaves still held their color against the steady work of the sun. The remains of the horse still turned the air green with the stench of rot. The exposed beams jutted from the buildings like freshly broken bones.

Miles summed it up simply by stating the obvious: "This is terrible."

We gathered again in the backyard of the American Information Center for a posttrip press conference, an event markedly different in tone than the one before we left. Everyone was tired and depressed and not a little bit confused about what, if anything, had been accomplished. Miles took the stage and summed up the day's events, reiterating that what we'd just done was symbolic (i.e., not effective). Future missions into the field would be done randomly, but with more or less the same goal: to stop and ask the soldiers what was happening. Everyone, he said, was enthusiastic about the trips, which signified an important step in figuring out what was happening in the countryside. Any questions?

Silence. Over 100 reporters stood in tight formation and not a single question came to mind. It was fairly clear to everyone that the day they'd just wasted signified absolutely nothing.

Three

We drove home in silence, the stereo off. Josip was morose; the trip to the Jashari compound had been his second. He had gone there the first time immediately after the attack, sneaking through tight Serbian security points by hiking through the woods. The ground had been bloodstained then, and the horse had still been alive, he said, although no one thought to free it at the time.

Josip's mother had sandwiches on the coffee table in the living room when we came in, even though it was late. Neither of us had an appetite, but to be polite we sank into overstuffed sofas and picked at the late-night snack while she took the opportunity to show off the house's one true treasure.

Stacked high on a shelf were several carefully bound volumes, one of which she gingerly extracted from its place and handed to me with great pride.

"What's this?" I asked.

Josip's mood improved immediately. "That's what my father did in his spare time. He translated all the works of Dostoyevsky into Albanian."

I could barely believe what I was hearing. "What do you mean 'all the works'?"

"Yes, everything. It took him fifteen years, but he finished just before he died. From skin cancer. He wanted Albanians to know different cultures."

His father had been a well-traveled journalist, Josip explained. In his "spare time," he also built the house we were sitting in . . . and apparently painstakingly translated Russian literature to Albanian. "Sometimes, it would take a month to find the right word for the Russian word in the book," Josip said. "My father was a great man. My mother doesn't think I'm as good as he was, because I am just a photographer."

"Why don't you start on Tolstoy?"

Josip snorted. "No, she thinks I am lazy and not good at doing things around the house. You know, I get the wrong kind of nails when something needs to be fixed. Things like that."

I looked at his mother, who confirmed everything with her eyes. "Tell her that being a photographer is important," I said, "especially with what's happening now. People need to know what's going on, and you're able to show them. Otherwise only the Serbs would tell their version."

Josip relayed this, but his mother wasn't hearing any of it, waving off her son's follies with a frustrated grunt.

Josip shrugged.

We finished the meal in silence, watching television with the sound turned off. Outside the house, Serbian helicopters churned the night air.

Four

The observer mission sealed my determination to travel out into the field on my own, if only for comparison's sake. There's nothing further from the truth than a choreographed press event, and if any of us had been thinking, we would have forged off on our own in the exact opposite direction from the ambassadors to gather some truly objective information. The next day, I dropped Josip at the office and made another swing by the hotel on the off chance that I would be able to catch a ride in a hard car. When that attempt failed, I gassed up and lit out, heading southeast.

I was bound for Malisevo, the main KLA stronghold about twenty-five miles from the city, alone again on the road. Few people encouraged traveling alone toward combat zones; the conflict had been going on long enough to spawn an entire genre of checkpoint horror stories from aid workers and correspondents. One photographer told of how the Serbs had ripped him and the people he was traveling with out of their car at a checkpoint that had recently come under fire from the hillsides. The muzzle of an AK-47 was pressed into his forehead while the car was searched and the translator was screamed at. Other passengers were held at gunpoint as well, the barrels of rifles shoved into their kidneys. The soldiers were not happy to see them, and the photographer said he thought he'd finally wandered into a situation he wouldn't emerge from. "There was absolutely no doubt in my mind that we were going to die," he said. But thanks to the quick work of the translator, they were shoved back into the car and pointed back toward the city.

And just a few nights before, Negative Face and his gang of malcontents had had a similar encounter at the main northern checkpoint, which they had made the mistake of trying to cross at night. They were detained and held at gunpoint for forty-five minutes, accused of being spies (an accusation that, in the case of Negative Face, was probably accurate). The translator was called a whore and a traitor. Things remained tense, but they were eventually released.

I'd given a lot of thought to where I was going before I headed out, not wanting to encounter anything even remotely similar. A Dutch reporter named Anders suggested Malisevo, where there hadn't been much fighting lately; at the time, it was the single largest KLA enclave in Kosovo. He'd been there and back with no problem.

I trusted Anders's advice mostly because I hadn't seen him in days. He and his photographer had immediately headed into the field the day after they had registered at the Grand Hotel and had ended up spending several nights with the KLA. They filed twenty articles with photos in the twenty days they'd been there, and the only reason I bumped into them at all in the media center was that they couldn't find a translator they trusted to take them to another story they wanted to pursue. I figured that of all the reporters in Kosovo, those who slept in the field rather than the hotel were apt to give reliable information. "Yeah, you should be able to get to Malisevo without any problem," Anders said. "I think."

The first several miles outside the city were deceptive: the day was hot, but a cooling breeze was waving the grain in the brown fields on either side. And the hazy outline of mountains that led to Montenegro to the west was just short of majestic. With *Let It Bleed* belting from the Escort's stereo, it was easy to forget where I was, but it didn't take long to be reminded. I took an exit from the highway that meandered through a sun-parched ghost town, the car kicking up a cloud of dust even along the main thoroughfare. I passed only two people, a pensioner struggling to mount a curb and a Serb cop who stood immobile on the side of the street in fatigues, staring at me as I rolled by. Lurking in a narrow alley were four or five blue-and-purple APCs.

Just on the other side of town, I rounded a bend and came suddenly on a military checkpoint, nothing more than a Yugo police car with all the doors open, a blue cold-war-era APC with an antiaircraft machine gun pointing down the road in the direction I wanted to travel and several Serb cops carrying standard-issue AK-47s with folding metal stocks.

The soldier on interrogation duty looked like Arnold Schwar-
zenegger, his rifle dwarfed against his muscles to mere pistol proportions. He was smeared with dark sweat in the heat and his camouflaged shirt was unbuttoned, revealing a Serbian cross tangled in his
chest hair. A crude tattoo on his forearm read, "JNA-1992."

I went through the typical routine of pantomime and map pointing, the shuffling of official papers, the search of the car, and the
warnings about death if I chose to continue. KLA snipers in the hills,
he motioned. Lots of fighting lately.

The warning had been given at so many stops by so many soldiers
that I regarded it as little more than a scripted requirement of anyone
guarding a road. But as soon as I drove through the barricade, I knew
that the soldier's admonition had merit. The landscape didn't change
in appearance—it was still the same bucolic countryside, red-dirt
fields hectic with skinny cattle, garish mounds of trash blown into
drifts on the side of the road, hills full of small trees zooming in
smooth slopes off to every side. But it changed in vibration . . . there
were no people on this side of the checkpoint, something genuinely
weird. No matter where you went, no matter how far you were from
the nearest village, there was always someone inexplicably walking or
standing on the side of the road, doing God knows what in the middle of nowhere.

Not here. There were no sounds of approaching vehicles, no buzz
of diesel tractor engines echoing from the fields, no sounds at all from
the empty, staring houses that huddled in the vales and glades. The
sense of pure vacancy was made all the more acute by the eerie suspicion that the hills were indeed quite full of human life—
camouflaged from sight, staring at the car through high-powered
binoculars. I drove very slowly, my seat belt off in case I had to leap
from the car if I came under sudden attack, both windows open to listen for the crack of a sniper rifle, but hearing only the high-pitched
hum my tires made on the fine washboard crinkle of the road,
evidence that a very heavy treaded vehicle had traveled through not
too long ago.

I passed a small village, too small to be indicated on my map,
though it hardly mattered now: it had been cleansed of inhabitants,
bullet holes freckling the surface of the stucco and plaster buildings
on both sides of the road. The minaret on the small but neat mosque
had been exploded by a rocket-propelled grenade or a tank shell and
was standing above the village like a stubbed-out cigar. Black smoke

streaks trailed from some windows, fading toward the roof, giving the eternal impression of movement, as if the fire were still raging. Again, it was the type of destruction that villages in Bosnia had suffered—the same dartboard facades, the same vacant windows speaking of the same type of horror. ("Vukovar, Sarajevo, Pristina. All same enemy," I remembered the Albanian café owner telling me.)

Past the village was nothing, nothing at all but a twisting, S-curve valley with high hills falling right down to the roadside. The turn to Malisevo was unmarked, but I could see the sandbagged checkpoint through the deep trees off to the right. I carefully steered the car through a rocky berm in the road, marked with a sign that read, "MINA!" When I came out the other side, I was staring down the pipe of a very long and very heavy-looking sniper rifle. A stern young KLA soldier stepped cautiously from behind the sandbags, motioning me forward, welcoming me, in his less-than-welcoming way, to KLA territory.

Five

Most of the Albanians living in Malisevo seemed to have the same job: selling black-market cigarettes to one another. The middle of town was nothing more than a central intersection crammed with tractors, grimy storefronts, and a large, empty lot that served as a booming, thriving marketplace. The market was short on tables, but long on Yugos and Zastavas with their trunks open and overflowing with crate after crate of L&M, Lucky Strike, Bond, and Marlboro cigarettes. No one seemed to buy anything, but the market was hip to shoulder with people nonetheless—Albanians who had fled their threatened or destroyed villages to join the KLA or to shelter their families under the rifles of the rebels rather than risk the dangerous and increasingly fatal exodus to Albania or Montenegro. They wore what they could find, nearly transparent button-down shirts, too-small American T-shirts donated to the Salvation Army (one featured a cartoon shark asking, "How about a BITE!?"), and colorless pants with patchwork holes. The heat was oppressive, radiating off everything—dirt, people, cigarette crates, the hoods of cars—creating an oven effect.

I was immediately the center of attention. It was hard not to notice a car announcing the driver's profession in big blue letters, especially in a place like Malisevo, where, because of a lack of gas, the streets were thronged with people rather than cars and I had to constantly lean on the horn to force my way through the morass.

I parked near the market and wandered around. Malisevo was a depressing little enclave, a thumb of territory surrounded on three sides by Serb forces and artillery pieces. The town itself was tiny . . . two main streets that met at the cigarette market. There was no electricity, no potable water, and more people than there were houses. An artillery attack couldn't have helped but inflict serious casualties. But that didn't keep people away. On the contrary, they flocked to Malisevo because at the time, it was home to the largest single group of KLA fighters in Kosovo. And apparently one of the largest groups of beggar children, who instantly surrounded me when I stepped out of the car. I fished out a dinar—which, the best I could tell, was worth about a dime—and asked one of the older kids where the KLA base was.

"Malisevo!" he blurted once he understood the question.

"Yes . . . but where are the soldiers?" I'd gotten very good at charades during the last week, and even though everyone in sight stared at me as if I were an idiot, I went at it enthusiastically, the children all looking at me as if I were a malevolent clown who was spoiling their birthday party.

"KLA?" the kid asked.

"Yes."

"I am KLA!"

But . . . never mind. I knew they were around somewhere; every morning in Pristina, we'd tune into EuroNews on the satellite to see what kind of footage our colleagues at the Grand Hotel had gotten the day before, and the most common background image during any report about Kosovo was a column of camouflaged rebels marching in formation up a barren hill near Malisevo. "Look!" Josip would yell, even though we'd seen the footage a hundred times. "Look at all those warriors."

"So why haven't the Serbs bombed them back to the Ottoman era if every one knows where they are?" I finally asked during one of these episodes.

"Because they're scared," he answered with a cocky smile.

"Scared of what?" I asked. "Even a shabby air strike could take out half that column."

"They would never do that because that's not the only group of KLA. All hell would break loose if the Serbs attacked Malisevo."

That turned out to be profoundly untrue. As it was, wandering around the stalls that were selling shriveled fruit and vegetables and the cars selling drinking water and black market gasoline by the liter, I was one of the last reporters to visit Malisevo before it was flattened by a massive government offensive. My visit came at more-or-less the height of rebel territorial control in Kosovo. It was estimated that the KLA held more than a third of the region, and there was serious talk among internationals that the group posed a legitimate threat to Serb control over the area. Kosovars were confident enough to call Malisevo the capital of their burgeoning nation and to make small strides toward establishing a grassroots government, including issuing improvised license plates.

But the KLA's utter lack of military aplomb was demonstrated weeks later during a three-pronged government assault designed to reclaim lost highways and parse the lands under rebel control to smaller, surrounded pockets. Part of this offensive included sustained armor and artillery attacks against suspected strongholds. One of the hardest hit was Malisevo. Because the KLA had lost every single set-piece engagement with the Serbs, there was disappointingly little resistance, so that Reuters was prompted to run an article with the headline "Whatever Happened to the Kosovo Liberation Army?" The article described the town in the aftermath of the fighting: "It is now a rubble-strewn expanse. Packs of hungry dogs, not guerrilla fighters, roam Malisevo."[1]

But at the time, it was a swollen, bloated village full of people with a lot of time on their hands. I escaped the heat at a crowded outdoor café, where I shared a table with three other men dressed in patchwork camouflage.

"What else can we do?" said one of the men at my table, the only person I could find who spoke a little English, when I asked why he'd come to Malisevo. "Our choices are to die running away or die trying to fight. I will never get shot in the back, I tell you."

Six

I spent three hours sitting in the café talking with the man, emerging with the equivalent of five minutes of conversation between people who can understand one another. He was twenty-six but looked sixty-six. "When all of this is over, maybe I will have to go work with some Serbs sometime," he laughed, explaining why he wouldn't give his name. His eyes stayed dark, suggesting that he only wished things would work out so well.

"I do not understand how I am here," he said. "I have never done anything to make me guilty. I am carpenter. Maybe someone would kill me because they do not like my work. But not because I'm Albanian."

He had lived near a place called Likoshan until he heard that the Serbs were raiding Albanian houses in the middle of the night and executing the people who lived there. As he was preparing his family—a young pregnant wife and their three children—there was a violent knock on the door. He said everyone froze, even the baby. He was sure, he said, that it was the last time they would see each other alive. But it was an uncle at the door, he said, not the Serbs. The man held a pair of beaten-up Uzi submachine guns in his hands and a sackful of bullets. "That's how I joined the KLA," he said. The women and children were put into the back of a truck with other relatives and sent in the direction of Albania. He went with his uncle and several cousins to Malisevo. He had yet to do any fighting—his job was to monitor highways with an unmounted rifle scope and a walkie-talkie that could have come from Radio Shack—and he was not even sure his Uzi worked, because he'd still never fired it.

"So do you think you could kill Serbs if you had to?" I asked.

"They will kill me," he said. "So no problem."

One standard of Balkan travel was not to go through any checkpoint when the soldiers were drunk, no matter which side they were on. And because the Serbs at the checkpoint between Pristina and Malisevo had been drinking when I first went through at 9 A.M. (as I drove past, a soldier was laid out in the grass in the shade of the APC, sucking languidly on a bottle of beer), I thought I should deal with getting back to safety sooner rather than later. I bid my friend farewell and good luck and nosed the car back out through the crowd.

I was driving fast back through the valley between the two forces, lulled into being less than completely attentive by the fact that the road had been empty when I'd come the other way. So I was completely unprepared for the sight that greeted me when I whipped around one of the many S-curves: two men stood in the middle of the road, wearing camouflage vests over their civilian clothing, aiming rifles at the windshield.

"Oh shit, don't shoot," I said to myself, coming to the dumbfounded realization that I was being ambushed. I hit the brakes and let go of the wheel to put both hands high. The rifles swung down slowly as the car rolled to a smooth stop. No one moved for several seconds. The only sound was the chirping of locusts, and other than me and the men with the guns, there was nothing in sight except forest, where several more men crouched; I could see movement out of the corner of my eye, but I didn't dare look away from the men who'd stopped me. Cautiously, I opened the door and, keeping my hands above my head, slid from the car.

In my most steady voice, I said, "I'm an American."

The shorter one, the one with no teeth and a healthy paunch, shouldered his weapon and, amazingly, extended his hand. "I'm Albanian," he said with a laugh. Then he asked for my papers.

Both KLA soldiers wore crusty civilian clothes and old sneakers. The only thing that made them identifiable was a red-and-black KLA patch sewn onto a Dallas Cowboys baseball cap one wore. Their weapons were so old it was almost hard to be scared; both carried bayonet-fitted M-1 rifles, state-of-the-art weaponry in World War II. And the short one obviously couldn't read because he was giving me trouble over the date of issue of my Yugoslavian visa, thinking perhaps that it had expired. Why he cared about a Yugoslavian visa when he was fighting for independence from Yugoslavia is anyone's guess, but we didn't get to debate the question. While I was trying to figure out how to pantomime "expiration," BBC's school-bus-yellow Land Rover ripped around the corner from the direction of Pristina, almost skidding to a stop at the sight of another press vehicle held up by men with rifles.

This caused a minor panic for the guerrillas. Now the two of them had to handle two vehicles full of reporters. While the tall one aimed his rifle at the TV truck, the other guy stuffed my papers back in my hands and motioned for me to beat it. I nodded to the BBC folks, leapt in the car, and floored it before anyone changed his mind.

Less than 500 yards away it happened again. This time I was coming so fast, I nearly ran over the dumb bastard who leapt from the trees into my path.

It was only after the car jolted to a screeching halt that I could raise my hands over my head, and it was only then that I noticed that there were more than a dozen men on both sides of the road, all of them staring carefully down the barrels of their weapons, ready to turn the car into a colander if I made a sudden move.

As soon as they saw my hands, the weapons came down.

The KLA soldiers at this impromptu checkpoint were obviously from a different unit from those just up the road. All wore camouflage uniforms with shoulder insignia and carried with them real hardware: a heavy machine gun, a dozen AK-47s with speed-taped ammunition clips for fast reloading, and a rocket launcher. Each soldier, from what I could see as I fumbled with my papers, carried a sidearm and a Rambo knife at the waist. One of them was a woman, a young girl, really, with badly dyed short red hair and a slight build.

Mercifully, this encounter was brief. The soldiers didn't even look in the trunk, and they waved me quickly on. Within a mile, I crossed the distance between the two forces, coming up on the Serb checkpoint. I had to wait while the soldiers searched a large cargo truck, the driver nearly hysterical with fear, gesturing wildly down the road and babbling nonstop. I assumed, correctly, that he'd also had a run-in with the KLA.

When it was my turn for interrogation, the car was surrounded by a half dozen Serbs, all of them chattering into their radios intermittently and fidgeting with their rifles while looking nervously down the deserted road. My papers were taken away and read carefully over the radio, as were my license plate number and vehicle registration documents. No less than four soldiers sternly poked questions at me; I comprehended nothing but "Ooh-chick-ah," which was the phonetic pronunciation of the Albanian initials for KLA. Their eyes were all the same, projecting a flat, dry stare that told me I was of no value to them whatsoever. It was the same look given to anachronistic machinery or a lifeless painting. No one was making any move to indicate I would be allowed to leave until I answered their questions, and for the first time, I noticed that the hillside was infested with small, individual sniper bunkers. I had no doubt they were trying to get information on the rebels' location down the road, and I pointed vaguely to the map they were thrusting at me. I'm no KLA loyalist, but I didn't want to give them information that could get somebody killed. I pretended not to understand and kept pointing to Malisevo, as if they were asking me where I'd been. They kept pointing to the place in the road where the guerrillas were. I kept shrugging.

This was a dangerous game . . . I could tell they were getting frustrated, and I knew it was only a matter of time before they would suspect I was being intentionally noncommittal and would decide to smack me around for conspiring with the rebels. Soon, a Yugo full of more soldiers blasted through and cut off on a dirt road leading to a high ridge. A Yugo is a silly-looking car in any situation, but it looks downright absurd packed with granite-faced men, rifle barrels poking from all the windows, as if in some sort of twisted Keystone Cops movie.

But I was in no state to appreciate the subtle humor of Serb military hardware. The Serb in charge handed me back my papers with a huge grin. Then, as if in slow motion, he snapped the bolt on his AK-47, ratcheting a round into the chamber, a sickening hollow sound I'll remember forever.

This is it, I thought. The end.

The soldier raised his rifle in the air and fired twice—*crack! crack!*—the hot shell casings ringing off the asphalt. His grin was gigantic as he looked at me. Seeing that I was about to go into a coma, he grabbed the passport from my hand and pointed to my birth date. Then he pointed to the date on his watch.

They were the same; it was my birthday. I had completely forgotten.

He even opened the car door for me, instructing me very carefully to report immediately to the media center at the Grand Hotel. He made me understand that there were people there who wanted to talk to me.

Seven

Needless to say, I never went anywhere near the Grand ever again. Though I didn't think anything sinister would happen, I wasn't about to find out for sure. I called Josip immediately, telling him what had happened. He listened to the entire tale without comment until I got to the part about the rifle shots. "It's your birthday? We'll have a party!"

A party. Terrific. In a way, it was fitting. Even though it was my birthday, it was also my last day in Pristina, a decision I had reached two seconds after leaving the roadblock. I suddenly saw the wisdom in something Josip had said to me when I first met him: "You've got to party while you still can. You never know when your partying days are over."

Yes, it was all very clear. I laughed hysterically in petrified, insane relief the entire way back to Josip's house.

We crafted a plan: we would collect as much money as we could find and speed around Pristina gathering the proper supplies and guests in time to watch the World Cup on television. We set off immediately, blazing through the softening afternoon light for several pounds of steak, a supply of peppers, a carton of onions, a jar of olives, a block of cheese, two cases of beer, a bottle of white tea, several refugees, and Josip's girlfriend.

It was a relaxing trip; in fact, it was one of the most relaxing times of the entire journey, my thoughts burdened only by the question of which team I wanted to see win the World Cup match, Brazil or the Netherlands. This relative euphoria was short-lived, however, when I realized that it came from the fact that I could drive my car away from Pristina in the morning; the people who would be celebrating my birthday could not. I was able to escape from the menacing glare of Serb soldiers on the street corners, from the disturbing presence of Albanian refugees digging through garbage heaps, from the death that was occurring at that very moment on the road between Pristina and Malisevo. (I had been told by a BBC technician that when he returned to the city thirty minutes behind me, instead of guerrillas on the road, there were hundreds of empty shell casings and the limbs of branches that had been blown off during a firefight.)

I suddenly wished I'd stayed at the hotel; I felt like the worst vulture of all, having pried too deeply into the lives of people who may well end up on such a lonely highway themselves. I hadn't given a thing in return. And tomorrow, I would be leaving them to their fate.

Back at the house, I sat at the kitchen table with others who were lingering around while the food was being prepared. Josip knelt in the middle of the kitchen floor, pounding the steaks with a tenderizer. The smell of sautéing peppers was sharp on the air, and the babble of Albanian voices as the women bickered over the sink floated in the soft night like the notes of a wind chime. The men were playing "impress the reporter," spinning wild tales while pouring small glasses of white tea. In that moment of perfect, beautiful, tender normality, I was struck with a deep melancholy. I envisioned a gang of reporters milling around a house that was filled with holes and carrion birds, fighting with each other for the best angle, stealing glimpses of family pictures that had been left behind and trampled in pandemonium. The things that had once been important had become detritus, littering a fire-scarred floor and providing material for refugees to pick through. The reporters didn't stay long . . . just long enough to burn through a roll or two before wondering where to go for better shots. They wandered away, and the house and its contents were left where they had fallen. In a corner of the house, buried under other items that had suddenly become less important than immediate escape, was a jumble of books: the collected works of Dostoyevsky, translated from Russian into Albanian.

At night, maybe, with the right kind of ears, a passerby would hear gentle laughter, the tinkle of glasses, and the steady thrum of a meat tenderizer on a hand-carved kitchen floor.

10 Gunboat Diplomacy

A war crime is a war crime. There is no justification for a war crime.

—James P. Rubin, Department of State
spokesman, May 19, 1999, responding to
a question as to whether criminal behavior
is justified if it occurs in retaliation
for an enemy atrocity

A world in which it is wrong to murder an individual civilian and right to drop high explosive on a residential area does make me wonder whether this Earth of ours is not a loony bin made use of by some other planet.

—George Orwell

One

A Serb policeman was shot and killed in the northern Kosovo town of Podujevo on December 21, 1998. Three days later, on Christmas Eve, the Kosovo Liberation Army announced that a cease-fire that had been agreed to in October 1998 was over and that the rebel force was again massing weapons in preparation for liberating Kosovo from Serbian rule. The day after Christmas, Serb police and KLA rebels engaged in one of the most significant gun battles since the truce, firing grenades, machine guns and mortars at each other near the town of Obranca in northern Kosovo, where Serbs were preparing to bury a Serb farmer who had been killed by the KLA a few days before. Two weeks earlier, Serbs and Albanians had engaged in a five-hour gun battle in southern Kosovo, shooting at each other across the Albanian border.

Refugees were once again on the move, this time through the snow. Hundreds fled the fighting in Podujevo, trekking for miles with their families through subfreezing temperatures to cram into safer houses in nearby villages that were already packed with refugees.

After two months of hope that the situation in Kosovo had cooled off with the coming of winter, international diplomats again returned to the embattled region to try to head off a war. The October 1998 cease-fire agreement had been wrung from the two sides when Milosevic apparently became convinced that NATO was going to keep its promise to bomb Serbian military targets if the fighting didn't stop. Soon after reaching the agreement, Milosevic withdrew a significant number of armor and artillery pieces and scaled Serbian troop presence down to only what was necessary to protect Serb civilians.

The international community had breathed a sigh of relief at this turn of events. From the beginning of the combat in February 1998 to the cease-fire agreement in October 1998, over 1,000 people had been killed and more than 300,000 displaced, mostly Albanian. The death toll promised to go much higher if the fighting persisted into the bitter Balkan winter because several thousand refugees were living in the mountains, afraid to return to their homes. Diplomats, led once again by U.S. envoy Richard Holbrooke, scrambled to head off what many said would be a "humanitarian disaster" if the refugees were left without shelter in the mountains. The diplomats' efforts seem to have paid off: the fighting slowed to a sporadic pace and the Serbs made steps to phase their forces out of the area. The cease-fire called for the Organization for Security and Cooperation in Europe (OSCE) to station 2,000 monitors in Kosovo to verify that Milosevic was cooperating with the rest of the provisions of the cease-fire agreement, provisions that included removing military hardware and stationing soldiers in their barracks rather than on the highways and in the villages. It was the largest undertaking for OSCE since its founding in the mid-1970s, and the mission was headed by a man used to chaotic environments: William Walker, the former U.S. ambassador to El Salvador.

There were the typical problems with the mission's implementation: for one thing, OSCE didn't have 2,000 people on hand and it took a few weeks before it eventually mustered up about 1,400 people. Critics griped that sending unarmed monitors to Kosovo was like giving Milosevic 1,400 hostages to guarantee that NATO wouldn't bomb his forces. Like the International Police Task Force in Bosnia, the OSCE "verifiers," as Holbrooke insisted on calling them, carried no weapons.

"It's all very nice, but what happens if the police refuse to go back to their garrisons?" John D. Fox, the Washington director of the Open Society, is quoted as saying in the *New York Times*. The Open Society is a foundation created by the philanthropist George Soros to promote democratic institutions in formerly Communist countries.[1]

But in comparison to many other international efforts in the Balkans, the plan seemed to work well at separating the forces—until the week before Christmas, when the violence broke out again.

Once the police officer was killed in Podujevo, Milosevic felt free to begin "limited" operations around the small village to arrest the perpetrators. Yugoslavia's state news agency, Tanjug, quoted police officials as saying that the Serb forces encountered "fierce" resistance and that they "liquidated . . . a number of terrorists who had attacked police."[2]

Pleurat Sejdiu, who had emerged as one of many political representatives of the KLA in the fall of 1998 and who was based in London, announced soon thereafter that the truce was being called off so that KLA rebels could defend themselves against what he characterized as a renewed Serb campaign against them. The KLA acknowledged to CNN that it was preparing for a sustained effort to wrest Kosovo from Serbia once and for all.[3]

The international community quickly got nervous that things would get out of hand. Albania's Foreign Ministry pleaded with NATO to intervene to "end the Kosovo drama," NATO Secretary-General Javier Solana told BBC television that Milosevic's "limited" operations were in direct violation of the October 1998 agreement and the supreme commander of NATO's southern forces, General Wesley Clark, repeated what had by then become a familiar mantra, that unless Milosevic ended the aggression, he faced military consequences.

On the ground, the international monitors met with both sides and traveled to conflict zones to try to preserve what was left of the truce. Their efforts worked for a time; although sporadic fighting continued, and threatened to escalate, outright warfare was held in check into 1999.

In January 1999, however, about forty-five Albanian bodies were found by reporters in a ditch near the village of Racak, evidence of the largest confirmed massacre in Kosovo to date. The death count rose to over 2,000.

Before entirely guttering out, the candle of hope sputtered to life once more with the announcement that Serbian and Albanian delegations would meet in February 1999 in France with Secretary of State Madeleine Albright and a multitude of European leaders, diplomats and envoys to discuss ways of permanently ending the conflict and coming to terms on a set of provisions the two sides could live with. Anyone who had watched the tedious, acrimonious, belligerent Dayton negotiations unfold held little hope that either side would concede anything that would lead to a peaceful compromise—the Serbs were talking about their own country this time, not some breakaway faction in Bosnia, and they hadn't even really begun to fight for what they believed was theirs.

The first several days of the negotiations were a total failure: both sides were at an utter stalemate, and at the end of each day of negotiation, Albright made it sound to CNN cameras as though the two delegations were simply being stubborn and refusing even to entertain discussions about various concessions.

But it later came to light that Albright was being disingenuous at best. The Serbs and the Albanians were disagreeing all right, but not necessarily with one another: they both refused to sign a document penned by the State Department that dictated the terms of a peace agreement that the United States wanted. The "talks" in France were far more an ultimatum delivered by Albright—who became so Pavlovian in threatening force that it no longer even made headlines—and much less a negotiated agreement that the Serbs and Albanians were hammering out themselves.

What came to be known as the Rambouillet Accords was a blueprint for ending the hostilities, but it also called for the de facto occupation of Yugoslavia by NATO, Yugoslavia's "reallocation" of its state assets, including the valuable Trepce and Stari Trn mines, and freedom for Kosovo within three years, when a referendum on the matter would be held in the province.

It was a weird document, to say the least. The first several provisions outline a potential constitution for Kosovo and lay out the judiciary and the executive branches of government. It then goes into lengthy detail about such minutia as police uniforms and police jurisdiction issues. Chapter 3 is an election schedule appointing the OSCE as monitor, and Chapter 4 discusses "economic issues," the most significant one being Article II, paragraph 1, which states: "The Parties agree to reallocate ownership and resources in accordance insofar as possible with the distribution of powers and responsibilities set forth in this Agreement, in the following areas: (a) government-owned assets (including educational institutions, hospitals, natural resources and production facilities)."

In other words, it sets out to privatize the single most valuable asset the Yugoslavian government owns: the billions of dollars' worth of minerals in the Trepce and Stari Trn mines. This provision—and everything preceding it—comes before a single mention of what the world had assumed the document was all about in the first place: the displaced and ethnically cleansed Kosovar refugees. Furthermore, the refugee provisions are included in "Chapter 4A," the only subchapter in the accords, as if they'd been tacked on at the last minute when everything else had already been decided and then someone noticed that they'd forgotten to mention human rights or refugees.

Neither side was terribly pleased with the bizarre document.

Though this was akin to NATO granting the KLA every wish it ever had, the KLA delegates were reluctant to sign the agreement because it didn't clearly outline the role the KLA would play in governing the region in the three-year interim before the referendum. The KLA also wasn't thrilled that independence wouldn't happen immediately. They didn't want autonomy, they seemed to be saying, they wanted independence. Hasn't anyone been listening?

For the Serbs, the situation was so much more dire as to be nearly comical. They'd gone to France thinking they were to discuss the future of Kosovo and what they were presented with was more or less a surrender document for all of Yugoslavia. Not only did the accords allow NATO to enter Kosovo, but Appendix B of the agreement also allowed the multinational force unimpeded access to all points within greater Yugoslavia and allowed unrestricted access to and use of railways, airports, highways, ports and associated airspace and maritime claims. Appendix B declared further that NATO personnel would be immune from arrest or prosecution for breaking local laws and that they could utilize "any areas or facilities as required for support, training and operations." The entire electromagnetic spectrum for communications and broadcast was NATO's to do with as it pleased and everything NATO brought into the country or took out was immune from taxation or Yugoslavian customs laws.

And of course, NATO could arrest anyone it wanted to.[4]

It's amazing that the Serb representatives didn't leave France the moment they finished reading the accords. NATO didn't just want an end to the Kosovo war, it wanted Belgrade as a trophy. If the delegates had signed the accords they would have gone down in history as the people who not only forfeited their sacred land to their sworn enemies but who had authorized an alliance of nineteen countries to take over Yugoslavia without so much as a shot being fired in defense. That the delegates would have been killed on the spot had they tried to return to Belgrade goes without saying.

In the face of the incredible one-sidedness of the Rambouillet Accords, the Serbs' efforts to negotiate can be seen as nothing less than fully valiant. But they were soon to discover that it was Albright who was impeding the negotiations by not allowing them to negotiate. The Serbs said they were willing to withdraw from Kosovo on the condition that the multinational force occupy Kosovo only and that it be under the command of the United Nations rather than NATO, and they wanted Russia to participate in the peacekeeping duties. By this point, Serbian promises proved to be about as reliable as NATO threats, but Albright wasn't about to give any quarter to test their sincerity. No dice, she replied, again threatening military force if the diplomats didn't sign.

The inevitable outcome of this standoff was war, but as the first of many dominoes began to tip over, it seemed the only person to grasp the reality of the situation was Milosevic, who gave up on the dog-and-pony show in France long before anyone else did. Turning his attention to preparations for what he knew was sure to come, he ordered soldiers and hardware to strategic positions along the northern Kosovo border.

European intelligence experts and the CIA quickly grew alarmed at the maneuver, and spies were able to detail Milosevic's plan, which was code-named Operation Horseshoe.[5] What was going to happen if the Rambouillet talks failed, they warned the diplomats, was a purge of ethnic Albanians on a level that had yet to be seen. Serb forces were going to push into Kosovo from the north like an inverted horseshoe, evicting or killing everyone in their path. The seismic wave of refugees that would flee south to Macedonia and Albania would likely crush both of those unstable nations unless measures were immediately undertaken to lessen the impact of what was shaping up to be one of the worse population displacements in Europe since the end of the Second World War.

No one in Rambouillet heeded the warning. Two CIA agents were so convinced that the international community's unwavering position at the negotiating table was going to end disastrously that they left the chateau in protest.[6]

Milosevic went about arranging his soldiers like so many game pieces, preparing for the endgame.

Two

Meanwhile, 21-year-old Florim Rashica and his family were preparing to run for their lives. The 141st Meha Uka Brigade of the Kosovo Liberation Army, which was fighting in the Shala of Bajgora, the shallow and picturesque valley east of Vucitrn that held a number of small farming villages, was having trouble holding off a Serbian military advance on two fronts, one from the south and one from the north.[7] Lately, in Florim's tiny hamlet of Studime e Poshtme, it was becoming increasingly dangerous to leave the house; Serbian snipers were close enough to send bullets smacking into the soft stucco and brick of the village's huddled buildings. For months, the Rashica family had been prepared to flee when the time came—they had their farm tractor hitched to a narrow wagon that was packed with food, clothing and whatever family valuables would fit into it. They had divided the family fortune of about 50,000 deutsche marks equally among them because if the rumors they'd been hearing were correct, they were going to need to bribe their way out of Kosovo if they were going to make it at all.

In late February, just as the two delegations in Rambouillet were preparing to reconvene after a two-week break, Serb police began advancing on Studime, hitting the village with mortars and heavy machine-gun fire. As if acting with one mind, the entire village simultaneously decided the time to flee had come. While his mother, brothers, sisters, aunts, uncles and several cousins packed into the wagon, Florim ran into the family's field under machine-gun fire to turn their livestock loose.

He never managed it. Waiting for him in the farmyard were five former friends, all Serbs from nearby villages. As if the shooting and the shelling hadn't been enough to convince the Rashicas that they weren't wanted in Kosovo, the five men beat Florim into a stunned, bloody mess, splitting his jaw, cutting his eye and opening an eight-inch gash in the back of his head. After five minutes of beating and kicking, the gang told him he had sixty seconds to get out of their sight before they shot him where he lay.

"So I left," Florim said. "I never knew I could crawl so fast."

Everyone else left too, though they didn't get very far. Florim limped back to his family's tractor, which was third in a line of hundreds streaming out of Studime. He tumbled into the back of the wagon with the rest of his family, crashing down next to a cousin who'd been wounded by sniper fire moments before.

En route to the main intersection at Vucitrn, which led to the road that could take them south to Macedonia, they passed a number of Serb police, paramilitary and regular army troops, some of them wearing ski masks to hide their identities. The soldiers were heading into Studime. Florim would find out later that they'd established a headquarters at a warehouse overlooking the main road through town.

The column was composed of tractors and wagons, some being pulled by horses or steers while others harrumphed clouds of acrid diesel smoke into the air, and it moved pitifully slowly, an easy target for harassing soldiers on foot. Florim and others in the caravan said that they were robbed and beaten intermittently as they fled their town.

The refugees finally came to a roadblock that they weren't allowed to pass through. Florim, in the third tractor, saw several police officers wearing masks stop the column and direct them to Drenica, a small village in southwest Kosovo, telling them that they'd be safe there. The road to Macedonia was closed, the police officers said.

The refugees at the head of the column quickly huddled to decide what to do. Not only did very few of them believe that they would make it to Drenica alive, none of them were very sure they wanted to. Rumors travel at the speed of sniper bullets in Kosovo, and everyone in Studime had heard horrific tales of concentration camps in Drenica and of mass killings and torture of Kosovars who were led there. But they obviously couldn't go back to Studime; it was apparent that most of the southern end of the Shala of Bajgora had collapsed before the Serb forces.

The best decision, it was hastily agreed, was to turn the caravan around, take narrow back trails around Studime and retreat north into the shrinking perimeter held by the KLA's 141st Brigade. Few people were thrilled at this decision: Serb forces were also threatening the KLA's northern front, and the small towns nominally under KLA protection were already swollen with refugees fleeing from other areas. The decision to pilot the slow-moving column through wooded trails to Studime e Eperme (Upper Studime), about six miles from Studime e Poshtme (Lower Studime), which they'd just fled, was a decision to be trapped in a pocket of refugees that was virtually surrounded by Serb forces.

Florim knew that they were only delaying their fates.[8]

Back in France, there had been a breakthrough—at least for Albright. The KLA had suddenly (so suddenly, in fact, that some members of Congress would later wonder privately who had been whispering in their ears and for what purposes)[9] changed their minds entirely and signed the Rambouillet Accords, even though everything they objected to about the agreement was still included.

This is exactly the course of events Albright had hoped for: she couldn't very well carry out her threat of force against the Serbs if the KLA themselves wouldn't sign a peace agreement.

As soon as the Kosovar delegation signed on the dotted line, everyone knew what was going to happen next. The Serbs hadn't been afforded anything they wanted out of the agreement and it was therefore impossible for them to sign. When the delegates packed up and left France that day, they were likely headed for bunkers in Belgrade: they knew they were going to war with the nineteen nations in the NATO alliance.

In Serbia, there seemed to be little reason to continue disguising Belgrade's actions in Kosovo as something other than ethnic cleansing. Within days—in fact, even before the KLA had agreed to Rambouillet's version of peace—Milosevic unleashed Operation Horseshoe, and wild rumors began circulating that the dreaded paramilitary commander Arkan was commanding his Tigers in Kosovo with orders to rob and evict the wealthiest Albanians first and send the spoils back to Belgrade. They were said to have lists of their targets.

William Walker, the head of the OSCE verification mission, saw very clearly the immediate future and ordered his people to get out of the line of fire.

Holbrooke attempted to pick up the pieces Albright had scattered on a last-minute, eleventh-hour flight to Belgrade. His attempts to avert war ended unsuccessfully less than twenty-four hours later, and Holbrooke left Belgrade for the last time on March 23.

On March 24, the bombing began and the floodgates were opened.

Three

While cruise missiles streaked across Kosovo's night landscape from the Adriatic sea and Stealth bomber pilots flying round-trip from Missouri delivered bombs with all the dramatic vocal inflection of a Bingo announcer, President Bill Clinton dropped a bomb of his own on his military strategists by announcing on television that NATO would not invade Yugoslavia from the ground.

The decision made sense in that Kosovo is horrifically unforgiving geographically and that the Serbs would be deeply entrenched and fully cognizant of the parallels to the Ottoman invasion of the 1380s. Fighting into Yugoslavia would be very bloody and very costly for NATO. But more immediately, there was really nowhere the NATO forces could enter Yugoslavia even if they wanted to.

Hungary is the only NATO country that has an international border with Serbia—and it was such a recent NATO inductee that its official membership plaque was probably still in the mail—but it has none with any other NATO allies. To get to a staging area in Hungary, troops and equipment would have to pass through Slovakia or neutral Austria, and neither of these countries was likely to grant permission.

The options to the south were no better: public sentiment in Greece was strongly in favor of the Serbs, as were the feelings of a substantial portion of the Macedonian population. Even if NATO forced the issue and staged from Macedonia, this country has only a 212-mile border with Kosovo, a narrow neck of an opening. It would be like a SWAT team having to storm a heavily armed compound through a single door.

Staging from Bosnia, where Republika Srpska borders Yugoslavia, was out of the question unless NATO wanted another simultaneous war in Bosnia. Romania and Bulgaria have borders with Yugoslavia, but they aren't in NATO. Asking either of them if they'd please allow the alliance to invade their neighbor through their common border would have been rude as well as unsuccessful.

Which left Albania, a pathetic country of bandits, mudflats and ports so polluted that going to the beach is a form of suicide. Military planners didn't want to do any maneuvers from Albania and therefore they didn't disagree with the president's position that NATO should only attack Kosovo from the air.

Many people *did* disagree, however, with revealing this news to the entire world, a strategy that made mission success—defined as the time when all Serb forces withdraw from Kosovo and all the refugees begin to return—all the more difficult. In fact, it stymied that success to such a degree that before long critics would accuse NATO of ethnically cleansing Kosovo itself. Since Milosevic was told that all he had to worry about from NATO was missiles and bombs—not soldiers and tank-killing helicopters—he poured troops into Kosovo and refugees poured out, which, of course, was the exact opposite of what the NATO offensive was meant to bring about.

On the ground in Kosovo, things had gone from bad to apocalyptic. Since the Serbs had only KLA ground forces to worry about, they were efficiently going about their task to completely eradicate ethnic Albanians from Kosovo with virtual impunity. Soon after the bombing began, hundreds of thousands of Kosovars began fleeing south to Macedonia and Albania. Only a week into the bombing, several thousand refugees arrived at the Macedonian border, only to find it sealed by the Macedonians.

Faced with an influx of untold thousands of Kosovars who would have to be fed and housed for an indefinite amount of time, the Macedonian government said, "No way," and ordered its border guards to shoot anyone trying to cross into their country until such time as Skopje received a wire transfer from someone else who would step up to pay for taking care of the refugees.

As a result, initially some 20,000 people were stranded in what became known as No Man's Land, a valley floor between two steep hills and within sight of the border station where they were without food or shelter. Some people died there, others gave birth. Dysentery was rampant. One reporter who'd seen the ungodly spectacle said the smell rising from the valley floor beyond the barbed wire erected by Macedonian authorities was like old meat and milk rotting under a summer sun. More people trudged into No Man's Land each day, walking single file along the railroad tracks that Serbs warned were mined on either side. Many carried their elderly relatives dozens of miles, seeking safety.

Finally, a deal was struck and the borders were opened. Non-governmental organizations, working miraculously fast, created the Blace Interim Camp in No Man's Land; Stankovac I and II were located a little farther into Macedonia; and Cegrane, the largest camp, which would eventually be temporary home to more than 40,000 people, was established outside Skopje.

In Albania, most refugees stayed at camps in Kukes, a medium-sized city miles from the Yugoslavian border. The people living in these tent cities had nothing other than what they had carried out with them—and they all had similar tales. Serbs came and forced them to leave immediately. Sometimes the fighting-age men would be taken away, perhaps to concentration camps, some said. Some people were forced onto trains for deportation to the borders, others drove their own cars, and still others walked or crammed onto overfilled carts and wagons being dragged by farm tractors. Many people had been robbed by Serbs they encountered at various checkpoints in Kosovo. Almost everyone was missing a loved one who was feared dead.

Pristina was emptied like the Krakow ghetto. Stem, Josip's brother-in-law, watched in horror from his twelfth-story apartment as the streets below him filled with Albanians being herded to the train station at rifle point by Serb soldiers screaming and kicking them along.

"As far as you could see, people were everywhere," he said. Photos smuggled out of the capital were like suddenly discovered color pictures of the Holocaust: an ocean of desperate, terrified people on the train platform crammed against the cars of an impossibly full train, arms reaching from the windows to the ground for one last touch of a relative or lover before the train pounded off into the unknown. Survivors of the journey told human rights workers that the frequent stops were the worst; that's when people were pulled off by soldiers and robbed or simply never seen again.

Stem stayed in the city because, he said, he figured it was no worse than wherever he would be forced to go. And as the head of an apartment filled with some two dozen relatives and acquaintances, he felt an obligation to do what he could to stay.

A surprisingly large number of Albanians braved the odds and stayed in Pristina. One man, a twenty-two-year-old waiter, stayed because his father was too feeble to leave. They never touched the permanently drawn curtains on their home, never lit a candle, and he only left at night to scavenge for food.

Others grouped together and formed independent militias to protect their families. One baby-faced sixteen-year-old boy said he and five armed friends only avoided certain death when a Serb patrol began house-to-house searches by hiding in a narrow tunnel dug into his basement floor. There they crouched in the pitch dark, single-file, Kalashnikovs aimed at the pale square of plywood covering the tunnel entrance, the only sounds their own ragged breathing and the knocking footsteps of Serbs as they pounded through the house looking for hold-outs. The boy, who was at the head of the line, said he was glad the Serbs never found the tunnel because he was as afraid of accidentally getting shot in the back by his fully cocked colleagues crowded behind him as he was of the Serbs.

Josip was lost for a time and I feared the worse. Coincidentally I called him from the United States several hours before the bombing started, but I screwed up the time difference and woke him up at 2 A.M. "Everything's quiet," he reported. "We're all just waiting." I tried to call him later that day, but an hour into the first stage of the bombing, there was no response on the cellular network.

I'd find out later that the Serbs stormed the offices of Josip's paper that day, killing the security guard, trashing the offices and planting booby traps throughout the building. Eventually, through a long network of contacts, I learned that Josip and his mother had abandoned the house, leaving it in the care of an Italian radio reporter. The reporter was evicted not long after by Serb soldiers who began trashing it as they kicked him out. The reporter escaped to Macedonia on one of the trains.

Josip surfaced later in Tetovo, Macedonia, where the newspaper's staff had somehow managed to revive their operations and print scaled-down issues of the paper, which were distributed to the refugees in the camps. His mother had stayed with friends and relatives in Kosovo.

Throughout the bombing campaign, more and more refugees flooded across the borders every day. On *Meet the Press* soon after the bombing began, Madeleine Albright reiterated that the bombing was succeeding in its efforts to protect civilians, end ethnic cleansing and remove the Serbian military from Kosovo.

Four

If the bombing campaign was succeeding at anything it was difficult to tell from the daily press briefings broadcast from NATO headquarters in Brussels. It's a rare public relations person who can stand before the world's cameras and say that the military efforts are having their desired effect when night after night television stations throughout the world report ever-increasing numbers of refugees fleeing a Serbian military machine that showed little sign of being affected at all by the nightly bombing raids. But NATO flack Jamie Shea gave it his best day after day.

Bad PR was destined to plague the military operation from the very start, stemming from the decision by NATO planners to bomb the entire country of Yugoslavia, not just Serbian military assets in Kosovo.

The list of targets included not only Serb soldiers and their tanks, but later included bridges, power plants, oil refineries, television relays, private homes of government officials and major highways throughout the country. The idea, Shea explained, was to crush the backbone of Milosevic's war machine, to ensure that any tanks that could still roll wouldn't be able to get oil, that all critical supply routes into Kosovo would be too crippled with cluster-bomb detonations to be navigated. And media outlets like the state-run radio and television networks were also defined as military targets, because, it was explained without a trace of irony, they were propaganda tools of the military—even though journalists are automatically considered noncombatants under the Geneva Convention.

It's unclear just how substantially bombing the state TV headquarters in Belgrade damaged the Serbian military in Kosovo, but it clearly damaged NATO's already questionable reputation in Serbia. Hundreds of thousands of Serb civilians, many of whom had never even been to Kosovo and couldn't care less if it was annexed by Albania or turned into a wildlife preserve, were left without power, transportation, access to food and medical supplies, jobs and—in far too many cases—homes.

The only early effect this strategy had was to totally galvanize the Serb population against the West. Milosevic suddenly enjoyed more popularity than ever in his country and Serb citizens held rallies and rock concerts on bridges they believed would be targeted by NATO planes. In fact, a black-and-white target quickly became the symbol of Serbian defiance and was found on T-shirts, ball caps, flags, banners, flyers and lapel pins.

Realizing, perhaps, that turning the entire population of Serbia against NATO wasn't such a good idea, NATO began leafleting Yugoslavia with messages saying that although their bridges, power plants, water treatment plants, places of work and, in some cases, their friends and relatives were all being repeatedly hit by cruise missiles and air-bursting cluster bombs, NATO had no beef with the Serb people, just their president. The leafleting seemed to have little effect.

Neither, in fact, did the bombing when it was actually directed at military targets. If the alliance, drawing on its experience in Bosnia—where the Serbs finally gave up and went to Dayton only after NATO jets hit military targets throughout the country—thought that it could pound the Serbs into surrendering after a week or two of bombing, it was sorely mistaken. It's true that Serbia's cold war–era military couldn't match the superior technology of the NATO members, but the Serbs were craftier than many military planners anticipated. For one thing, the Serbs rarely used their rather potent multiple rocket–launcher (or MRL) air-defense systems. Therefore, since they didn't shoot at NATO planes, NATO largely didn't know where they were and the Serbs managed to keep many MRLs intact.

Serbs also managed to keep many of their tanks through the decidedly low-tech strategy of parking them in civilian barns and gutted houses, hiding them from satellites and drone planes.

And then the Serbs shot down a U.S. F-117 Stealth-equipped fighter plane over the city of Novi Sad, using old-fashioned antiaircraft guns. The Stealth is a piece of machinery that's supposed to be completely invisible to radar. It's unclear whether the jet was downed with a very lucky shot or whether the Serbs employed some sort of ingenious trick to locate the plane, but it hardly mattered. Though the Serbs were having their country leveled by missiles fired from two miles in the sky or hundreds of miles off the Adriatic coast, they were also schooling the NATO alliance in the amount of determination they had, and downing a supposedly invisible airplane gave a boost of adrenaline to the Serbs' already high national morale.

In fact, the world was getting a full treatment of the character of the Serb people: proud to be the eternal underdogs in the fight against imperial powers intent of crushing their culture and their people, a perception that was helped every time an errant NATO bomb—and there were many—missed its target and blew up whole residential blocks. The Serbs also displayed a never-die sense of humor: when the Stealth fighter went down, someone made a poster for the lenses of CNN cameras that said, "Sorry, we didn't know it was invisible." More than once, a Serb representative said that every Serb will fight to the death before giving up Kosovo, less because they all loved Kosovo so much than because they all suddenly hated NATO.

The Serbs also seemed to be using their weapons better than NATO: at least they weren't killing people they didn't intend to kill. If the military campaign began rather oddly with one side sharing its battle plans with the other, it quickly grew tragic. Air campaigns are difficult to manage with complete success, it soon became clear. "Smart" weapons turned out to be more autistic than cognitive as heat-seeking CBU-97 cluster bombs continually succeeded in finding vehicles filled with warm Kosovar civilians rather than equally warm Serb soldiers. The list of NATO misfires in which civilians were killed grew so long so quickly that even dogmatically liberal radio talk show hosts in the United States began wondering, on the air, whether we were actually killing all these innocent people—whom we were trying to protect—on purpose.

Very little of the information about NATO's civilian "collateral damage" was verified by independent sources. Most figures on civilian deaths came from the Serbian Foreign Ministry, and, except on very rare occasions, journalists were escorted to death sites by Serb officials to film bodies of innocent victims of the air campaign. There-fore, the number of actual deaths is disputed and will likely never be known. NATO, for one, isn't going to start an investigation into the matter.

"We have not been able to do this in the past, we can't do it at the moment and we won't be able to do it in the future," NATO spokesman Jamie Shea told reporters in Brussels. "NATO simply doesn't have the personnel on the ground with ballistic and other ex-perts to determine the truth. But I think it is clear to everybody by now that Serb TV and President Milosevic is [sic] not a very reliable source in these matters."

Nevertheless, a general consensus has emerged about some events, based on news reports and eyewitness testimony:

Only two weeks into what would be a seventy-eight-day offensive, NATO missiles landed in a residential neighborhood a half mile from their intended target in Aleksinac, destroying apartment buildings and a pharmacy. The number of dead is estimated at between twelve and seventeen. Two days later, NATO missiles "may have overshot" the state-run telephone switching station in Pristina, killing at least five.

In mid-April, NATO admitted its planes blew up a railroad near Leskovac, scoring a direct hit on a passenger car filled with civilians. A following car plunged off the rail into the canyon below. Somewhere between 10 and 70 dead, depending on whom you ask. A day later, on the road between Pec and Prizren, near the city of Djakovica, NATO planes inexplicably dropped cluster bombs on a column of refugees not once but repeatedly, blasting unarmed Kosovars into fine clouds of bone and hair. At first NATO said there were military vehicles in the convoy, although they somehow managed to escape the carnage, because none were found in the wreckage. The attack killed at least eighty people, none of whom coincidentally were Serbs—but survivors insisted there were no military targets, just horses and tractors. NATO leaders then suggested that the Albanians had been killed by Serbs. When they could produce no evidence for that explanation, they came out with the Monty Python–style excuse that a Serbian MiG-29 had somehow managed to buzz the column completely undetected by NATO's forces and had blown up the refugees at the precise moment that the NATO planes were bombing the still-missing Serbian vehicles they insisted were interspersed in the column.

NATO finally admitted responsibility.

A week later, NATO deliberately destroyed Serbian radio-television headquarters in Belgrade, killing and wounding journalists and media personnel. Then a cluster bomb hit a busload of civilians on the Luzane bridge in Kosovo, north of Pristina, killing about twenty-three. Some survivors reported that a second run on the bridge attacked the ambulance team that came to the rescue. Then, a day after arduously winning permission to use Bulgarian airspace, NATO accidentally shot a missile into a residential neighborhood near Sofia in what was actually the fourth misfire into Bulgaria.

The list continues; NATO seemed on pace to rack up more confirmed civilian kills than the Serbs.

But Shea eloquently defended the accidents during his daily press briefing at NATO headquarters:

> [I]n the last two months, Milosevic's forces have intentionally killed thousands of civilians. Our conservative estimate, and this really is conservative, is that over five thousand people have been summarily executed, and this is not a result of an accident, this is a deliberately planned, carefully orchestrated campaign of ethnic cleansing in which over eight hundred thousand men, women and children have been expelled from their homeland; another half a million are living in the woods and mountains of Kosovo as internally displaced persons; the homes of hundreds of thousands of people have been destroyed or severely damaged; we know there have been rapes of hundreds of women; and this systemic abuse is not simply documented by NATO, it is documented by the people who really know about these things—the United Nations and a number of human rights organizations. And of course, Belgrade has made sure that none of this, none of these pictures of this murder, deliberate murder, ever get out of Kosovo to be seen on our TV screens. I continue to believe that this campaign is the most accurate, precise military campaign in the history of human conflict.
>
> Now you are going to ask me, are innocent people going to die in a conflict like this one? The answer is undoubtedly yes. But Milosevic kills and terrorizes civilians, not by the dozen, but by the hundreds of thousands, and it is a matter of policy for him to do that.[10]

The Chinese would surely disagree with the "most accurate, precise military campaign" part of the analysis: only weeks before Shea made these passionate comments, a small flock of NATO missiles blew up the Chinese embassy in downtown Belgrade, killing three Chinese citizens. The CIA sheepishly admitted that the embassy wasn't on its maps, even though it had been open for business at its fatal location since 1996 and its correct address was available on the Internet.

All hell broke loose when that happened. For nearly a week, the American ambassador in Beijing was trapped in his embassy, which was rocked by stones, vegetables and some of the most virulent anti-American epithets heard since the Vietnam war. Clinton apologized repeatedly, trying to place the blame on Milosevic for forcing NATO to use missiles at all. Russian and Chinese diplomatic ties to the United States were more strained than at any other time since the cold war.

Then The Hague named Milosevic as a war criminal, playing the international community's best—and final—card, officially removing any incentive that Milosevic would have had to fly the white flag. If he's going to be tried for war crimes, why negotiate for anything?

Five

The Rashica family didn't make it to Macedonia after all.

On May 2, the KLA's 141st Mehe Uka Brigade ran out of ammunition. The mixed Serbian forces of a commander known to KLA field officers only by the code name Iber-3 punched through the northern perimeter and fought their way south, hoping to join with the southern Serbian forces that held ground in Studime e Poshtme (Lower Studime). Hysni Ahmeti, the 141st's commander, called for his men to retreat, and he sent word to the refugees in Upper Studime that they should head for Vucitrn.

But those from Studime knew what lay between them and Vucitrn: a warehouse filled with Serbs. But they were completely surrounded and the KLA had just left. There was nothing else to do. Gunfire and mortar detonations lent an air of panic to the villagers' retreat.

The winding dirt track between Upper and Lower Studime was quickly jammed with tractors, horses, wagons and about 1,000 terrified people. The column was at least two miles long and got nowhere because, as expected, the Serbs in Lower Studime stopped the refugees at gunpoint, killing a horse at the head of the column. Before long, Serb soldiers had made their way into the column and began looking for men young enough to fight with the KLA.

Florim and his family were stuck in the middle of the column, next to a narrow creek that followed the dirt road. He said everyone was mortified with terror, unable even to breathe properly, waiting to see what would happen now that they'd been effectively captured by the Serbs. Florim's mother hid his seven-year-old brother under her skirt.

Before long, three Serb officers approached Florim's wagon. One of the men he recognized: it was Vucina Janicevic,[11] a former chief of the Vucitrn police force, and he was obviously in charge of the other Serbs, one of whom slashed the wagon's tires with a big knife and another of whom jerked the men out onto the dirt road demanding money.

The chaos must have been mind-numbing. Florim's aunt said that there was so much shouting going on between the soldiers demanding money and the Kosovars trying to give it to them that no one understood the other for a period.

Then about ten Serbs started beating Florim after they'd taken 1,500 deutsche marks from him. He said he thought for sure that he would be beaten to death, and he might have been, had one of the Serbs not tried to assault Florim's twelve-year-old female cousin, who was sobbing on the wagon. When the soldier grabbed her, trying to pull her off the trailer for purposes that can only be guessed, she went berserk, screaming hysterically. At that, the girl's father, Florim's uncle, burst from where he was hiding behind a tree near the creek and begged the soldier to leave his daughter alone, offering a wad of cash by way of bribery.

The soldier took the money.

Then he shot the uncle at point-blank range with his Kalashnikov, filling him with holes from pelvis to head.

Florim didn't see which one of the soldiers pulled the trigger because he was curled into a fetal ball at his uncle's feet, blood filling his eyes from numerous lacerations on his head. The bullets kicked his uncle about ten feet down the road and in the ensuing confusion and deafening panic of nearby Kosovars who were sure they were next to be executed, Florim managed to crawl under his family's wagon. When he was able to open an eye, he saw Janicevic again, standing with a group of soldiers, one of whom was probably the one who shot his uncle. Other members of Florim's family and several KLA officers watching the carnage on a small hill overlooking the dirt path also identified Janicevic and his lieutenant Dragan Petrovich as being in charge of the Serbs.[12]

As the sun fell, the pace of the executions picked up, including one that involved several victims who were first robbed and then machine-gunned by a number of soldiers who walked several feet away, turned suddenly and randomly opened fire into the crowd.[13]

Eventually, the column of refugees, who were by now shell-shocked with terror, were led to Vucitrn, where they were stuffed into a warehouse for the night, and then were sent on to Albania— "where they belong," Florim said one soldier told him.

On May 3, Ahmeti and a group of KLA soldiers crept to the massacre site shortly before dawn, gathered more than 100 bodies from the dirt road, the creek bed and nearby fields and prepared them for a proper Muslim burial.

One hundred and ten were interred together in a mass grave next to an existing Muslim cemetery.[14]

Six

The week before the massacre in Studime, there was a huge party in Washington, D.C., to celebrate NATO's fiftieth birthday, but it was a strained affair. The refugee numbers were around a half a million and climbing. Civilian casualties were mounting. Wes Clark kept calling for more and more air power so he could bomb twenty-four hours a day. There were increasing numbers of anti-NATO demonstrations happening all across Europe, mostly in NATO countries, especially in Italy, where jets left with bombs and returned empty to Aviano Air Base around the clock. Sixteen Apache helicopters were supposedly en route to Albania from their base in Germany but after much fanfare of their imminent arrival, there was still no sight of them. The Russians had rediscovered their Andropov-era personality, and anti-Western demonstrations were held in Red Square. It all added up to a huge wet blanket on what should have been a hell of a celebration for an organization poised to enter the twenty-first century having won the cold war without firing a shot.

Instead, the best NATO leaders could pull off was a grim-faced show of solidarity, insisting that they were all in this until the bitter end and that the bombing campaign had to—just *had* to—work eventually, even though it showed no sign whatsoever that it would before Kosovo was totally empty of Albanians.

Things were quite bleak and they weren't even close to over. The bombing campaign wouldn't end until June 10, and not because the Serbian military had been mortally wounded. In fact, once the smoke eventually cleared, Pentagon analysts began slowly coming to the conclusion that NATO had done very little to the Serbian military and that what had contributed more to breaking Milosevic's will was when the military blew up industrial plants and bridges, targets that affected the population more than the army.[15]

Richard J. Newman, a reporter for *U.S. News and World Report,*
wrote on September 20, 1999:

A NATO team that visited 900 "aim points" targeted by NATO in
Kosovo found carcasses of only 26 tanks and similar-looking self-pro-
pelled artillery pieces; after the war, NATO claimed it destroyed 110.
The discrepancy seems sure to cause lasting controversy. Some NATO
analysts think pilots hit many more decoys than at first thought—including some that were inflatable—and that the Serbs may have set
damaged tanks out to be struck over and over. The Air Force has de-
duced from pilot reports, cockpit video, and intelligence sensors that
measure the plumes from explosions on the ground that they really destroyed at least 75 tanks, according to a NATO official. That would
mean the Serbs, for some reason, took blown-up tanks with them when
they left Kosovo in June.[16]

The Serbian military had never been graded below "fully operational" by the Pentagon. NATO planners were coming to the uncomfortable conclusion, wrote Newman, that "the attacks that hurt
the citizens of Yugoslavia the most were the catalyst that induced
Milosevic to give up."[17]

Indeed, the Serbs had more than enough morale and equipment to
fight their war, which wasn't against NATO but rather against the
KLA and the Albanians the KLA sought to protect. When all was
said and done, relief agencies estimated that 90 percent of the
dwellings in Kosovo had been destroyed and 800,000 ethnic Albanians—nearly half the prewar population—had been driven out of the
country. There are no firm estimates on how many either couldn't or
didn't leave and were displaced within Kosovo, but it's reasonable to
assume it's also in the high thousands.

What was most likely another key factor in Milosevic signing a
peace agreement with NATO on June 10 was the fact that Russia
weighed the long-term pros and cons of defying NATO.

The Russians turned out to be one of the most critical players of
the entire campaign. The day the bombing began, Russian Prime
Minister Yevgeny Primakov was over the Atlantic in a jet en route to
a scheduled meeting with U.S. Vice President Al Gore. When he received word that NATO was firing into Belgrade, Primakov turned
his plane around in midflight and returned to Moscow, an ominous
sign of what was to come. Throughout the bombing action, the Rus-

sians were vehemently opposed to the NATO strategy and incensed that the alliance would circumvent the Security Council. Russian President Boris Yeltsin openly sided with Milosevic, vowing to violate the trade embargo on Yugoslavia by sending oil via the Black Sea if necessary. Russian mercenaries were rumored to be fighting with the Serbs in the Kosovo hills.

It seemed all of Europe was dangling by a thread and everything NATO had accomplished in its fifty years was hanging in the balance over Kosovo.

To keep the crisis from deepening, a series of intense behind-the-scenes meetings took place between State Department officials and Russian representatives to find a way to keep the Soviet bear in hibernation. What emerged was the de facto appointment of Russian envoy Viktor Chernomyrdin as a middleman between Milosevic and the West. This was seen as a positive step on American editorial pages: though the Russians were still very pro-Serb, opening a channel between NATO and Belgrade was widely regarded as the first step in talking about the terms of an eventual Yugoslavian surrender.

That the Serbs would eventually give up was a foregone conclusion: for one thing, there's simply no mathematical way that a single country can outlast the air forces of nineteen, even if it meant the alliance had to bomb Serbia into a parking lot to win. But more important is that the reason for Belgrade to remain defiant was rapidly becoming less and less compelling—the goal of crushing the KLA resistance, ethnically cleansing Kosovo and obliterating the Kosovars' defiant will seemed to be at hand. Under the jets, bombs and cruise missiles of the strongest military force assembled on Earth, the Serbs with their thirty-year-old equipment had managed to drive 800,000 people out of the country in eleven weeks and internally displace and kill untold others. They may not have been winning against NATO, but they were certainly winning where it mattered to them.

But public support in Yugoslavia was beginning to wane, as expected. Serb civilians were suffering greatly and voices calling for Milosevic's head on an iron spear began to be raised from within Serbia itself. And the Russians, knowing that the Serbs couldn't hold out forever, realized that they were backing the loser.

The Russians were in a bind: after all the hoopla, they couldn't well desert the Serbs now that the writing was on the wall . . . but they also couldn't afford to totally alienate NATO, which would be around far longer than the Milosevic regime in any event. They needed a way to save face.

With Chernomyrdin, they got it.

Milosevic "gave up" in June, and the terms of the deal Chernomyrdin brokered were laughably similar to those Albright had rejected out of hand in Rambouillet three months and a million refugees ago: the multinational force would occupy Kosovo only, not all of Yugoslavia; the mission would be a joint NATO-Russia endeavor under UN mandate and the matter of Kosovo's freedom through referendum was dropped: Kosovo was still part of Yugoslavia.

The one thing the Serbs and the Russians didn't get, officially, was a Russian sector of responsibility in Kosovo, an area that would come under Russian command within the UN framework. Out of the question, replied Strobe Talbott, the deputy secretary of state, who, curiously, took over delicate negotiations from Albright for undisclosed reasons. The Russians wanted their own sector to ensure their seat at the decision-making table in matters over Kosovo and the Serbs wanted them there to provide security for Kosovo's Serb civilians.

Thinking it still controlled the situation, the West rejected the idea.

Seven

At the end of the war, an estimated 1.5 million people in Kosovo were refugees and few observers even wanted to estimate the number of dead. Most of the buildings had been destroyed. Macedonia, Albania and Bosnia sheltered the majority of more than 800,000 Kosovars who'd been driven from Kosovo. Russian and Chinese relations with the United States were at an abysmal, dangerous low. The Serbian military had remained largely intact. And President Milosevic was still in power, as close to being put on trial for war crimes as he was of winning the Nobel Peace Prize.

Yet Albright danced victoriously with refugees in Stankovac and President Clinton gave a speech on national television that turned another dubious mission in the Balkans into a rousing success. The speech called for peace and reconciliation between Kosovo's different ethnicities and congratulated the multinational alliance that had persevered through criticism and international land mines to emerge victorious.

He announced the particulars about the joint NATO-UN mission and described the coming deployment of the multinational peace-keeping force, predictably termed KFOR for Kosovo Force.

With his words still echoing around the world, and while pundits and news producers were already beginning to look for the next big story, the Russians dropped the other shoe: about 200 Russian soldiers stationed near Tuzla in Bosnia gassed up their tanks, broke camp and motored all night through Serbia and directly into Kosovo in flagrant defiance of NATO's orders that they not arrive in the area before the other international troops, which were still days away from being ready to deploy. The soldiers chugged slowly down the main drag in Pristina on their way to the city's airport, the most militarily strategic position in Kosovo. The Russian armored vehicles, some repainted to say KFOR, were covered in Serb-tossed roses from the cheering throng of Serbs and they were flying the Serbian flag next to their own, an image that was broadcast world-wide on the same networks that had carried Clinton's speech only hours before.

"Peace" and "victory" were clearly terms that were open to interpretation.

11　Epilogue: Gnjilane, July 1999

Meet the new boss, same as the old boss.

—The Who

One

Two weeks after Clinton made the announcement that the war in Kosovo was over, I was ducking sniper fire in the eerily quiet city of Gnjilane on a rubble-strewn street lit only by arson flames that were licking at empty buildings.

Photographer Chris Hondros and I had been sitting at a lone table outside the city's only open café, which had the good fortune of being directly across the street from a command post of the 82nd Airborne Division and was allowed to stay open past the 8:30 P.M. curfew because the soldiers pulling late-night guard duty needed a good source of coffee. We were sipping beer and listening to classical music echo from the shopkeeper's stereo through the open doors and up the abandoned street. We grew bored watching the soldiers stop the odd car or two that crept along the shattered boulevard in violation of the curfew—in a manner that made us sympathize with those being stopped; we were both familiar with coming upon a sudden checkpoint with men pointing rifles and shouting orders in an indecipherable language—and we decided to wander up the street to take another look at the arson fire that turned the night sky orange over the low buildings and sent a steady wake of crimson sparks floating heavenward.

We moved slowly up the middle of the street . . . the presence of the soldiers a few hundred yards away little comfort in a city that was rocked nightly by violence and gun battles. The street was narrow and lined with storefronts that came right up to the road. Although we were the only people in sight, we were fairly certain that every blacked-out window held eyes that watched our progress; before the curfew settled over Gnjilane, the street had been packed with people, as if the local team had just won the Super Bowl. We were pretty sure that all those folks simply melted behind the walls and stayed close to the windows so that they could see whatever was inevitably going to happen that night.

We didn't get far, just around the dogleg in the road that brought the burning Serb business into sight, when shots rang out—*crack! crack! crack!*—just overhead and to the right, the unmistakable sound of an AK-47.

The good news is that we didn't hear the whiz of passing rounds or hear them smack into nearby walls, meaning that either we weren't the sniper's targets or he was a miserable shot. We hugged the walls nonetheless and began jogging back the way we'd come.

The U.S. soldiers were fanned out around the street, night-vision goggles and rifles aimed at the rooftops, Lt. Matt Farmer whispering into his radio. A soldier they referred to as Gonzo one block over was reporting that the rounds had smashed into the street near his sandbag bunker.

"How close?" I asked the lieutenant.

"Close enough for him to keep his head down," he replied. He quickly assembled a squad of six to march up the street and hunt for the sniper.

Hondros and I tagged along—we'd been hanging out with the soldiers at headquarters long enough through the night to have developed a good rapport. That, two cases of Coke and two cartons of Marlboros had put us in their good graces, and no one said anything as two reporters in shorts and T-shirts fell in with a squad of armored and heavily armed American soldiers.

The squad fanned out on both sides of the street, snapping rounds into the chambers of their M4A assault rifles, everyone communicating either through barely audible whispers or hand signals. The only sounds were the crunch of gravel underfoot and the crackling of the fire we were slowly approaching.

On the right was a deep alley buried in the shadows cast by a rare operating street light out on the main boulevard. Another fire was starting in a building halfway down the alley, but it did nothing to penetrate the pitch murk that turned us blind.

"Night vision," whispered Farmer, sliding his helmet-mounted gear into place over his eyes. The M4As were equipped with infrared laser sights sitting snugly under the barrel. Their beams are only visible through night-vision gear, so as we moved down the alley, the soldiers scanned a narrow corridor awash in a green glow, as if it were under the sea, punctuated with the tiny blue dots of the team's infrared sights dancing like deadly fairies on the walls.

For me and Hondros, though, the journey into the alley was a lesson in pure blindness. We followed only the soft footfalls of the soldier directly in front of us, bumping into sweaty body armor when the team stopped. Farmer motioned for everyone to crouch and listen . . . According to Gonzo's best estimates, the sniper was in a second-floor window directly above us . . .

No sound at all . . . It was so quiet it was easy to believe that you could actually hear the rhythm of eight hearts beating double-time, the occasional snap of flame-ridden timber from the burning house making me jolt involuntarily.

After several long minutes, Farmer decided to call off the search. We'd heard nothing, seen nothing; emerging into the relatively brighter gloom of the main street, the soldiers cleared their weapons.

"It sure is a quiet night tonight," Farmer said to no one in particular. It didn't start out that way . . . I'd gone to Gnjilane with Hondros and the freelance reporter Cabell Bruce thinking it was going to be something of a day off. We'd been rocketing around Kosovo in a faltering car rented in Pristina, making grim comparisons to the first days of the Dayton Accords, smelling sweet death lingering in the air as we drove through decimated villages, getting harassed by Serbs in Mitrovica and trying to avoid an untold number of unseen land mines and unexploded NATO ordnance. After a week of this, we thought it prudent to visit the sector controlled by American forces, maybe shop at the PX and speak English for a change.

And indeed, pulling into Gnjilane it seemed that we were in for a slow day. The city is poky and doddering, seeming to have avoided the fate of less fortunate villages that were empty of everything except yet-to-be-discovered corpses of Kosovars in wells and ditches. The first sight to greet visitors arriving from Pristina is a carefully painted mural of flags of the NATO nations and earnest, if misspelled, prayers of thanks to the city's armed saviors.

"Boy, the Americans sure got the cushy assignment," someone said. While the French were trying to figure out what to do about Mitrovica before it became another Mostar; the British were busy shooting drunken revelers bobbling AK-47s from atop cars in Pristina; and the Germans were dodging grenades and chasing arsonists in Prizren, it seemed that all the Americans had to do in this city that few had ever heard of was sip coffee and learn Albanian from local children. Gnjilane had a relaxed air that made it seem as if we'd somehow driven from Kosovo into some other country, one that was actually peaceful.

None of us noticed the smoke on the horizon.

An hour later, a section of burning roof from a Serb business that had been firebombed in broad daylight within sight of an American military outpost collapsed and fell on my head.

It was nothing serious, but enough to make my skull ring and to cover me in a fine dusting of ash.

I'd been standing outside an Albanian-owned café directly next door, watching the brave but nervous Kosovar firefighter trying to douse the flames while a gang of several hundred fellow Kosovars milled around gawking, some of them throwing stones and bricks at the burning building.

I had just gotten the official propaganda on the fire—"The Serbs set this fire themselves to make you think the Albanians did it"—when the roof fell apart and crashed at my feet, blasting chunks of dirt into my face and whipping an overhead high wire down across the top of my head.

Those in the crowd quickly stepped forward to pat out a part of my shoulder that had caught fire and dust me off. The owner of the café looked genuinely concerned—he'd just shown me the spot inside the café where he said the former owner of the burning building had thrown a grenade at him and his friends during the war. He'd spent a great deal of time pointing out all the shrapnel marks, and now he was concerned that I would get knocked out and not write about his experience and the fact that he had *not* set this fire, which had gotten the attention of a legitimate mob of people. Why would he set something on fire that would threaten his own business? It must be the Serbs, he concluded, who'd set the fire themselves . . . They were obviously determined to see his business fail at any expense to themselves.

I shoved my way through the crowd, still choking up soot, looking for Hondros and Bruce, no easy task given that KFOR had blockaded the street and established a perimeter manned by nervous teenage Americans with assault rifles. The roadblock created a logjam of cars and bodies that did nothing but increase the curiosity factor and attract more people and cars.

But it made sense to seal the street while they still could; things were getting a little out of hand. In a matter of minutes, the quiet street had taken on the air of a pending riot. One minute, we were making small talk with Farmer in his command center at the local post office and the next there were no less than three arson fires within fifty yards of one another and a crowd of people beginning to feed off the mayhem.

Across the street from the café, a group of people were trying to batter down a corrugated metal door. Smoke was rising over the small wall it was set into and word was that two old Serbs were trapped inside, victims of a Molotov cocktail thrown from a speeding car. Finally, an Army captain smashed his way through, rifle at arms, and I followed him into a courtyard where Vera and Blagoje Simonovic, both sixty-nine, were trying to contain a fire that was already eating into the roof. The Army captain, Glenn Tolle of the 96th Civil Affairs Division, grabbed a rubber garden hose and began doing what he could against the fire. I stood off to the side, watching the Simonovics pace in a manner I'd grown to know well.

It wasn't actually pacing, but rather the motions of someone whose entire understanding of the world has collapsed without warning and who has no idea what to do, say or think. First, Blagoje began babbling at other American soldiers who'd arrived to see what was happening, then he moved to a straight-backed chair as if to sit, then he changed his mind and bellowed at me that he needed to leave for Serbia, but the goddamned Albanians had stolen his car two days ago and no one would help him move his possessions. He didn't know anyone there anyway, he said; he'd been born in Gnjilane and never expected to leave. Vera was going through the same contortions, bouncing around the inner courtyard, finally settling on, of all things, the activity of vacantly picking crab apples from overhanging branches and stacking them in the crook of her folded arm.

Tolle, losing the fight against the fire, was about to suffer the same fate that I just had. Timbers began falling around him and finally he tossed down the hose and angrily commanded me to look in the charred bedroom.

"There's a crib in there for chrissake," he said. "What if there'd been a fucking baby in there?"

At that moment the roof let go and landslided into the house. When the roar died down, all that was left was a sound that pushed Tolle over the brink: laughter and cheering from the crowd watching from the street.

He snatched up his rifle and strode from the courtyard with purpose, zeroing in on the first Kosovar he saw wearing a smile, shoving him, screaming in his face.

"You think this is funny! What if this was your house?" he shouted, momentarily forgetting that this was, in fact, the condition that many Kosovars had found their houses in. "You need to stop this," he shouted to the whole crowd. "This is accomplishing nothing."

Yet another fire had broken out about a half a block away, the smoke rising slowly and inconspicuously at first, then gathering momentum to the point where it was finally noticed by Sgt. First Class Mark Eubanks, who ran to investigate. The house burning was down the narrow alley that we would later explore for the sniper. Eubanks found an entire first-floor room totally engulfed in shooting flames— but he thought he could still save the rest of the house. Shouldering his rifle, he quickly found two large plastic pails.

But there was no water. And no one to help him find any. Sputtering in furious frustration, Eubanks yelled at an elderly man who was standing to the side watching the house burn with his hands clasped behind his back, trying to make him understand through sheer volume that he needed water, *water!*

The only apparent source of water, however, was up the street at the café, where about a dozen Albanian children splashed with a hose, warding off the hot sun and the ambient heat of the burning building they were playing next to. So in ninety-six-degree heat, spurting sweat under full body armor, he double-timed between the hose and the fire no less than a dozen times and managed to keep it contained until the haggard Albanian fireman could arrive to extinguish the blaze.

Once the fireman took over, Eubanks unshouldered his rifle and stood belligerent guard over the entrance to the alleyway.

"Cocksuckers!" he screamed at the gawking mob.

Later that night, after we'd given up trying to find the sniper, someone sneaked through the night and reignited the house. It burned to the ground.

Two

Fading into sleep that night on the hard floor of the 82nd Airborne's post office—near the main counter, which still had local mail stacked in cubbyholes in anticipation of long-gone residents coming to retrieve it—I could barely manage to contain a fit of morbid laughter: having leaped at the first opportunity to return to Kosovo, I had taken a two-week job with an NGO called Operation Kosovo, which works on international legal issues. My job was to write a report about, of all things, the state of the rule of law in the first thirty days after the bombs stopped falling.

From what I'd seen so far, my assignment was going to be easy: there was no rule of law at all.

As if following some universal mathematical equation as irrevocable as two plus two equals four, Albanians began ethnically cleansing Serbs from Kosovo within days, if not hours, of the minute the last bomb fell, and there were precious few who seemed capable of stopping the inevitable.

The calculable trouble was accelerated by the astounding rate of refugee repatriation. Roundly ignoring the pleas of international leaders to stay in their refugee camps until mines and unexploded ordnance could be cleared, the refugees flooded back to Kosovo at a pace that astonished even the most optimistic human rights observer. Most of the Kosovars simply walked home.

Macedonia's Stankovac I, the most well-known of the refugee camps because it was the cleanest and most well-organized and therefore the most photogenic—it played host to Hillary Clinton, Tony Blair and Madeleine Albright on their various publicity tours of the misery—was empty of its 30,000-plus refugees in two weeks. Ed Joseph, an aid worker for Catholic Relief Services, the NGO that ran Stankovac I, was there to say good-bye to the last refugee family as they left the camp.

"It was weird," he said. "I felt like saying, 'Thanks for coming. I hope you enjoyed your stay.'"

For a brief time, some NGOs tried to maintain control of the borders, to keep track of who was entering the crippled province, but it soon proved futile owing to the sheer volume of people wanting to get back in. There was nothing to do but open the borders entirely and allow anyone and everyone to flood north, and hope for the best.

The sudden reverse surge of refugees created problems: because the Russians had grabbed the airport, NATO had to discard its original plan of gradual integration into Kosovo and simply deployed everywhere at once. First in were British Gurkhas, tough Nepalese soldiers who parachuted miles within the province's borders to secure the narrow mountainous passes that characterize the first dozen miles of the road from the Macedonian border. Fearful of mines and ambush, the column of tanks, troop transports and armored personnel carriers moved at a maddeningly slow pace—once they squeezed through one of only four southern entry points, which were clogged with returning Kosovars—arriving in Pristina hours after many journalists and even some refugees.

The force then fanned out into its five "brigades," or different multinational areas of command, deploying so fast that in some towns there were three military forces maintaining a presence at the same time: NATO, the KLA and the Serbs who hadn't pulled out yet.

Add to this tense mix hundreds of thousands of refugees returning to Kosovo—as well as an unknown number of suspected Albanian gangsters simply interested in a little ethnic cleansing of their own— and the result was near pandemonium.

It didn't take long at all for the tables to turn 180 degrees on the Serbs: once the returning refugees saw what was left of their towns and their families—places like Lodja were not only destroyed and burned down, but Serb forces had even gone to the trouble of bringing in earth-moving equipment to completely level every building— the first urge was to burn something Serbian.

In a matter of days, Serbs had gone from victimizer to victim. And the ethnic Albanians had been transformed from oppressed freedom fighters into the terrorists Belgrade had accused them of being in the first place.

In Gnjilane, the city's 20,000 Serbs, about 20 percent of the total population of about 100,000, were instantly terrorized, as were pockets of Serbs in Prizren, Pristina, Vucitrn, Pec, and other towns. One of KFOR's first tasks in Gnjilane was to engage in a standoff with a platoon of KLA soldiers who attempted to march through the city wielding assault rifles. When told that they would have to surrender their weapons, some KLA members took up combat positions in the woods. Only the most delicate of negotiations by the U.S. soldier in charge averted a fire fight.

But the KLA quickly learned a tactic employed by the Serbs in Grbavica so long ago: to effectively terrorize your ethnic enemies in the presence of international troops, strip off your uniform, and blend into the general population. Thus, when a grenade was thrown it was impossible in most circumstances to determine innocence or guilt unless someone was caught red-handed.

Disturbingly, the retribution violence wasn't conducted against cells of die-hard Serbian paramilitary resistance. Most of those Serbs who had actively engaged in ethnic cleansing had retreated to Serbia—or Mitrovica, we soon discovered—and those left to defend themselves against invisible murderers were usually elderly.

In Prizren, 200 victims of Kosovar retaliation found temporary sanctuary behind the too-low walls of the Orthodox Bagoslavia seminary, which was run by a Serb rector who received at least one death threat a day. Those seeking revenge weren't necessarily discriminating: one of the residents of the seminary was an eighteen-year-old Albanian teenager with an eight-month-old baby girl. Her crime was that her brother-in-law had worked in a clerical position with the Serbian police force before the war. Therefore, after the bombing stopped, a gang of Albanian men killed her husband with an ax. A few days later, she was gang-raped by five masked men speaking Albanian while her infant daughter lay in a crib in the same room.

Another resident was, like the Albanians, a Muslim, but she was from Bosnia and her Serbo-Croatian language was enough to get her beaten up while her husband was kidnapped. After the assault, she had nowhere to go and slept on the street in front of a German KFOR checkpoint, until she heard she might be safe at Bagoslavia. Pacing the seminary courtyard smoking one cigarette after another, a fist-shaped shiner bruising her left eye, certain that her husband was dead, she was throughly at a loss as to why fellow Muslims would turn on her.

The vast majority of Serbs at Bagoslavia were old peasants and all of them had similar stories. One seventy-two-year-old woman's fine white hair was still stained with blood from where Kosovars had cracked her skull; a sixty-nine-year-old man had watched his house burn from his hilltop field where he'd gone to cut hay. He'd left his wife inside the house when he went to the field, and now he didn't know whether she was dead or alive.

Dawn Schellenberg, an American woman in her mid-twenties who ran the seminary for International Relief Kosovo, an NGO, said that although those within Bagoslavia's walls were safer than if they were wandering the streets, it was only a question of degree. Surrounded on all sides by tall buildings and hilltops, the open courtyard was clearly visible to potential snipers, who would be able to take aim easily without so much as a telescopic site. A single RPG or well-tossed grenade would be catastrophic.

More worrisome was the fact that those in the seminary represented only about 1 percent of the estimated Serb population in and around Prizren and the sanctuary was already over capacity.

"My concern would be what do you do when all the houses are down?" Schellenberg said. "Because they're going down systematically."

Three

If it was hunting season for those of Serbian descent, it was a surprisingly good time to be of Albanian descent in Kosovo. The pain and grief of those who returned only to find that everything they held dear had been destroyed and defiled was as overwhelming as I expected it to be, but alongside the torturous emotions that accompany surviving ethnic cleansing, there was a distinct vigor. It took me awhile to identify it as a sense of victory.

When we first arrived in Pristina, it was difficult to know how to feel; as we crested the hill from the south, the city's squalor was scattered out below us, partially hidden in the smog of burning garbage. The immediate emotion was depression. The city was awash in gray—it was hard to tell where the smoke ended and the sidewalks began. But you quickly noticed an incredible vibrancy among the people inhabiting it. Unlike the previous year, the Kosovars in

Pristina bore with them something distinctly resembling hope: as shattered as it was, they considered Pristina the capital of their new nation. But in the schizophrenic character of the days immediately following the bombing, the mania of freedom was often quickly replaced with the stabbing melancholy of the price paid to achieve it. Pristina's dual realities were literally written on its walls.

The PTT building, for instance, had housed the state-run telephone service and citywide switching station until it was hit with a Tomahawk missile. Now it housed chunks of plaster and bits of paper debris, a black-charred hole in its side where the missile had entered like an explosive fist. From a distance, the PTT building seemed like a perfectly good example of NATO's skill at surgically delivering ordnance from afar to specific targets: the building is dead center in the middle of the downtown district, surrounded by little shops and non-target buildings.

On closer inspection, however, one saw that the shops had been vaporized by the impact, and a building next door that was twice as high as the PTT building teetered uncertainly over its rubble-strewn plaza, every window blown out from being too close to the target, the walls of its ground-floor cinema completely gone.

"What's that building?" I asked an OSCE representative who had a perfect view of the destruction from her sixth-floor office. The damage to the taller building was so acute, I was certain it was deliberate.

She shrugged. "Collateral damage."

If they were ever upset about it, the people of Pristina seemed to have gotten over it. The rest of the city was undergoing its renaissance, undoubtedly seeing more new construction and remodeling than at any other time in its existence. In fact, the pace of reconstruction was so impressive that without having been there to actually witness it, I would barely have believed it.

Tony's Spagetteria, for example, arguably the most popular restaurant in Kosovo before the bombing, was once again the most popular destination, despite the fact that it had been utterly eviscerated by Serbian guns only weeks before. Hondros had to produce a photo he had taken of its decimated facade before I would believe that the destruction had been as bad as everyone said it was. I looked at the picture while sitting on the restaurant's freshly swept outdoor plaza under a brand-new forest-green market umbrella, nibbling tortellini carbonara and sipping an imported Budweiser.

The reason for this incredible pace of reconstruction is clear enough: the Kosovars have waited for so long to run their own lives that they couldn't see the logic at all of sitting in a refugee camp for another day when they could be back home preparing to open for business. They've hungered and fought so long for a free Kosovo that sweeping up broken glass and arduously hauling new furniture and panes of glass on a tractor from Albania were only small steps in claiming what they believe is rightly theirs.

Some things didn't require fixing at all, just a change in ownership. For instance, the Grand Hotel was under new management, but it was hard to tell. In the days following the peace announcement, the KLA had come into the low lobby and announced that operations would be conducted by Albanians from that point forward. Any Serbs who wished to remain and work were free to stay, or so we were told. Apparently, none took that option, however, and every position was staffed with Kosovars. Those who ran the government media center left without even packing up their computers.

Immediately after announcing the Grand's new ownership, KLA soldiers liberated the hotel bar and poured drinks for reporters, a PR turn so astute in a city without so much as a lukewarm beer for sale that the AP reporter was compelled to write a story about it.

But under the Kosovars, the only real thing that changed was the language spoken by those behind the desk: an Albanian providing "security" stood guard at the front door next to the pair of permanently stationed British paratroopers, all money paid for anything went directly into the pocket of whoever was charging you, whether it was for a room or a Coke, and the chicken served in the restaurant had the texture of a boiled football.

The Grand was adopted as the unofficial headquarters/social club/party nexus of the Atlantic Brigade, a group of young American-Albanians who'd volunteered to fight for the KLA during the NATO bombing campaign, having departed from their gathering place in Yonkers, New York, with much fanfare. Although the tales of teenage kids from Brooklyn fighting in Kosovo, many of whom have never been outside New York, were initially entertaining, the constant preening of slick-dressed American KLA fighters who couldn't speak much Albanian quickly grew tiresome.

For instance, Florim from the Bronx, a sniper whose first several shots at the enemy turned out to be aimed at a forward KLA unit because he couldn't tell the good guys from the bad, constantly harangued us into visiting his recently acquired penthouse in Pec, where he wanted to show us the collection of Kalashnikovs, RPGs and Dragonav SVD rifles he'd kept hidden from KFOR.

According to the peace agreement, Security Council Resolution 1244, the KLA was supposed to demilitarize and turn in all of its weapons to KFOR, but when I asked about a dozen members of the Atlantic Brigade whether this was likely to happen, the question was met with derisive laughter.

"The KLA is never going to disarm," said Florim. "How can we disarm when we're still part of a country whose president has been indicted for war crimes?"

As it became more and more apparent that the KLA wasn't complying with the disarmament clause of the resolution, KFOR went into a huddle, and when it emerged it had created something called Kosovo Corps, a KLA force that isn't mentioned anywhere in the peace accord. No one seems to be very sure what the role of the Kosovo Corps is supposed to be, however; it has been described alternately as a rapid reaction military force, a fire-fighting unit, a humanitarian agency, and a "natural disaster" response team. Critics, especially Russian and Serb critics, decried the move as a way for KFOR to avoid the matter of forcing the KLA to disarm.

But the creation of Kosovo Corps was at least an acknowledgment of reality: many Kosovars had yet to stop and consider that Kosovo wasn't yet free, at least not in the sense that they've always wanted it to be. It's still a part of Serbia, after all, and the United Nations and KFOR ostensibly run the entire province, from law enforcement, such as it is, to managing state assets.

But if the Kosovars have thought of these things, then they are simply ignoring them. They had succeeded in creating a de facto parallel government under oppression and violence at the hands of the Serbian leadership, so now, pushing the definition of freedom further than international peacekeepers intended was small potatoes: it isn't much of a stretch to begin instituting a parallel government under the conflicting wishes of the UN, either. Kosovars will do what they want.

And the things they wanted the most in the months immediately after the bombing were to rid their "country" of Serbs and to establish with certainty that they were in charge.

KFOR's choices were to try and mitigate the results of this through concessions like the creation of Kosovo Corps or to go to war with the KLA, something no one wanted to do just yet.

Besides, the KLA wasn't giving anyone much choice in the matter . . . they'd begun taking control of the province long before the UN had even decided on a headquarters building in Pristina.

Since the vast majority of Kosovo had suffered greatly during the war, the KLA, which had fought against great odds for Kosovo's freedom, was seen by many as the government, regardless of what the UN said.

And the KLA continued winning the hearts and minds of its constituents with aplomb, taking advantage of KFOR and the relatively slow implementation of the United Nation's Mission in Kosovo (UNMIK) to establish control in areas that wouldn't see an NGO or a KFOR vehicle for weeks.

"There's a vacuum for law and order," said Sandra Mitchell, the outgoing human rights director for the OSCE. "KLA civil control is filling in the gaps."

In Pec immediately following the end of the bombing campaign, the KLA "liberated" the city's electricity substation from the Serbs who'd run it previously and handed over its operation to Albanians, who worked without pay to turn the lights on. Pec had power long before many other cities in Kosovo. They also seized the Pecko Brewery and began producing their own beer; it was the same stuff, but it was now called Union.

If one overlooked the KLA's tacit approval of ethnic cleansing, the system seemed to be working relatively well. Other than theft and drug trafficking, intra-Kosovar crime seemed low or nonexistent compared to the crimes Serbs were suffering, and the KLA operated a jail in Srbica for those who were caught committing more serious infractions. The KLA had convinced KFOR to allow certain high-ranking officials and their aides to carry sidearms and wear their uniforms in public, and in each city of any size, the KLA had a municipal headquarters where Kosovo's future was debated in cheaply paneled rooms under a cloud of cigarette smoke.

The KLA "government"—for lack of a better term—operated with only a passing nod to UNMIK and its decrees and far outpaced the international community in establishing, or at least laying the groundwork for, civil rule. While those under the UN umbrella were still looking for office space and lodging, the KLA was patrolling street corners and turning on utilities.

When we arrived in Pristina we were very minor cogs in yet another giant wheel that had been put into motion by a Security Council resolution. The city was overrun by diplomats, journalists, NGO
staff, UN personnel, KFOR soldiers, opportunistic cab drivers and
translators from Macedonia, drug runners from Albania and an innu-
merable number of peculiar hangers-on—college students and re-
tirees with photo hobbies who had nothing better to do than spend
their vacation or summer break in Kosovo.

The UN document outlining the goals and mandates of the peace
agreement was a carbon copy of that in Bosnia except it wasn't
named after a middle-American city. Security Council Resolution
1244, like Dayton, called for the establishment of two commanding
bodies, the United Nation's Mission in Kosovo (UNMIK) and
NATO's KFOR. UNMIK was in charge of implementing the civilian provisions of the resolution, things like creating a judiciary, figuring out what laws were going to be enforced, overseeing the creation and deployment of a civilian police force that would be
identical to the IPTF creating and filling the position of ombuds-
man, appointing commissioners and so on. KFOR, in charge of military security, was led by British general Michael Jackson, who insisted all reporters refer to him in their dispatches as "Mike"
Jackson to avoid any uncomfortable confusion with the pop singer
of the same name.

One big difference between the UN mission in Bosnia and
UNMIK was that KFOR was dead serious about its role, even if
that role was open to interpretation by individual soldiers on a case-
by-case basis. A week into their deployment, two British paratroopers emptied their magazines into a car filled with Kosovars in
downtown Pristina during one of the many nighttime rallies that
brought traffic to a standstill. The vehicle had been circling the district repeatedly, its occupants waving huge Albanian flags from the
windows and firing a Kalashnikov into the air through the sunroof.
On its fatal pass, a man sitting on the roof raised the rifle to crank
off another burst and the paratroopers opened fire, dicing the car to
pieces, killing the man on the roof and another passenger and
wounding the others.

Even though the car had reportedly been driving away from the
soldiers at the time, they reported that they felt in imminent danger
from the man, believing that he was taking aim at their positions.
KFOR spokesmen used the incident as an opportunity to show that

the multinational force was the sole authority in the region and wouldn't stand any tomfoolery with weapons and such. But it also quietly shuffled the offending soldiers off stage left and began investigating the incident.

In other areas, KFOR soldiers actively arrested anyone they felt even vaguely threatened by and locked suspects in the brig.

Everything else, however, was so similar to Bosnia that it was easy to get the impression that the UN machine was really a traveling sideshow that set up camp in different Balkan cities from time to time and trotted out the same starched gas bags that had been at the last location.

"This is like Dayton II," said Sandra Mitchell of the OSCE. "Dayton worse," she added.

The UN headquarters, located at the old municipal police station next door to the Grand Hotel, was ringed with barbed wire and salt-and-pepper-haired Europeans with huge jowls, pencil-thin mustaches and tales of their years of previous service to other UN missions.

The thing that was most remarkable about the UNMIK operation was how they managed to be in Kosovo and still operate as if they were in a vacuum. Very few high officials seemed to notice that the KLA had taken over Kosovo under their noses. The most striking example of this phenomenon was in the person of Sven Fredrickson, the Norwegian commissioner of the UN Civilian Police, whom I literally bumped into in Mitrovica outside the offices of the French Gendarmerie. Not having seen a single CivPol officer in the week I'd been in Kosovo, I took the opportunity to ask him how well he thought an IPTF model would work in Kosovo. Fredrickson had been CivPol commissioner in Bosnia from 1993 to 1994 and had worked with IPTF for two and a half years.

Frederickson assured me that everything would work out fine, that one can look at any situation and see "difficulties," whereas he chooses to see them as "challenges," et cetera.

"Well you know," I said, "I've been in a lot of these towns around here and most of them seem to have a KLA police force already up and running. Most of them are armed and they obviously have the respect of the citizens. Do you think independent police forces like the KLA will pose a problem for your mission?"

He smiled and confidently twirled his mustache. "My boy, there will be no police acting independently of *me*, I assure you."

At that, an aide opened the commissioner's Range Rover door and he was whisked away. Exactly five minutes later, I was in a restaurant interviewing a uniformed KLA commander who gave the name Tyson. He and his bodyguard carried firearms and had been strolling the market checking up on the armed KLA military police stationed throughout the city. The market is about six blocks from where I'd been standing talking with Fredrickson.

When I told him about the commissioner's comments, Tyson said, "The KLA is the police, everybody knows. How can you have police without the KLA?"

Mitrovica, an industrial city north of Pristina, turned out to be good source of ironies. About every other building was a charcoaled hull and it was jam packed with impoverished refugees. The whole reason we were there was because of a bridge that was quickly approaching infamy status. It was a wide, four-lane affair that spanned the Ibar River, which divides the city into northern and southern halves. The neighborhood north of the bridge was filled with Serbs from across Kosovo: common civilians, refugees fleeing Kosovar retribution and, if the rumors were correct, paramilitary and police officers who'd been active during the war, including Dragan Petrovich and Vucina Janicevic,[1] the Vucitrn police officers who Florim Rashica's family said commanded the soldiers who committed the massacre at Studime.

Indeed, even some French KFOR soldiers guarding the bridge said that many of the men gathered on the Serb side of the river drinking beer and brandy at the outdoor café were paramilitaries and they suspected that there was likely a large cache of long-barreled rifles within easy reach.

But despite knowing, or at least strongly suspecting, this, the French did little about it. Nor did they do anything about the series of evictions and ethnically motivated beatings and robbings happening daily on both sides of the river. And despite the fact that the bridge hosted confrontations every day between the Serbs and the Albanians that often involved gunfire and rock tossing, the French maintained only a skeleton crew of soldiers on the bridge.

Chris Hondros and I decided to see one of these confrontations for ourselves. In fact, we may have even started the whole thing without quite knowing it. When we arrived at the bridge from the Albanian side, we wandered over to a tightly packed group of people speaking with high animation. We strolled up to see what was happening and immediately we were the center of attention. Anyone with a camera and a brace of notebooks is usually surrounded within two or three minutes of pausing to rest in Kosovo, and this situation was no different. Everyone had a gripe that they needed to tell a reporter and they all proceeded to do so at the same time in increasingly louder voices in order to be heard above what was becoming a babbling din. The commotion naturally attracted more people, and within minutes, Hondros and I were in the eye of a hurricane of people begging to tell their stories.

Finally, our overwhelmed interpreter, an eighteen-year-old kid named Bezman, decided to ignore all but one story; he told us about a woman nearby with a newborn child who had been sitting in the hot sun all day waiting for the French to escort her to her apartment on the other side of the river.

She'd just returned to Mitrovica from a refugee camp in Kukes, but what should have been a joyous homecoming to a city ostensibly under NATO control had turned out instead to be a continuation of the nightmare that had driven her to out of Kosovo and to Albania in the first place. Her apartment was less than 100 yards inside the Serb half of Mitrovica and she was too scared to walk over there by herself.

Just as the crowd was pointing the woman out, our substantial gathering had gotten the attention of several French Gendarmerie officers. The Gendarmerie had the same military status as the KFOR soldiers, but they were charged with civil control until CivPol took over the task. The 100-man force was charged with looking into lootings, robberies and other crimes that were less serious than murder and arson, and included breaking up suspicious-looking gatherings like the one we were in the center of.

The crowd had worked itself up into the type of indignation that threatened to turn into violent action over the perceived injustice of the mother and her child forced to sit in the sun for three hours awaiting French escort to an apartment she could see from her perch near the bridge. It was clear, however, that the officer in charge was having a tremendously difficult time understanding the turbulence, and finally, Hondros broke in and told him what all the fuss was about.

Wisely, the young officer immediately called for a jeep to take the mother across the bridge, hoping to defuse the situation. This seemed to appease the crowd for the time being, but the prospect of the woman going over into the Serbian neighborhood made me more nervous than if she had simply found a place to stay on the Albanian side of the bridge. Hondros and I started walking to the other side of the river with a small contingent of reporters, all of us eager to see how she was going to be received.

There was a minor problem, however. Our interpreter didn't want to go. He was sure he'd get beaten up by the Serbs. So we dressed him up with Hondros's KFOR press card, turned with the photo facing in, and gave him an extra camera to sling over his shoulder so that he would look like just another reporter.

Walking across the bridge was a tense affair. Directly ahead, the road continued up a hill past a broad plaza that was filled with people loitering on the planters, mostly young men in what's been described as the "Balkan uniform": polyester jogging pants and matching windbreakers. To the left was a café with several outdoor tables that were packed with people more ominous-looking, older men whose considerable five o'clock shadows, tangled hair and hefty muscles made it very easy to believe that they were Chetnicks or paramilitary members.

The Gendarmerie ruined any gains in public relations they'd made by giving the mother a quick lift to the other side when they dropped her off directly in front of the café and then sped away before she could even gather all of her belongings. We were close enough to hear one of the men at the table shout out, "Where do you think you're going, bitch?"

She immediately speed-walked past the café, carrying her little bald baby, as a short column of reporters and photographers followed. Bezman and I had the misfortune of being at the end of the line.

Utilizing some sort of internal radar that was far more fine-tuned than I ever imaged, three Serbs leaped from their chairs as we strode by, blocking our way. They weren't interested in me; but one of them reached for the KFOR card clipped backward to Bezman's shirt, turned it over, clearly saw that the photo wasn't him.

Without saying a word, one of the Serbs grabbed him forcefully by the shoulder and began to hustle him away.

"Hey, hey, it's OK, he's with me," I said.

"It's not OK," said one of the Serbs in broken English. "He is Albanian."

They were trying to shove Bezman somewhere and I knew that if they got him into an alley or a doorway, it would be all over for him;

the best he could hope for would be a terrible beating. So I also grabbed him and started pulling in the opposite direction, trying to defuse the situation with my best "everything's cool" tone.

It didn't work. As soon as I grabbed Bezman's shirt, about ten more Serbs from nearby tables jumped up and surrounded us. I looked over my shoulder, but Hondros was gone, along with all of the other reporters, who had followed the mother and her child into their apartment. I was suddenly so flooded with adrenaline that I began shivering with chills: I was going to get my ass kicked along with Bezman, I thought. Within sight of French soldiers, no less.

But the Serbs just punched him hard once in the kidneys and told him to get back to his own side of the city.

A day later, Hondros, Cabell and I decided, for some reason or another, to drive our rented Opel Kaddett across the bridge to see how far the northern half of the city extended beyond the river. We'd rented the car from someone in Pristina and it wasn't exactly the best investment any of us had ever made: it often had to be push-started and sometimes in the morning, a small mushroom cloud of yellow flame would explode from the carburetor when the engine cranked over. The brakes barely worked, the tires were bald and out of alignment and the chassis rode nervously low on its suspension. The only advantage the car offered was that it was unlikely to get stolen.

But it was a big disadvantage in Mitrovica: not only hadn't we taped "PRESS" or "TV" to the sides, but it also had a license plate from Urosevac, a largely Albanian town. When we cruised across the bridge and past the mob of Serbs hanging out at the plaza, every head turned as we drove past. We followed the road up the hill, through a tall canyon of relatively nice brick apartment buildings that seemed to have been spared a large degree of ethnic cleansing and on through to the other end of town, about a mile from the bridge.

"I think this is as far as it goes," Cabell said. "Let's go ahead and turn around." I looked in the rearview mirror to see if I could U-turn in the middle of the road and noticed a VW Golf riding my bumper. The car was packed with young Serbs.

I made a right turn into the parking lot of an abandoned gas station and turned around. The VW kept going straight.

Heading back toward the bridge, we were moving slowly, like tourists, staring at the sidewalk vendors selling shriveled vegetables, cigarettes, toiletries and every other imaginable gimcrack. One man was selling a collection of metal parts that couldn't have been anything other than the disassembled engine of his car.

Halfway back to the bridge, I glanced in the mirror again. The Volkswagen was back, inches from my rear bumper, and the passenger made a pistol motion at me with his thumb and index finger.

"Oh shit," I said. Before I could explain myself, the car whipped around on the passenger side and then jerked violently directly in front of us, practically colliding into our front end. The Serb driver stood on his brakes, forcing us to a screeching halt in the middle of the road. Three passengers in the backseat stared at us.

"OK, be cool," Cabell said. "They think we're Albanians."

I very slowly tried to drive around them in the oncoming lane, which was empty, but the Golf bucked into our path and again blocked the way.

"We'd better not fuck with them," Cabell said. "Let's get out and talk to them."

Fuck that, I thought. The moment we get out of the car is the moment we get shot. Before we had an opportunity to debate it, however, the Golf jerked forward and careened ahead. I threw the Kaddett in gear and sped after it, heading for a KFOR APC that I knew was parked around the corner.

As we pulled into the shelter of the vehicle, the Golf turned around and slowly drove past again, the passenger once again pointing his index finger–gun barrel at me. Then they were gone.

So it was pretty clear to us that northern Mitrovica wasn't a place that was friendly to Albanians. The Serbs had not only effectively partitioned the city, but they also clearly guarded one of the main roads to northern Kosovo as well. Not coincidentally, the road north from the bridge also leads directly to the mines in Trepce and Stari Trn.

But everyone in a position of authority I spoke with about the situation seemed to think the reports about Mitrovica were overblown and that it could be worked out sometime in the future, an opinion clearly not held by anyone on either side of the bridge. The UN's solution to the Mitrovica problem was to assign Sir Martin Garrett as the city's administrator.

Garrett had held the same position in Mostar.

Four

The one bright spot in the implementation of the Kosovo security resolution was provided by Michael Pedersen, the rule-of-law director for the OSCE. From an office with a view of the former secret service headquarters, which had been rendered skeletal by a cruise missile that had scattered the glass of its windows on rooftops for blocks around, he outlined the considerable progress he'd made in attempting to bring some legal order to the chaos.

The progress was considerable because he'd accomplished more, nearly single-handedly, than anyone else I had encountered in two weeks. When we met, he was celebrating the fact that he had recently been granted six staff members instead of two and that his project of identifying and recommending for reinstatement Kosovars who'd been judges prior to 1989 was off to a banging start.

Finding the judges hadn't been hard, he reported. Most of them had stayed in Pristina even after they were forced to find a new line of work when Milosevic removed the province's autonomy. In the thirty days since the bombing had ended, he'd interviewed more than 253 judges, cataloging them according to their former area of legal specialty, such as property rights laws, criminal law, etc. Once identified, the judges were presented to a panel of seven that included one representative each from UNMIK, the OSCE, and UNHCR (UN High Commissioner for Refugees), a Serb, two Albanians and another citizen obliquely referred to only as a "Kosovar Muslim."

The panel screened the applicants and made recommendations to Dr. Bernard Kouchner, the special representative of the secretary-general and the man in charge of UNMIK. As of mid-July, Kouchner had appointed thirty judges, whose duty it was to travel to the headquarters of the different multinational brigades and conduct detention hearings for the people arrested by KFOR.

This development was comparatively miraculous when compared with Dayton's pace at the same stage of its implementation.

But the crushing fact was that it was likely too good. For one thing, no had yet decided on precisely what laws would be enforced. Pedersen said that officially, the Yugoslavian criminal code was still in effect, though not entirely. There were some measures in the code that were woefully undemocratic, he said, such as the fact that people can be detained for up to seventy-two hours before they're charged with a crime. Therefore, only some of the code would be enforced.

Sadly, to the best of his knowledge, Pedersen was the only person who'd done a full accounting of the Yugoslavian code to determine which parts were enforceable and which weren't. But he hadn't released his analysis yet because it was still in its draft stage, he said. Therefore, no one on the ground—including the KFOR soldiers who would be doing the arresting—had any idea what laws were in effect. The most obvious consequence of this became apparent one night when we happened across a squad of paratroopers in Pristina who'd stopped a suspicious van with Albanian license plates. The van's bay had been gutted and the bay and the inside of the doors had been retrofitted with thick Styrofoam, making it perfectly soundproof. One soldier said he spotted what he thought might be dried blood splattered on the floor, but in the weird rays of the overhead sodium-vapor streetlight it was hard to tell. The soldiers also found a five-pound block of hashish in the personal possession of the van's two occupants.

To a reporter, the situation certainly seemed like one that would result in an arrest, but the soldiers weren't sure. Obviously drug trafficking was illegal . . . right? And if so, was it KFOR's job to arrest them?

These questions were posed by radio to the squad commander, who then consulted with someone higher up the chain of command. The word came back that no one was sure what to do with the two Albanians. So they kicked them loose and confiscated the dope.

Another problem had to do with the judges themselves. Since no comprehensive code had been adopted yet, it was unclear what standard the judges would apply to determine whether a detainee deserved to remain in jail pending trial because the hearings were closed to the press and members of the public.

And if they did agree to keep a suspect locked up, no one could say for how long because there wasn't yet a trial system.

Perhaps most ominous, though, as Pedersen admitted, was that no one had strenuously screened the applicants for anything other than their legal experience. None of the applicants were asked whether they were members of the KLA.

"If you look close enough," Pedersen said with a weary shrug, "you'll find blood on everyone's hands."

That much was clear no matter where you looked. In the short period of time I was in Kosovo after the bombing, things seemed to get gradually more and more out of control. Before long the French began taking sniper fire in Mitrovica, and it could well have come from either side. Gnjilane remained a nightmare for the Americans and it grew downright hellish once the Russians scattered themselves across the other brigades; they were instant targets and one was shot in the thigh in Gnjilane less than a week into their deployment. Near Lipjan one night at sundown, more than a dozen Serb farmers were massacred with assault rifles as they worked in their fields. The Associated Press reported that in August, at least one Serb was murdered every day in Pristina alone. Also in Pristina, a bomb detonated in front of a huge partially built Orthodox church; it was unlikely that it would ever be finished. Kosovars cleansed Serbs as systematically, and just as ruthlessly, as the Serbs had cleansed Kosovars. Homes burned every night.

When I left Kosovo for the last time in mid-July, it was as much a retreat from the danger as it was from the overwhelming frustration of watching a murderous cycle gain momentum, despite everything that had happened up to that point. The pain of Kosovo was stupefying, anesthetizing.

So it was only appropriate that due to the traffic at the Macedonian border, Hondros had to drop me off about a mile away to avoid being stuck for hours. I shouldered my bags and trudged through the dust toward the border crossing, weaving through trucks and clouds of diesel smoke, blending into a procession of others moving between the two countries for reasons of their own. I walked past a factory of some sort that looked as though it had been empty for some time. It was hard to say whether it had been damaged during the war or had just decomposed under communism.

Underfoot was a river of human detritus abandoned a couple of months ago by refugees staggering toward the uncertain safety of the border . . . children's toys welded into the dirt by hundreds of truck tires, empty water bottles scattered like seashells, colorful but unidentifiable scraps of clothing flapping on barbed wire like Sherpa prayer flags. And beyond the wire, the weird valley floor called No Man's Land, empty of everything but discarded or used-up possessions that had once been deemed valuable enough to grab in retreat but that now were useless garbage. A white horse wandered in the middle of the field.

Passing me in the other direction, on their way into Kosovo, some for the first time since they had been driven out, was a steady stream of Kosovars dragging overstuffed plastic garbage bags or battered luggage, their eyes dead; they were not shocked by anything anymore.

They didn't seem to look at much as they began their long trudge into their homeland, they just turned their heads down with a determination I'd come to know well, one that would be invaluable as they righted the overturned pieces of their lives and attempted to forge a state and a government from the smoldering ruins of ethnic cleansing.

But the nationalism that was necessary for embracing the reconstruction was also demonstrating how easily and transparently it crossed the line from tool of peace to weapon of war and back again.

For many returning to Kosovo with nothing waiting for them but what they had carried out—their nationalism—it was their most valuable possession.

As everyone has seen, it's also the most deadly.

Notes

Prologue

1. United Nations Security Council Resolution 1031, para. 5.

2. United Nations High Commissioner for Refugees spokesman Ron Redmond, press briefing, March 19, 1996, Sarajevo.

3. Dayton Peace Agreement, Annex 1-A, Article IV, para. 4 (b).

4. Peter Maass, *Love Thy Neighbor: A Story of War* (New York: Alfred A. Knopf, Inc., 1996), p. 145.

5. Suada Kapic, *Sarajevo Survival Map* (FAMA: Sarajevo, 1997), "Snipers."

6. Maass, p. 111.

7. Kapic, "Introduction."

8. UNHCR press briefing, March 19, 1996, Sarajevo.

9. Richard Holbrooke, *To End a War* (New York: Random House, 1998), pp. 335–336.

10. UNHCR press briefing, March 19, 1996, Sarajevo.

Chapter One

1. International Criminal Tribunal for the Former Yugoslavia, indictment of Dragan Gagovic et al.

2. Ed Vulliamy, "Middle Managers of Genocide," *The Nation*, June 10, 1996 (accessed at www.thenation.com).

3. International Criminal Tribunal for the Former Yugoslavia (ICTY), indictment of Goran Jelisic et al.

4. Human Rights Watch, *Bosnia-Hercegovina, The Fall of Srebrenica and the Failure of UN Peacekeeping* (New York: HRW Publications, October 1995).

5. Richard Holbrooke, *To End a War* (New York: Random House), pp. 159–160.

6. Captain (Canada) Tom Mykytiuk, First Battalion of the Royal Canadian Regiment Battle Group, interview, July 1, 1998.

7. Human Rights Watch, *Bosnia and Hercegovina: Beyond Restraint: Politics and the Policing Agenda of the United Nations International Police Task Force* (New York: HRW Publications, June 1998), p. 30.

8. Ben Jillett, United Nations Civilian Police Commander, International Police Task Force, Drvar station, interview, July 1, 1998.

9. Captain (Canada) Scott McCorquedale, Administrative Officer, First Battalion of the Royal Canadian Regiment Battle Group, SFOR Camp Drvar, interview, July 1, 1998.

10. Office of the High Representative, "Human Rights Report," para. (3), April 1998.

11. Ibid., para. (2).

Chapter Two

1. Captain (Canada) Scott McCorquedale, Administrative Officer, First Battalion of the Royal Canadian Regiment Battle Group, SFOR Camp Drvar, interview, July 1, 1998.

2. Richard Holbrooke, interview on *Firing Line*, August 1998.

3. Richard Holbrooke, *To End a War* (New York: Random House), pp. 221–223.

4. Ibid., p. 216.

5. McCorquedale, interview, July 1, 1998.

6. Ibid.

7. NATO/SFOR LANDCENT, Transcript: Joint Press Conference, Coalition Press Information Centre, Tito Barracks, Sarajevo, April 27, 1998.

8. Ibid.

9. War Criminal Watch, www.wcw.org (accessed August 15, 1998).

10. ICTY indictment of Dr. Radovan Karadzic and General Ratko Mladic.

11. Rezak Hukanovic, *The Tenth Circle of Hell* (New York: Basic Books, 1996), p. 44.

12. Ed Vulliamy, "Middle Managers of Genocide," *The Nation*, June 10, 1996.

13. UN Security Council Resolution 819.

14. Human Rights Watch, *Bosnia and Hercegovina: The Fall of Srebrenica and the Failure of UN Peacekeeping* (New York: HRW Publications), pp. 11–21.

15. Ibid., pp. 31–32.

16. Ibid., pp. 35–48.

17. Holbrooke, *To End a War,* p. 71.

18. PeaceWatch, *Bosnia in the Balkans* (Washington, D.C.: U.S. Institute for Peace, April 1998).

19. Amnesty International, *AI Report 1998: Bosnia-Herzegovina* (New York: Amnesty International Publications), January 1998.

20. Office of the High Representative, "Human Rights Monthly Report," April 1998.

21. Amnesty International, *AI Report: 1998.*

22. Dayton Peace Agreement, Annex 11, Article III, para. 1 (a)–(c).

23. Ibid., Annex 11, Article VI, para. 1.

24. Human Rights Watch, *Bosnia and Hercegovina: Beyond Restraint: Politics and the Policing Agenda of the United Nations International Police Task Force* (New York: HRW Publications), June 1998, p. 30.

25. Ibid., pp. 28–29.

26. Ibid., pp. 27–28.

27. Ibid., pp. 2, 10.

28. Ibid., p. 23.

29. NATO/SFOR LANDCENT Transcript: Joint Press Conference, Coalition Press Information Centre, Tito Barracks, Sarajevo, April 27, 1998.

Chapter Three

1. Robert D. Kaplan, *Balkan Ghosts: A Journey Through History* (New York: Vintage Books, 1993), p. 22.

2. Ibid., p. 31.

3. Ibid., p. 25.

4. Ibid., p. 33.

5. Charles Ingrao, "Touring the Military Frontier," *Purdue Liberal Arts Magazine,* 1996–1997.

6. J.F.O. McAllister, James L. Graff, Andrew Purvis, and Bruce van Voorst, "When to Go, When to Stay," *Time,* October 4, 1993, p. 40.

Chapter Four

1. Peter Maass, *Love Thy Neighbor: A Story of War* (New York: Alfred A. Knopf), p. 122.

2. Colin Soloway, "How Not to Catch a War Criminal," *U.S. News and World Report,* December 9, 1996, p. 63.

3. War Criminal Watch, www.wcw.org (accessed August 15, 1998).

4. David Rohde, "Eyewitnesses Confirm Massacres in Bosnia," *Christian Science Monitor,* October 5, 1995.

5. Richard Holbrooke, *To End a War* (New York: Random House, 1998), p. 69.

6. Charles Ingrao, interview, August 1998.

7. Human Rights Watch, "Failure to Arrest: Common Excuses Answered," Arrest Now! Campaign, 1997 (www.hrw.org).

8. Ronald H. Bailey, *Partisans and Guerrillas* (New York: Time-Life Books, Inc., 1978), p. 148.

9. Robert D. Kaplan, *Balkan Ghosts: A Journey Through History* (New York: Vintage Books, 1993), pp. 5–6.

10. Holbrooke, pp. 39, 42.

11. Ibid., p. 23.

12. Warren Zimmerman, *Origins of a Catastrophe: Yugoslavia and Its Destroyers* (New York: Times Books, 1996), pp. 120–121.

13. Ingrao, interview.

14. Confidential source, interview, 1998.

15. Rebecca West, *Black Lamb and Grey Falcon* (New York: Viking Press, 1941), p. 482.

16. David Rieff, *Slaughterhouse: Bosnia and the Failure of the West* (New York: Simon & Schuster, 1995), p. 138.

17. Maass, p. 181.

18. Ibid.

Chapter Five

1. Human Rights Watch, "Failure to Arrest: Common Excuses Answered," Arrest Now! Campaign, 1997 (www.hrw.org).

2. Ibid.

3. Colin Soloway, "How Not to Catch a War Criminal," *U.S. News and World Report,* December 10, 1996, p. 63.

4. Ibid.

5. The Balkan Institute, "Dayton at Two Years: The Latest in a Series of Balkan Institute Updates on the Implementation of the Dayton Accords," Washington, D.C., January 1998.

6. Richard Holbrooke, *To End a War* (New York: Random House, 1998), pp. 218–219.

7. Ibid., p. 217.

8. Richard Holbrooke, interview on *Firing Line,* August 1998.

9. Dayton Peace Agreement, Annex 1-A, Article VI, para. 3 (a).

10. Ibid., para. 5.

11. Holbrooke, pp. 332–334.

12. Mark Milstein, "Task Force Eagle: The Return of American Forces in Harm's Way," *Soldier of Fortune,* March 1996, p. 42.

13. Holbrooke, p. 324.

14. Charles Ingrao, interview, July 29, 1998.

15. Human Rights Watch, "Failure to Arrest."

16. Soloway, p. 63.

17. PeaceWatch, *Bosnia in the Balkans* (Washington, D.C.: U.S. Institute of Peace, April 1998).

18. Soloway, p. 63.

19. Stacey Sullivan, "Bosnia's Most Wanted," *Newsweek,* July 21, 1997, p. 41.

20. Gilles Delafon and Thomas Sancton, "The Hunt for Karadzic," *Time,* August 10, 1998, pp. 68–70.

21. Ibid.

22. Holbrooke, p. 348.

23. Sullivan, p. 41.

24. Richard J. Newman, "Hunting War Criminals: The First Account of Secret U.S. Missions in Bosnia," *U.S. News and World Report,* July 6, 1998, pp. 45–49.

25. Ibid.

Chapter Six

1. Human Rights Watch, "Failure to Arrest: Common Excuses Answered," Arrest Now! Campaign, 1997 (www.hrw.org).

2. Rebecca West, *Black Lamb and Grey Falcon* (New York: Viking Press, 1941), p. 1009.

3. Rob Siebelink, "Radovan Karadzic, the Psychiatrist Who Became the Most Wanted War Criminal," *Drentse Courant/Groninger Dagblad,* April 1997 (Accessed at http://www.nord.bart.nl/~papafinn/karal-gb.html).

4. Peter Maass, *Love Thy Neighbor: A Story of War* (New York: Alfred A. Knopf, 1996), p. 158.

5. Siebelink.

6. Maass, p. 161.

7. Samantha Power, "The World of Radovan Karadzic," *U.S. News and World Report,* July 24, 1995, p. 44.

8. Siebelink.

9. Maass, p. 161.

10. Richard Holbrooke, *To End a War* (New York: Random House, 1998), p. 338.

11. Human Rights Watch, *Bosnia and Hercegovina: A Failure in the Making: Human Rights and the Dayton Agreement* (New York: HRW Publications, June 1996), p. 2.

12. Holbrooke, p. 344.

13. Associated Press, "Second National Election After Bosnian War Seems Confusing," September 9, 1998.

14. Ibid.

Chapter Seven

1. Robert D. Kaplan, *Balkan Ghosts: A Journey Through History* (New York: Vintage Books, 1993), p. 40.

2. Elez Biberaj, *Albania in Transition: The Rocky Road to Democracy* (Boulder: Westview Press, 1998), p. 14.

3. Ibid.

4. Lord Kinrose, *The Ottoman Centuries: The Rise and Fall of the Turkish Empire* (New York: Morrow Quill Paperbacks, 1977), pp. 58–59.

5. Biberaj, p. 18.

6. Kaplan, p. 34.

7. Biberaj, p. 248.

8. Kaplan, p. 40.

9. Biberaj, p. 248.

10. Richard Holbrooke, interview.

11. Richard Holbrooke, *To End a War* (New York: Random House, 1998), p. 357.

12. Paul Taylor, "U.S. Special Balkans Envoy Robert Gelbard: 'Without Question a Terrorist Group,'" Reuters, London, March 9, 1998.

13. Biberaj, p. 254.

14. Kaplan, p. 42.

Chapter Eight

1. Confidential source with knowledge of the peace negotiations in both Bosnia and Kosovo.

2. Ibid.

3. Tom Hundley, "Outdated or Disorganized, Kosovo Foes Ill-Equipped for War," *Chicago Tribune*, July 8, 1998.

Chapter Nine

1. Reuters, "Whatever Happened to the Kosovo Liberation Army?" September 9, 1998.

Chapter Ten

1. Steven Lee Myers, "2,000 Monitors to Go to Kosovo, but Their Power Is Unclear," *New York Times*, October 15, 1998.

2. CNN, "Serb Offensive Heats Up in Kosovo," December 27, 1998 (www.cnn.com).

3. Ibid.

4. Rambouillet Accords, Appendix B, Para 21.

5. Brian Duffy, "Heartbreak in the Balkans," *U.S. News and World Report,* April 12, 1999.

6. Ibid.

7. Hysni Ahmeti, Brigade Commander of the KLA 141st Mehe Uka Brigade, interview, Vucitrn, July 11, 1999.

8. Ibid.

9. U.S. Rep. Rod Blagojovic, interview, Washington, D.C., May 1999.

10. Jamie Shea, NATO spokesman, daily press briefing at NATO headquarters, Brussels, Belgium, June 1, 1999 (NATO transcript).

11. Florim Rashica, Desarta Rashica, Fatima Rashica, Shehide Rashica, interviews, Studime e Poshtme, July 12 and 14, 1999; and Ahmeti, interview, July 11, 1999.

12. Florim Rashica et al., interviews, Studime e Poshtme; Hysni Ahmeti and four officers of the KLA, interviews, Vucitrn and Mitrovica, July 1999; Human Rights Watch, "Separation of Men and Mass Killing Near Vucitrn," Human Rights Flash #40, Kukes, Albania, May 20, 1999.

13. Romeau Ventura, War Crimes Investigator for the International Criminal Tribunal for the Former Yugoslavia, interview, Studime e Poshtme, July 9, 1999.

14. Account reconstructed from eleven interviews on five occasions in Studime e Poshtme, Vucitrn and Mitrovica with those involved in the incident or investigating it, July 1999.

15. Tim Butcher and Patrick Bishop, "Nato Admits Air Campaign Failed," *The Telegraph* (London), July 22, 1999.

16. Richard J. Newman, "Attacks on Serbian Troops in the Field Were Ineffective. So What Won the War?" *U.S. News and World Report*, September 20, 1999.

17. Ibid.

Epilogue

1. Hysni Ahmeti, Brigade Commander of the KLA 141st Mehe Uka Brigade, interview, Vucitrn, July 11, 1999.

Bibliography

Amnesty International. 1997. *AI Report 1997: Bosnia-Herzegovina.* New York: Amnesty International Publications. January.

_____. 1998. *AI Report 1998: Bosnia-Herzegovina.* New York: Amnesty International Publications. January.

Associated Press. 1998. "Second National Election After Bosnian War Seems Confusing." Sarajevo. September 9.

Bailey, Ronald H. 1978. *Partisans and Guerrillas.* New York: Time-Life Books, Inc.

The Balkan Institute. 1997. "Dayton Implementation: A Mid-Term Report Card." Washington, D.C. April 24.

_____. 1998. "Dayton at Two Years: The Latest in a Series of Balkan Institute Updates on the Implementation of the Dayton Accords." Washington, D.C. January 5.

Biberaj, Elez. 1998. *Albania in Transition: The Rocky Road to Democracy.* Boulder: Westview Press.

Central Intelligence Agency. 1997. "Serbia and Montenegro." *World Factbook.* Washington, D.C.: CIA.

Cigar, Norman, and Paul Williams. 1997. "War Crimes and Individual Responsibility: A Prima Facie Case for the Indictment of Slobodan Milosevic." Washington, D.C.: The Balkan Institute. August.

Delafon, Gilles, and Thomas Scancton. 1998. "The Hunt for Karadzic." *Time,* August 10.

Drezenga, Vinka. 1998. "Croatia Approached the EU." *Croatia Weekly* (Zagreb), July 3.

Drozdiak, William. 1998. "Rise of Kosovo Guerrillas Puts NATO Powers in a Bind." *Washington Post,* July 8.

Gelbard, Robert S. 1998. "Statement Before the Senate Armed Services Committee." Washington, D.C. June 4.

Gjelten, Tom. 1995. *Sarajevo Daily: A City and Its Newspaper Under Siege.* New York: HarperCollins.

Goodgame, Dan. 1991. "In the Gulf: Bold Vision. 'What If We Do Nothing?'" *Time*, January 7.

Graff, James L., Bonnie Angelo, William Mader, J.F.O. McAllister, and Michael Montgomery. 1993. "Srebrenica Succumbs." *Time*, April 26.

Hedges, Chris. 1998. "U.N. Stymied by Resistance to Easing of Bosnian Partition." *New York Times*, February 2.

Holbrooke, Richard. 1998. *To End a War*. New York: Random House.

Hukanovic, Rezak. 1996. *The Tenth Circle of Hell*. New York: Basic Books.

Human Rights Watch. 1995. *Bosnia and Hercegovina: The Fall of Srebrenica and the Failure of UN Peacekeeping*. New York: HRW Publications. October.

_____. 1996. *Bosnia-Hercegovina: The Continuing Influence of Bosnia's Warlords*. New York: HRW Publications. December.

_____. 1996. *Bosnia-Hercegovina: A Failure in the Making: Human Rights and the Dayton Agreement*. New York: HRW Publications. June.

_____. 1997. *Bosnia and Hercegovina: Politics of Revenge: The Misuse of Authority in Bihac, Cazlin, and Velika Kladusa*. New York: HRW Publications. August.

_____. 1997. *Bosnia and Hercegovina: The Unindicted: Reaping the Rewards of Ethnic Cleansing*. New York: HRW Publications. January.

_____. 1997. "Failure to Arrest: Common Excuses Answered." Arrest Now! Campaign.

_____. 1998. *Bosnia and Hercegovina: Beyond Restraint: Politics and the Policing Agenda of the United Nations International Police Task Force*. New York: HRW Publications. June.

_____. 1998. *World Report: Bosnia and Hercegovina*. New York: HRW Publications. July 28.

Hundley, Tom. 1998. "Outdated or Disorganized, Kosovo Foes Ill-Equipped for War." *Chicago Tribune*, July 8.

Ingrao, Charles. 1996–97. "Touring the Military Border." *Purdue University Liberal Arts Magazine*. Winter.

_____. 1997. "Bosnia's Day of Judgment." *Brown Alumni Monthly*. February.

_____. 1997. "Bosnia's Leaders Fight Own Past." *Newsday*, October 24.

_____. 1997. "Myths Against Sound Reason." *Tages-Anzeiger* (Zurich), October 21.

_____. 1997. "Reviving the Balkans' Multiethnicity." *Providence Journal*, October 21.

_____. 1998. "Judging the Criminals: An Independent, International Criminal Court as Deterrent." *Weltwoche* (Zurich), June 25.

_____. 1998. "What the World Needs Now Is a New Court." *Newsday*, June 16.

Kapic, Suada. 1997. *Sarajevo Survival Map*, "Snipers." Sarajevo: FAMA.

Kaplan, Robert D. 1993. *Balkan Ghosts: A Journey Through History*. New York: Vintage Books.

Kinross, Lord. 1977. *The Ottoman Centuries: The Rise and Fall of the Turkish Empire*. New York: Morrow Quill Paperbacks.

Krauthammer, Charles. 1993. "The Greatest Cold War Myth of All." *Time*, November 29.

Lupic, Zeljko. 1997. "Croatia—Hrvatska: History." *Journal of Croatian Studies.* New York: Croatian Academy of America.

Maass, Peter. 1996. *Love Thy Neighbor: A Story of War*. New York: Alfred A. Knopf.

McAllister, J.F.O., James L. Graff, Andrew Purvis, and Bruce van Voorst. 1993. "When to Go, When to Stay." *Time*, October 4.

Milstein, Mark. 1996. "Sarajevo 'Olympics': Pillage, Rape, Burn and Bug-Out." *Soldier of Fortune*, July.

_____. 1996. "Task Force Eagle: The Return of American Forces in Harm's Way." *Soldier of Fortune*, March.

Naegele, Jolyon. 1996. Bosnia: "Once A Serb Town, Drvar Has Become the Croat Stronghold." Radio Free Europe/Radio Liberty, Inc. September 4.

Nelan, Bruce W., James Carney, J.F.O. McAllister, and Bruce van Voorst. 1993. "No-Guts, No-Glory Guys." *Time*, November 22.

Nelan, Bruce W., James L. Graff, J.F.O. McAllister, and Bruce van Voorst. 1993. "Blood Threats and Fears." *Time*, August 16.

Newman, Richard J. 1998. "Hunting War Criminals: The First Account of Secret U.S. Missions in Bosnia." *U.S. News and World Report*, July 6.

NATO/SFOR LANDCENT. 1998. Transcript: Joint Press Conference. Coalition Press Information Centre, Tito Barracks, Sarajevo. April 27.

Office of the High Representative. 1998. "Human Rights Monthly Report." April.

_____. 1998. "Interview with the High Representative: European Melodies Are Getting Louder." April 22.

O'Rourke, P. J. 1994. *All the Trouble in the World: The Lighter Side of Overpopulation, Famine, Ecological Disaster, Ethnic Hatred, Plague, and Poverty*. New York: Atlantic Monthly Press.

PeaceWatch. 1998. *Bosnia in the Balkans.* Washington, D.C.: U.S. Institute for Peace. April.

Power, Samantha. 1995. "The World of Radovan Karadzic." *U.S. News and World Report*, July 24.

Reuters. 1998. "Bosnia Envoy Doubts NATO Can Police Kosovo Too." September 9.

_____. 1998. "Bosnian Elections Could Cement Fragile Peace." September 9.

_____. 1998. "Bosnia's Leading Political Figures." September 9.

_____. 1998. "NATO Could Put 50,000 Troops in Kosovo If Cease-Fire." September 9.

_____. 1998. "Whatever Happened to the Kosovo Liberation Army?" September 9.

Rieff, David. 1995. *Slaughterhouse: Bosnia and the Failure of the West.* New York: Simon & Schuster.

Rohde, David. 1995. "Eyewitnesses Confirm Massacres in Bosnia." *Christian Science Monitor*, October 5.

Siebelink, Rob. 1997. "Radovan Karadzic, the Psychiatrist Who Became the Most Wanted War Criminal." *Drentse Courant/Groninger Dagblad*, April.

Soloway, Colin. 1996. "How Not to Catch a War Criminal." *U.S. News and World Report*, December 10.

Staresina, Visnja. 1998. "A Hague Message to 'Small Fish.'" *Croatia Weekly* (Zagreb), July 3.

Sullivan, Stacey. 1997. "Bosnia's Most Wanted." *Newsweek*, July 21.

Taylor, Paul. 1998. "U.S. Special Balkans Envoy Robert Gelbard: 'Without Question a Terrorist Group,'" London: Reuters. March 9.

United Nations. 1998. "Report on the Human Rights Field Operation in the Region of the Former Yugoslavia." New York: United Nations Publications. April 30.

U.S. Department of State. 1995. "General Framework Agreement for Peace in Bosnia and Hercegovina." November 21.

U.S. Department of State. 1997. "Bosnia and Herzegovina: Country Report on Human Rights Practices for 1996." Released by the Bureau of Democracy, Human Rights, and Labor. January 30.

Vulliamy, Ed. 1996. "Middle Managers of Genocide." *The Nation*, June 10.

West, Rebecca. 1941. *Black Lamb and Grey Falcon.* New York: Viking Press.

Zimmerman, Warren. 1996. *Origins of a Catastrophe: Yugoslavia and Its Destroyers.* New York: Times Books.

Index

Printed in the United States
118791LV00001B/220-267/A